WHEN FORMALITY WORKS

WHEN FORMALITY WORKS

Authority and Abstraction in Law and Organizations

ARTHUR L. STINCHCOMBE

THE UNIVERSITY OF CHICAGO PRESS • CHICAGO AND LONDON

ARTHUR L. STINCHCOMBE has been a fellow of the American
Academy of Arts and Sciences and is professor emeritus of
sociology at Northwestern University. His book *Constructing Social
Theories* (1968, 1987) won the American Sociological Association's
Distinguished Scholarly Publication Award, and his *Information and
Organizations* (1990) won the association's Weber Award.

The University of Chicago Press, Chicago 60637
The University of Chicago Press, Ltd., London
© 2001 by The University of Chicago
All rights reserved. Published 2001
Printed in the United States of America
10 09 08 07 06 05 04 03 02 01   1 2 3 4 5

ISBN: 0-226-77495-3 (cloth)
ISBN: 0-226-77496-1 (paper)

Library of Congress Cataloging-in-Publication Data

Stinchcombe, Arthur L.
    When formality works : authority and abstraction in law and
organizations / Arthur L. Stinchcombe.
        p.   cm.
    Includes bibliographical references and index.
    ISBN 0-226-77495-3 (cloth : alk. paper) — ISBN
0-226-77496-1 (pbk : alk. paper)
    1. Sociological jurisprudence. 2. Legal authorities.
3. Formalities (Law) 4. Abstraction.   I. Title.

K370 .S75 2001
340'.115—dc21

                                            2001027409

⊗ The paper used in this publication meets the minimum
requirements of the American National Standard for Information
Sciences—Permanence of Paper for Printed Library Materials,
ANSI Z39.48-1992.

CONTENTS

ACKNOWLEDGMENTS

I conceived many of the elements of this book while applying for an unpaid visiting appointment to the American Bar Foundation. Labor market processes require matching what one wants to do and is competent to do with the mission of some organization. Reexamining what one has become in the light of what one might be able to do in some social system is the central problem of identity. An imagined American Bar Foundation, an imagined law and social science community of scholars, and an imagined future stream of work for myself were central to creating the line of conduct that has resulted in this book.

Three people were central to maintaining this imaginary future in the reality of the subsequent four years: Bryant Garth, Carol Heimer, and Robert Nelson. Bryant Garth defended me from the body of law and social science peers who thought it was unlikely that this work should amount to anything. He found the odd corner in the allocation of space, the unallocated bit of summer salary, the odd bit of textbook chapter writing I could do easily with what I had already learned, which did not have to pass peer review. Carol Heimer managed knowing more about the subject I was writing about, and the audience I was writing for, with a hard-headed nose for intellectual sloppiness but a keen view of what could be made of it if I straightened it out. Only the best intellectual companions can do that. Robert Nelson was the buffer between Northwestern University and me during the process of my retiring. His assurance, backed by work and money, that I was basically the sort of scholar that graduate students should learn from sustained me against the uncertainties of not having a real job.

In an Australian interlude at the Australian Research School of the Social Sciences, John Braithewaite and Robert Goodin welcomed me into the intellectual community and gave cues that all was perhaps not hopeless with this undertaking. I have several aborted books for which neither others nor myself supplied sufficient conviction on that matter. Braithewaite gave me detailed, occasionally scathing, but always kindly suggestions on chapter 2. These shaped my fundamental revision of that chapter as it appears here, to which I was further persuaded by penetrating comment on intellectual organization by an anonymous referee for the University of Chicago Press. Goodin welcomed an early draft of chapter 4 as a submission to the *Journal of Political Philosophy*, arranged for penetrating referees, and forced me to deepen the argument substantially.

Bruce Carruthers is the senior author of chapter 5, and of its predecessor as a paper in *Theory and Society*. In a certain sense his authorship is recognition enough, and praise from a junior author to a senior author for knowing more, thinking faster, and working harder is out of place. I will therefore make no mention of that, or of my wisdom in choosing him as co-author.

Richard Lempert persuaded me that I had gotten off on the wrong foot in a subproject on the law of evidence. The general approach of this book should be at its best when addressing this part of the law, because the attempt to formalize the transition from common-sense facts to legal facts is at the core of my argument. I think Lempert was right to persuade me my attempt did not do the job, but I still think somebody should do it.

Critical help on particular parts of the work were given by Janet Gilboy on chapter 3, Jack Heintz on the general approach, Fred Schauer on an early draft of chapter 4, participants in a Law and Society Convention session where I presented an early version of chapter 3, participants in an American Sociological Association session where an early version of chapter 6 was presented, and many members of the American Bar Foundation with whom I had frequent casual intellectual conversations.

I think I successfully navigated the troubles I had writing the book and that, in the end, it holds water. That is, of course, up to the readers and future research to decide. It is, however, my own responsibility if errors of fact, reasoning, or choice of problems still mar the work, and not of all those who helped and encouraged me.

The institutional source of support that heads the list is TIAA-CREF. My retirement pension ought instead to be called TIAA-CREF Emeritus Professorship in Whatever I Please. The office space and welcome of the American Bar Foundation were essential to the work. I don't know what a square foot of office space is worth at 750 North Lake Shore Drive in Chicago, but they provided me with about two hundred of them for several years. It was an ideal place to work on a project like this one. Australian National University provided me an office in the Research School of the Social Sciences, where I wrote the first drafts of chapters 3, 4, and 6. The Lochinvar Society provided both physical and psychological support.

I gratefully acknowledge the kind permission of Blackwell to reprint parts of chapter 4, previously published in the *Journal of Political Philosophy* 7(3) (September 1999): 209–24; and of Kluwer Academic Publishers to reprint parts of chapter 5, previously published in *Theory and Society* 28 (1999): 353–82.

Kai and Per Stinchcombe, my children living at home during this project, were a joy. I do not imagine that improved the book much, but it sure helped make life worthwhile while I wrote it.

CHAPTER ONE

INTRODUCTION: WHY IS FORMALITY SO UNPOPULAR?

Perhaps the subtitle for this book should be: "How and Why Formality Works, If and When it Does." This means that the book is about how one can build formalities so they work, and tend them so they continue to work. That of course does *not* mean that I think formality works all the time. It would not be complicated enough to write a book about how it can work, if it always worked. And much of the time formalities are designed to be rituals, and not to work. Very often they are perverted from their intended purpose to serve corrupt purposes for which they were not designed. I will try to remind the reader from time to time that I do not believe formality always works.

This book is akin to one that explains how a healthy liver works without mentioning cirrhosis, or diabetes, or liver cancers, or jaundice, or blocked bile ducts. A physiologist discussing how a liver must look if it is to serve its functions would hardly be considered a hopeless utopian—a Pollyannish functionalist—merely because he or she did not write about the pathologies. It is however a much more serious matter for a sociologist, even one who has written at some length about how formalities were invented by former slaveowners after emancipation in the British Empire so as to reconstruct a system as close to slavery as possible without the formality of owning slaves (Stinchcombe 1995, chap. 10). These formalities were invented to evade the implications of the formalities dictated by parliament. Spanish colonials were more explicit about it, in the phrase: "I submit, but do not obey," when they thought a law unwise.

Because the gut reaction of sociologists is that formality is all a fraud, I am led to write a book emphasizing that formality can work and that one can tell whether formality satisfies the criteria that can make it work.

Sometimes it is built to work for purposes I think are basically bad ones, such as the rightlessness of aliens in American immigration law, which I analyze in chapter 6. My purpose there is to show that formal rightlessness can work for the purposes for which it was designed, even though I would want no part of the designing. It is as if an oncologist were to write about why and how a cancer of the liver could satisfy the purpose of growing and metastasizing; chapter 6 analyzes a cancer on due process of law.

Formality is central to the distinction between law and the rest of social life, and the controversy over formality is prevalent within law. Formality used to be a central criterion for the differences between "formal organizations" and other kinds of social structures. Our naming or definitional conventions no longer emphasize the formality of organizations, because in our theories the formality has become epiphenomenal.

I believe that much of the difficulty we have in dealing with formality is that we lack a nuanced definition of what we are talking about, a typology of its varieties, and a theory of the mechanisms by which it is caused and has its effects. In particular, I think Max Weber—and the whole tradition following or supplementing him that contrasts formality with informal social organization—got it wrong. I propose to study several cases of formalization, by which I mean creating an abstraction in such a way that it can be taken as a "fact," so that most people, most of the time, do not have to go behind it. My purpose is to develop the theory of formalization, by which I mean analysis of the conditions under which formalization as I will define it occurs, the effects that people hope for from it that sometimes follow it, and its pathologies. Most of chapter 2 is an essay on the definition of formality and formalization. In this introduction, I write more briefly about why it is important to get clear about what formality is and about some of the difficulties with defining it in the way we have done in the past. I also outline the chapters that follow.

My basic argument then is that formality is unpopular because it has been misconceived as consisting mainly of its pathologies, while its virtues have been thought to obtain only in those rare cases where substance does not matter. I argue that a clearer understanding of how formality works to accurately and usefully reflect substance will allow us to see, in a variety of specific instances in the book, that at its best it does better with the substance than we could do informally.

THE IMPORTANCE OF FORM

I suspect that law (or mathematics) would be impossible without formalization, but to explain why, for example, "informal law" will not serve we have to build the theory of form *so that it does not necessarily contradict sub-*

stance. If the formality of law is useful, it must be useful because it sub-stantively achieves something. When form does not represent substance, formality is a pathology, will not have the desired effects, and so will, in the long run, be unstable.

I believe, then, that the best intuition to follow is that formality and formalization have to do with abstraction *so as to preserve what is essential in the substance.* When formalization works well, its purpose then is *the same as* the purpose of all the substance. But it has been transformed into an abstraction (for example, the blueprints of chapter 3) so that that sub-stance (say, the client's intentions about a building) can govern the activ-ities of others (contractors and craftsmen and craftswomen). Further, that formality of the blueprint is written into a contract so that, if that governing of others' activities goes wrong, the difficulty can be taken into court to have it put right (or bargaining can go on in the shadow of what would happen in court). Just as gasoline, jet fuel, lubricating oil, and Vaseline are not the opposite of crude oil but refined versions for spe-cialized uses, so formality, when it works,[1] is not the opposite of the in-formal substance but a refined version (or versions) of it. I think under-standing formalization is central to understanding the relation of law, or mathematics, or formal organization to the rest of social life. My argu-ment is that when law (or mathematics, or organization) works, it is the same substance as the rest of social life, but formalized for one purpose or another.

The basic dependent variable I want to explain is "formalization," a process. Unless formality is seen as active, as a direction of change, one cannot understand how it can grasp a rapidly changing reality. One main kind of formalization is creating a socially valid rule, such as a law, that applies a set of abstract requirements (for example, "Thou shalt not kill," with the appropriate exceptions for accident, war, self-defense, in the course of duty as a policeman, abortion in the first trimester, and so on) to a large number of concrete cases. Formalization entails the develop-ment of an abstraction of a large amount of concrete data (as a "guilty of murder" verdict and a sentence are abstractions of the evidence brought to court, certifying among other things that the various excuses for vio-lating the commandment are not satisfied), arrived at in such a way that further social action (such as a course of action by the penal system) is governed by that abstraction, without in general going back to the orig-inal data. "Abstraction," "governed by," and "not going behind" are mat-ters of degree, and so "formalization" is a variable; from this point of

---

1. I expect to define "when it works" by showing variations in the degree to which it works in future chapters, a definition by example.

view, the tablets brought down from the mountain were not fully formalized, with all the excuses and adaptations to a changing reality of "Thou shalt not kill" that God later allowed to Moses.

The analysis of formalization begins in this chapter with defining Our beginning comment on formalization in this chapter will first define the different sorts of informality that formality is contrasted to. Then in chapter 2 I analyze abstractions by which formalized action is governed to see what features they must have to be good for governing, and what features that the government of social action must have to make good use of good abstractions so developed. Some of the features of abstractions that make them useful for government (for example, "correctability") require that sometimes one has to "go behind" the abstraction in order to improve it. In its turn, that means that, to be a good representation of the substance, a process of formalization has to have provisions to allow people to go behind the formalities to help improve their grasp of the substance. It is of the essence of formality that most people most of the time do not have to go behind the formality to the substance, *because someone else can be trusted to have done so already and to do so again when necessary.*

It is exactly this substantive rationality embedded in the formalization (and reformalization) process that Max Weber quite missed in his analysis of "rationalization," and so led us astray. In particular, in his sociology of law, he tried to characterize formality (in the sense of certainty of the meaning of a rule in the law) without paying attention to formalized debate about that meaning (for example, in appeals courts). My basic argument in this case (analyzed in more detail in chapter 4) is that certainty of meaning amounts only to various current resting places in a process of improving that certainty by substantive debate, in appeals courts, in legislatures, or in administrative implementing regulations. I undertake a reanalysis of Weber on rationalization and formalization in the final chapter.

But this means that if sociologists want to contrast the formal meaning of the law with, for example, substantive justice, they have to outthink the appeals court judges and the legislators who make their living improving the fit between law and substantive justice. Or (perhaps more often) such sociologists have agreed with a dissenting opinion that one of these improvers of formalities has already expressed. But for a sociologist to have a minority opinion on how to make the formality just is not the same as the sociologist being on the side of substance against formality. We must not confuse unjust formality (by some sociologist's standard) with formality ineffective for the standard of justice it holds itself to.

The same applies to organizations: before a sociologist can show in publications how to improve formality for the substantive purpose of the organization, the formality is very likely to have changed in the direction he or she recommends. If not, the investigator may find, after a close look at his or her interviews, the recommendation appearing in the opinion of someone in the organization who failed to get it adopted. But to understand this dilemma, it is better to set up a typology of ways of being informal that have different relations to the formality, so as to keep it straight.

THREE KINDS OF INFORMALITY

Formality is, of course, the high end of a variable, so its meaning depends on what it is contrasted to. Part of the problem here is that "informality" has a strong meaning in sociology, Habermasian philosophy, and much of the humanities: a world of warm personal relations subverting formal purposes and rules, a world of feuding and uncontrolled power struggles in the back room, a world of sexual harassment, or of the fraud and force or white collar crime, of union busting, and of conspiracies in restraint of trade. By the traditional sociological argument, informality is to formality as machine politics, with its warm personal relations within ethnic neighborhoods and corruption in appointments and contracts, is to "good government."

Much of the informality in this book is quite the opposite—loose joints between different kinds of formality. In chapter 4, for example, we take up the fact established by Karl Llewellyn (1960) that in about 9 percent of appeals cases the appeals court decides on the basis, not of the reason for the decision in the precedent, but of a reason in the "other reasons" (*obiter dicta*) given as legitimate in the precedent. That is, there is still, even in the decision to overturn a formality, reasoning that was there in the precedent. The appeals court does not go all the way back to the analysis of raw social life to find the reasons for its decision, but only back to what appeals courts of the past gave as legitimate reasons. But the precedent has mentioned more than one valid reason that applies in cases like the one the precedent decided. Thus the precedent itself is (or at least becomes, in the text of the opinion of an appeals court) a mixture of different formalities.

It is then at the discretion of the appeals court, in the case being appealed this time, to choose among those previous reasons. The appeals court cannot, except in extraordinary circumstances, go "outside the law" for its reasons. But the precedent had not only the *ratio decidendi*, the deciding reason, in its case, but also numerous other reasons that applied to the previous court's analysis of that case. The form of the "informality" or "discretion" of the appeals court is to appeal *to a different part of the formalities* of the precedent, in some 9 percent of the cases. In most of the other 91 percent, the appeals court simply affirms the precedent. "Overturning" a precedent is very rare; distinguishing the present case from the case of the precedent, using another of the reasons applicable from the precedent, is the usual "informality" of the appeals court authorities. I want to distinguish the kind of informality that chooses among embedded formalities by a somewhat informal process from anarchical formality that pays no attention to the system.

I call this sort of informality "informally embedded formality." That is, there is nothing un-abstract or un-governing about the appeals court overturning a lower court decision. Appeals are almost invariably more abstract than the case being appealed—and have more impact on the overall government of activity by the, possibly new, legal abstractions—than any particular lower court case is likely to have. But the contingency of an appeal is in the informal background of the lower court, in the anticipated process of an attorney deciding to appeal and drafting the writ of error, and of that writ's being accepted by the appeals court. That is, the writ of error is much of the time part of a process of formalizing a new distinction in legal reasoning, based on previous legal reasoning. Further, in the relevant 9 percent of the cases, the appeals court is not committed to following the formality of the precedent, but instead has decided it is willing to go behind those formalities to see if they are right. So the embedding of the higher court's authority in the lower court process is informal, even though according to my definition given above, the appeals court is nearer to the essence of the formality of the system as a whole: it is improving that system so it can be formal in more different situations without as much uncertainty.

Informally embedded formality has two main forms. The first is the hierarchical form that we see in the lower court–appeals court example, where the embedded formality provides for review by "superiors" who have greater authority in any particular case, and wider authority over many cases of different kinds. The second is a division of labor form that we see in an electrical contractor taking on the responsibility of meeting the electrical standards of the building code, of the Underwriters' Laboratories testing of the components, and of the standards of the skill, workmanship, and technical adequacy embedded in the world of electricians, electrical workers' unions, electrical engineers, and electrical contractors' associations. The authority is embedded and not formally governed by the architect because it is specialized, and can be better embedded correctly in the design of the building by letting the electrical contractor and electrical engineer, and ultimately the electrician, manage the details.

The appeals court example leads immediately to another sort of informality that occupies much of this book and that I call "formality being constructed." The book's basic idea is that formality works best when it is based on an abstraction of reality that is effective for the purpose at hand. Either of two sorts of informality tend to happen, however, when the abstraction proves to be out of accord with the situation: one that constructs a more formal, or better, formal system, or one that simply patches up the mistakes that formality would lead to. In this sense, informality can take the form of discussion, experimentation, distinguishing cases, writing memos (or briefs to a higher court)—attempts to locate the problems in the abstraction and discern what change or adaptation could grasp the substance sufficiently well for further action—all in the interest of improving the abstraction. Or informality can take the form of deviant action aimed at achieving the ends that the abstraction failed to achieve.

For example, an essay examination for a degree, common in the British higher educational system, is intended to abstract from the competencies of the student a grade summarizing his or her overall competence. If a student has missed the instruction that said to answer one out of three questions, and has answered all three, then each question might be said to measure one-third of the relevant competence, and their sum would be an adequate measure. But the abstraction for grading the examination did not give any instruction of how to grade an answer that covers one-third of what is expected, nor how to add three inadequate answers to get a whole one. A university might invent an informal method of dealing with the particular problem at hand, inventing a retest because the test as it turned out was not really the test they had intended, or asking the examiners to pretend that they had asked for three answers and grade it on that basis. One sort of informality, then, is making a patch on the system to get the right result for the case at hand, but not modifying the system of abstractions for future formality.

Or the university might try to invent a routine for the future that would force students first to copy the question they intend to answer, so that particular problem would not happen again. The ritualistic (and stupid) answer is simply to ignore the fact that the candidate took a different test than the others, and to pretend that the answer to the first question (because it was "chosen" first) is an adequate abstraction of the talent and learning being measured. Any of these is an informal response to the inadequacy of the abstraction for the particular case in hand; but some are true to the purpose of the original abstraction, others are not. Some address the error with the purpose of getting the right answer in this case; others with the purpose of improving the examination procedure henceforth.

The third kind of informality is that part of social life that is left out of the governing formality, which I will call "classical informality." Sometimes that can be simply everyday life lived during time at work or influenced by the work setting, irrelevant (in principle) to the activities governed by the formality. Often sociological interest in such informality is to show that it is indeed not irrelevant after all, that friendships can be the basis of a conspiracy to undermine governance by the formality (for example, by setting upper limits on the amount of work to be produced). Sometimes it can be systematically subversive of the formal order, as in informal secrecy about bribery, or a mobilizing conversation for a wildcat strike that looks, from the outside, like friendly conversation. Sometimes it can be the very first stages of improving the abstraction system, as when a conversation at a professional meeting suggests a new and more accurate way of making the first cut in the set of applicants for a position. In any case, the general point is that the formal system never pretended it was going to govern the activity in question, so it is informality by default.

If one discovers that the classical informality by default is after all important to the organizational outcome, it would show an imperfection of the system of formality. The imperfection might be either that the abstraction of reality by the formality is not adequate to its purpose, because it did not abstract all the relevant causes of outcomes, or that the government by the abstraction, the monitoring and incentives, is not as effective as it needs to be.

Formality as defined by these contrasts, then, is a variable whose value is determined simultaneously by three criteria. First, a practice is more formal when the abstraction it represents, rather than some other abstraction, governs the activity in question, when the formality that governs an activity is not "informally embedded formality." Thus when we find that the craftsmanship of the electrician is not represented in the blueprints or in the specifications, but instead in a publication in general electrical standards and in the local building code, we say that this import of external formalities is brought into the construction process "informally" by the electrician. In particular, it means that the architect and the client have nothing to say about that aspect of the matter at hand, because the formality that they govern cannot trump the electrician's importation of "superior authority" of the codes. It is because the abstractions in the code are presumptively adequate and presumptively authoritative that the architect and client ordinarily need not, and perhaps cannot, go behind them. They therefore need not put them into the blueprint. This does not of course mean that it would be better to embed all the electrical standards in the blueprint, hoping that the architect is after all a better electrician than the electrician is.

Second, a practice is more formal when most of the bugs have been worked out of it, so that it is not preliminary. After a bill in Congress has been through the committees of both houses and has been bargained out and analyzed there, has been subject to debate and amendment in both houses, bargained out again in a conference committee of the two houses, and passed in the same form by both, then it is no longer preliminary except that it has to be signed by the president. Before that time it is still informal in the second sense of informality. When that period of correcting the proposed formality comes to an end, one does not need to go back to the testimony in the substantive committee to find out what bill is going to the president; the law passed by Congress has been worked out as far as Congress can do it, and the law that goes to the president is formalized to a very high degree, in the sense of formality being constructed.

Third, a practice is also formalized to the degree that it is set apart from the interests of everyday life, from fear or favor among individuals, from backroom power struggles, and from conspiracies controlling the agenda to keep outsiders' interests from being represented. Thus the practice of a secretary's meeting her boss for dinner may be informal unless brought under organizational jurisdiction by a complaint of sexual harassment, or favoritism, or padding the expense account to pay for the dinner. Since all those are rare occurrences, the dinner is "presumptively informal," and any resulting divorce is also outside organizational governance. A sexual harassment policy, or central allocation of secretarial personnel to avoid favoritism, or a policy on an upper limit on the expense of a working dinner all may formalize what had been informal before. Except in totalitarian systems or total institutions, people do not usually try to formalize the whole of people's lives. When they do, they regularly fail. And in particular, in pursuit of the impossible goal of formalizing everything, they then often fail to formalize the things that really matter.

A central task of this book is to explain when formalities are serious. In none of the cases of formality studied in the separate chapters of the book are the objectives of the system of formality intended to be totalitarian, so we will not be much concerned with the fact that none of them govern the whole lives of the people subject to them. We will therefore be primarily concerned with the first two definitions of the degree of formality, the degree to which substantial parts of the governance of the activity is left to other systems of formality "informally" brought into the system, and the degree to which the abstractions and the attached monitoring and incentives to make them effective have been "completed," so that they are beyond the debugging stage and do not have to be constantly gone behind to see what is going wrong.

FORWARD IN SEQUENCE TO THE BOOK

Chapter 2 is a theoretical chapter on the definition of "substantively rational" formalization. I outline a number of dimensions that differentiate the abstractions in formality, and several more that differentiate how abstractions are made authoritative so they can govern activity. I hope this chapter helps us understand the mechanisms involved in making formality that works, formality with substance, so that the cases of formalization studied in the succeeding chapters will show theoretical unity. The main argument is that, if formality is to govern a part of the substance of social life better than informality could, it first must have mechanisms that make the abstractions in it an effective representation of the problems and solutions in an area of social life. In particular, it first has to have mechanisms that increase the cognitive adequacy, meaning the accuracy of the abstractions, cognitive economy so the abstractions are easy to work with, sufficient to represent all the causes of all the relevant effects, and wide enough in scope so that it covers most of the situations in the area of life it is supposed to govern.

Second, to govern effectively formality must have mechanisms to assure communicability, so that the governing cognitions are not sealed off from the people who actually have to manage the situations. An architectural blueprint must communicate to the client what the building will look like and what it will be useful for, to the subcontractors for the basic structure what they must do for the building to stand up and be of the right size, and so on. An abstraction system of formality then has to be transmissible and correctly interpretable by the people who have to do the activity. It has to be transparent in the sense that inside conspiracies do not distort the abstractions. It has to be durable so that noise or forgetting does not destroy the message before it can be used.

Third, an abstraction system has to have a trajectory of improvement so that it can track changes in the world, increase its scope, and correct its errors.

For people to trust such a system enough to believe that they need not (at least not usually) go behind the formalities to the raw substance, there have to be mechanisms in the governance system to assure people that the above criteria are satisfied. Formal validations are often enough: if a law has been adopted by Congress, for example, the legal, technical, administrative, and balancing of interests has already been done, as best it can be done for the present, so it is ready to be implemented. Such mechanisms include formal validations (such as signatures), risk assumption (such as title insurance in real estate transactions), procedures for making sure attention has been paid to the main problems (such as the debate behind the congressional votes), and formalized standards or protocols (such as the welding standards in construction discussed in chapter 3) that assure procedures known to be acceptable to the best experts. One can in general trust abstractions without going behind them when trustworthy people or institutions have already gone behind them in a routine way, to make sure they provide a satisfactory picture of the reality for the purposes at hand. A formal validation by an incompetent who does not listen to the evidence is "informal" in the bad sense of that word, and produces ineffective governance.

The scheme just outlined is further considered in chapter 2. It is designed to be appropriate for functional analysis. For example, if a curriculum in, say, French is so laid out that at the end students can read, write, and speak French, then it satisfies the criteria for substantively effective formality laid out above. If the abstractions of that curriculum, as represented in the textbook and the knowledge of the teacher, are accurate renditions of French grammar, vocabulary, and phonetics, the resulting French competence of the students will be serviceable for its purpose. This means that we would expect such abstractions to govern because they were indeed effective, a functional explanation. But any other protocol that produced the same end, such as an immersion course simulating a child's learning, could be explained by the same function.

An accidental sequence, such as the old one of learning Latin grammar and vocabulary first, then redescribing both English and French as variations on Latin, might be sustained by the same function of becoming competent in French. But it might have come about because of Latin's function in the Christian religion, which had no particular relation to the function of learning French. It caused people to learn misdescriptions of both grammars and misdefinitions of words with Latin roots. But these in turn shaped the language of educated people, so that in time Latin was not as dysfunctional. In this case we would have a functional explanation of a common dysfunction of formal grammar, namely, that it often misdescribes the actual grammar because it was fitted to a different language. If such misdescription is not corrected by the institutions for formal learning, then people will have to find other ways than the formal ones to learn to understand, speak, read, and write French. The formality of Latinized French and English grammar, then, is not explained by its effectiveness in its function.

The strategy throughout this book is to analyze different systems of authoritative abstractions so as to sort out when their relation to government of activity is of the sort to produce, on the average and in the long run, good abstractions. This means we will look at processes of rendering abstractions authoritative, especially by making it socially unnecessary to go behind them to the less abstracted "reality," to see whether the authorized abstractions are of the sort that would represent reality better in the long run.

Chapter 3, the first example (construction blueprints) after the theoretical introduction, is a study in the formalization of technology. Much of construction technology is routines that may once have been abstractions, but are now embedded in the skills of workers or in implicit operating tactics; it is the same with other technologies. They have often been improved by ideas of the workers about how to cut a corner here, cut another bit of time off there, a habit of adapting to variation in the raw materials at still another point. But in building construction the special features of the technology of a particular building have to be specified in advance, so as to describe the performances of contractors and subcontractors in the contracts. These have to be described well enough so that the contractors can bid on them, and so that the interdependencies of the products of several crafts and contractors fit together and build a solid and functional structure.

The formalities of blueprints, then, have to be good enough abstractions of the substance of a building not yet built so that concrete foundations poured in accordance with them will hold up the building and its contents, so that the partitions into which plumbing and electrical wiring are to be put are wider on the inside than the pipes and conduits that go into them, so that the windows ordered in advance can be fitted into the rough enclosures left by the bricklayers, so that the furnaces fit between the relevant part of the floor and ceiling of the basement, and so on. The argument here is that the function of the formality of blueprints is to reduce the variance in the meaning of technical facts (and the corresponding technological acts that cost money) between what the client transmits to the contractors and what contractors understand, and that one can tell which technical facts matter most by which ones are most formalized in the prints.

I also show that the reduction of ambiguity in the description of the performances of the contractors is created not only by the blueprints, but also by the extensive formalization of the meanings of the technical language of construction (including standards, materials specifications, building codes, apprenticeship textbooks, as well as conventions of blueprint reading) by institutions of the construction industry. Many people make their living by making sure that the substantive formalities of performance description in construction contracts mean the same thing, ultimately, to the craftsmen who weld steel beams together and to the clients who want the building to stand up.

From the point of view of the book as a whole, chapter 3 is intended to be a clear example of a functional argument for serious formality and an intensive analysis of informally embedded formality. gravity causing buildings to fall down is clearly not an arbitrary social definition, but a force of nature, formality should be more developed where gravity causes more problems. The abstractions in it should be related carefully to the substance. Both these facts, if substantiated, will strengthen the argument that formality is sometimes useful.

This allows us to turn to more problematic cases to add more substance to the theory. Easy cases support theory; hard cases improve it. And we can go on to more problematic "needs" in the functional theory without perpetual worry about the social constructionism of "needs," because this one stops convincingly with Newton's laws of gravity.[2]

Chapter 4 is organized around Karl Llewellyn's analysis of the improvement of the abstractions in the law by appellate review of difficult cases (Llewellyn 1960). This is a convenient place to start the analysis of the formalization and reformalization of formal systems, what I have called the "trajectory of improvement." I show how Max Weber's analysis of formal law misses a crucial aspect of trajectories of improvement of formalities, partly by analyzing abstraction badly. I argue that every abstraction can be considered either as a category defined by the features of instances classified within it, or as the complete collection of analogies among instances. Then I argue, with Llewellyn, that often creating modified abstractions by intensively analyzing hard cases is crucial for the rationalization of law, because it helps update the abstractions.

I show Llewellyn's argument to be that one may improve abstractions better by examining the analogies between cases than by asking whether the cases belong in one or another category. New features of the contracts in highly liquid markets, for example, may be better studied by close examination of what a market maker actually "relies on" to conduct its business than by asking whether some particular interpretation of a signal in an auction satisfies the usual legal definition of a reliance. In fact, many of the cases Llewellyn uses hint at the problem we treat more generally in chapter 5. If the reader has trouble with chapter 5, he or she may sympathize with the appellate court judges Llewellyn shows struggling with fraudulent bills of lading as security for credit, or the bankruptcies of foreign exchange dealers all of whose contracts were agreed on by telegraph.

---

2. Newton was actually quite dissatisfied with his causes "acting at a distance," but hoped someone would find a way around it later on. Instead we have got used to it. So the social construction of gravity was more of a problem on the scale of planetary orbits than in architecture, where arches were an ancient invention. If heavy things are harder to hold up than light things, that is enough for exogeneity of the "need" for solid foundations and beams.

The larger purpose of chapter 4 is to show how local disequilibria in social action, due to local bad fit of abstractions and reality, can produce a system for correcting the abstraction system. The appellate court system is exactly one for picking out bad matches between concepts and facts (or between legal conceptual results and "justice" in a given factual situation), and for improving the concepts by analyzing the analogies and distinctions among cases.

Chapter 5 studies cases where formalization is central to social flexibility and responsiveness of a formal system, to what I call "robustness." It is here that we take issue head-on with the tradition that implicitly urges that formality implies rigidity, which then informal devices may render flexible. Liquidity in financial markets has among its purposes making it possible for investors to change their investments easily or to get their money quickly out of their investments for consumption purposes. Formalization can make a great many concrete investments (such as shares in corporations that are a claim on the constantly changing flow of material assets and financial instruments owned at a given time by a corporation) "formally equal" to each other. This equality (the central element of more general commensurability of investments) is central to the liquidity of investments in the financial markets. We (the paper on which the liquidity part of chapter 5 is based had Bruce Carruthers as senior author) study especially the market in secondary mortgage bonds and how heterogeneous assets like houses can become formally equivalent shares of pools based on the mortgages.

I then turn to the way in which budgets, combined with hierarchical arrangements of budget authority, make flexible responses by formal business and nonprofit organizations possible. Without a formalization that bears some resemblance to what happens to concrete assets that turns them into stocks and bonds, the constant reallocation of resources within the firm would be much more difficult. And without formal budget authority within the limits of its spending authorization, each separate department or division would not be able to commit itself, so as to achieve its objectives, until all the uncertainties in other parts of the organization were resolved.

Without formal divisions of spending authority, then, to render responses at the bottom formally "liquid," formal organizations would be as rigid as a market where all the wealth was buried in hoards under people's houses. Because such spending authorities create the right kind of rigidities, to allow the organization to respond by changing budgets or by allowing spending up to budget figures, the organization as a whole is rendered flexible. We will develop the analogy between the flexibility of formal organizations and the flexibility of liquid markets by showing how continuously revised prices and continuously changeable budgetary allocations have the analogous foundations.

The basic argument of chapter 6, on the formal structure of immigration law, is that a formal classification of aliens at the border by the *a priori* probabilities that the agent might find an admissible immigrant, or an alien with a defensible claim to a right of entry or residence, is also a classification by how much payoff there will be to collecting information carefully. Investigating impossible hypotheses is not an efficient way to advance knowledge, whether they are hypotheses in science or in administration. If the hypothesis that a Spanish-speaking person caught swimming the Rio Grande would be an admissible immigrant is sufficiently improbable that "impossible" is a close approximation, then it does not pay an administration to investigate the case with much "due process." Formalization of inattention, by abstract predictions of *a priori* negligible probabilities of being an eligible immigrant or an alien with substantial rights, is then a cruel rationalization of citizenship.

Of course such authoritarian administration and lack of appeal to due process is a dangerous business in a democracy. The citizen and near-citizen population have a great interest in not being caught up by accident in a category that gets no hearings, just "repatriation." Thus the formalization of *lack of access* to due process protections has to be formal because the United States wants to protect citizens and near-citizens. The formalization of rationally grounded willingness to be irrational by not paying attention is itself surrounded by a contrary formalization of rights to an administrative hearing, appeals to the courts, and the like. Thus the meaning of authoritarian carelessness with the rights of people who *a priori* have no right to due process is defined by care (not as much as I would like, but that is a different matter) for those who *do* have an *a priori* case that they are people with rights.

Chapter 7 discusses the semiformal stratification of bits of knowledge in science, with a focus on theorist Imre Lakatos (1978 [1980], 1976a [1961]; Koetsier 1991). Unlike the law, science as such only values a piece of knowledge insofar as it leads to new knowledge. A fact may be true but not matter if it cannot be used to produce new knowledge. This does not, of course, deprive that fact of its engineering usefulness.

Lakatos argues that at any given time, there is a "core" of knowledge in a field of research that is giving rise to new knowledge, and a "periphery" that is too uncertain to rely on, or does not lead anywhere, or otherwise is not as useful for further advance. Thus Einstein's early innovations in quantum mechanics (on black body radiation) were not useful because no one but he knew what to do with them. They became central as quantum mechanics was extended to new findings in specific heat (by Einstein himself), absorption lines in radiation from the sun (by Bohr), and the internal structure of atoms (by Schrödinger, Feynman, and others). One might say that the core moved to incorporate Einstein's results because they were producing new knowledge. Their usefulness then made their perceived incompatibility with interference patterns of radiation into an anomaly; these patterns had been part of the core of the wave theory of radiation, and the anomaly eventually led to the wave theory of subatomic particles. As long as the incompatibility of the quantum theory of black body radiation was not in the core that led to new knowledge, according to this approach, contradictions were not really anomalies.

The stratification by usefulness into core and periphery bears varying and uncertain relations to the epistemological distinction between probably true and uncertain, or between uncertain and probably false. Refereeing and related formal processes for a science are therefore fairly uncorrelated with the stratification of the same knowledge into reliably useful in engineering versus "cutting edge"—into "still research" versus "in development," in turn versus "in pilot plant stage" and "in commodity production." The complexities of these two kinds of stratification of scientific and technical knowledge do much to explain the recurrent conflicts between "pure" and "applied" science. There is then a conflict about the formalities between pure scientific stratification systems that formally have to publish Einstein's early work (that everybody "knew was wrong"), to engineering stratification systems that cut the budgets of impractical speculations like Einstein's.

The conclusion, chapter 8, unifies the theory of the book by contrasting it with Weber's treatment of his distinction between formal law and substantive justice, and by analyzing the interpenetration of formal government of details by abstractions and details not so governed in concrete interaction situations. The continuous variation in the degree to which activities in situations are governed by abstractions makes it a mistake to talk about informal structures and formal structures. Instead we must talk about formalization processes, involving abstraction from details in the situation and validation of government by those abstractions. But in any given situation, some of the actions and interactions escape these processes, or have them to different degrees.

The power that goes with government by abstractions tends to be concentrated on those who can create validated abstractions and make them govern. But I argue that many, probably most, conflicts between "formal" and "informal" aspects of a situation are actually conflicts between different abstractions that might govern, and are misconceived as conflicts between informal and formal ways of proceeding. Many misinterpretations of social life have to do with not looking far enough for abstractions to see where "informal" social life came from and how it came to be justified in a different part of the formal tradition.

FORMALITY AS SOCIAL INTERESTS
RIGHTLY UNDERSTOOD

The upshot of this argument, then, is that the unpopularity of formality in social life is due to the fact that it has been understood by its pathologies. When it works properly it achieves the ends it was built for, the substantive ends that people have decided to pursue. When formality pursues ends alien to us, it is in general because those are the ends of others. It is not the formality that is at fault, but the politics that delivers formal powers to others.

CHAPTER TWO

A REDEFINITION OF THE CONCEPT OF FORMALITY

ANALYZING ABSTRACTIONS

My purpose in this and the next three sections of this chapter is to analyze abstractions, by which I mean to describe important variables that differentiate abstractions and systems of abstractions. In particular I want to so describe those variables that I can relate them to the variations in formality outlined in chapter 1 and, consequently, to the different types of informality also identified there. For example, in this chapter I describe different features of abstractions that describe the *cognitive adequacy* of abstractions to grasp the social life they purport to govern: their accuracy in description, their sufficiency to grasp all that is necessary to govern the action, their cognitive economy that makes them easy to work with, and their scope so that they can govern a wide variety of situations. Cognitive adequacy is the first of the three main variables that make formalization based on the abstractions effective.

I will then want to say what the degreee of cognitive adequacy—high or low—implies for the role of "informally embedded formality," one of the types of informality I mentioned in the introductory chapter. For example, if blueprints governing the construction process are in the course of development, they may be able to be formalized faster if the architect can depend on skills, formally embedded in plumbers' apprenticeships, being informally incorporated into the dimensions of the piping connections; then the architect will not have to specify them. I will also want to say when the system of abstraction just being formalized, another of the types of informality outlined above, has a low (or high) amount of cognitive adequacy. And I will want to know how the classical informality of everyday life and personal relations excluded from the formalized gov-

ernment of activity may supply cognitive adequacy in interpersonal relations on the job, so that the organization's standard operating procedure
need not say when one should say please and thank you.

That is, this and the following three sections have two simultaneous
tasks. They develop a way of describing the abstractions embedded in
formalities so that we can tell whether the abstractions are good enough
to be "serious," in the sense used in this book, in the formal government
of activities. And it describes simultaneously the different ways we should
look for these features of formality when the formality is embedded in
different kinds of informality.

Thus we will expect the electrician governed by the building code, informally embedded in the blueprint of a construction project, or the appellate judge, informally embedded in the process of the lower court by
the possibility of a writ of error, to have a different impact on the system
of action governed by the respective formalities. But this informal embedding of skills and authority in the formalities of the blueprint, and of
the contract of which that blueprint is a formal part, and the different
embedding of the higher court's formality in lower court procedure will
produce different kinds of informality. That informally embedded formality will be directed by different processes from the informality of
judges' and electricians' having, in everyday life, other judges and other
electricians among their friends and colleagues. And both of these will be
different still from the implications for cognitive adequacy of such recent
developments as making formal contracts over the Internet. For example, the "legal fact" of a contract having been "finally signed" has not
been adequately worked out. The formalization of consent that makes a
negotiation over the Internet into a contract is in the process of formalization, and someday a new Karl Llewellyn will have to tell us how the
common law ended up having made such "final signing" clear (see chapter 4).

This introduction to the theory in this chapter is meant to warn the
reader that things get worse before they get better. Each of the major categories of qualities that describe those abstractions good for governing
activities (cognitive adequacy, communicability, and a trajectory of cognitive improvement over time) have various aspects or components that
also must be described so that the variable has some concreteness. But the
units whose formalization we want to diagnose are systems of governing
that have different levels and kinds of informality: they have informally
embedded formalities from elsewhere, or are in the process of developing new formalities, or are embedded in everyday life happening in the
same times and places as formal interaction, but excluded from its government. We have to look into those varying situations, varying ways of

being informal, to see what implications they have for cognitive adequacy, communicability, and trajectory of improvement, and conversely what these different types of relations of informal social life to formal social life mean for the content of the informality.

This is too many things to do at once. The purpose of the case studies of systems formalized in different ways in the rest of the book is in large measure to give repeated concrete expositions of the intersecting variables sketched out in the next three sections.

The three sections that follow, then, consider what I call "cognitive adequacy," "communicability," and "improvement trajectory." The basic idea of the first is that, in order to so grasp the relevant reality that it can be governed effectively, the abstraction system must itself be cognitively adequate to grasp that reality: it has to abstract in a way that is sufficiently accurate that it does not misdescribe the situation being governed and sufficiently economical that it grasps only the part necessary and does so cleanly enough and in an orderly enough fashion that one can think about it easily. The abstraction system must also describe the causes and effects situation fully enough so that it is sufficient for governing, and its reach must be of sufficient scope to cover enough activity to be worth the while. So in describing variations in abstraction systems that make them more or less cognitively effective at a given time, we need to describe what makes them accurate, economical, sufficient, and of wide scope.

The basic idea of the section on communicability is that in social activity, an adequate system of abstraction has to be communicated to those parts of the social system that deal with each part of the reality. It is therefore not enough that some one person have an adequate cognition of the situation; the abstraction has to be communicable, in an adequate form, to the organizations or persons who do the job. The blueprint abstraction of a future building that is cognitively adequate for an architect has to also communicate to the client the purposes the building can serve, for the client has to approve the building before its components are put out to tender. The blueprint has traditionally been translated into a perspective drawing for that purpose. But that blueprint has to communicate also to the subcontractors and craftsmen who pour the foundation so the building will stand up. Classes on reading blueprints would not be offered to both clients and craftspeople if it were sufficient for the architect alone to understand how to build the proposed building.

I argue that to be communicable, an abstraction has be to transmissible to and interpretable by the people who have to do the activity being governed. It also has to be transparent (in the sense of "transparent markets"—a continuous auction makes the current price a transparent reflection of market value, for example), so that people along the path of communication do not have motives or capacities to conceal and distort the abstraction. And it has to be durable in the sense that noise, error, or passage of time do not erase the message in the abstraction. To describe abstraction systems by communicability, then, we need to describe what makes the communication of abstractions through the relevant social system possible in such a way that they still adequately describe the situation: the variables that determine whether an abstraction is transmissible, transparent, and durable.

The section on the trajectory of improvement argues that as the reality changes, or varies over its normal range, the most effective abstraction system for grasping that reality also must change. Thus the question is whether the trajectory of the system improves the grasp of the situation, and especially whether it at least changes fast enough to keep up with changes in the world it is trying to govern. So unless a system of abstraction has embedded ways of improving the abstractions, it will soon not be adequate, and in particular will not be as adequate as other, informal, ways of dealing with the situation.

Much informal social life in organizations reflects an abstraction system that lags behind changes in the world, or that did not grasp it correctly in the first place and formalized its own ignorance. For example, the efficiency of technologies in the average manufacturing firm or farm seems to improve, in recent U.S. history, by about 3 percent per year, about 2 percent by reducing real costs and 1 percent by improving quality. Unless the abstractions in the formal system improve accordingly, in twenty-three years half of the governing system will have to be informal because half of the activity will no longer be grasped by the abstraction system. The three variables by which we describe the improvability of a system of abstractions are correctability in the sense of a system for diagnosing and reviewing mistakes, the development of algorithms that can be perfected or can have options added to them, and the development of robustness, so that the system can continue to abstract correctly under a greater variety of circumstances.

COGNITIVE ADEQUACY

By the cognitive adequacy of a system of abstraction, I mean the likelihood that application of the system to a situation in the social or physical world in which action is required will yield a picture that can guide action. This means (1) that it accurately portrays the world in a manner that (2) is cognitively economical (it does not have much noise and is not difficult to grasp) to work with to yield the correct diagnosis and the correct remedy, (3) that the description is full enough to include all the aspects of the situation relevant to the action to be taken, and finally (4) that the scope to which the abstraction system applies is wide enough that most situations that have to be acted on are included. An abstraction system that is high in accuracy, economy, sufficiency, and scope is then high in cognitive adequacy. A system of formality that is low in cognitive adequacy will not be good enough to govern action effectively, and so formalization without cognitive adequacy will not be serious. The explanation of formalization with abstractions that have low cognitive adequacy, that are "ritualistic," will therefore be explained by different theories than those developed in this book. For example, as mentioned in chapter 1, the formal system for deluding the members of the British empire that slavery was abolished, while creating "labor markets" that left very few decisions to the former slaves, was not meant to be sufficiently cognitively accurate so that the English public could know what was really going on.

Accuracy

By accuracy I mean that there is not much error in the abstraction. Llewellyn (1960, 195) formulated this criterion for law as follows: "Besides economy and efficiency, the rule of law requires rightness. The situation must be rightly grasped, the criterion rightly seen, the effect neatly devised to purpose, else neither clarity nor economy of language can serve true beauty."

Criminal convictions are, for example, a poor measure of the crime rate ("an inaccurate abstraction"), because most crimes do not lead to arrest and most crimes cleared by arrest do not produce convictions. So while a criminal trial is relatively transparent in the sense that it is very clear where the decision came from and that it was, in principle at least, dispassionate and objective, and that decision is easily communicated to the prison system or to the appeals court if necessary, it ordinarily has low accuracy. We hope that not many innocent people are convicted, but know that many of the guilty go free.

Victim surveys that do not depend on connecting a crime to a given offender are much more accurate in estimating the crime rate and show much higher crime rates than do convictions. A victim survey is more formalized than the average conversation, but much less formalized than a criminal trial, or even than a plea bargain. But it does not abstract the right part of the evidence—whether a particular person has been proved guilty, is not hedged about with the right of the person charged to defend themselves, and the like—that can put someone in prison. The error in conviction rates is largest for crimes such as burglary that are hard to pin on an offender but that leave clear traces that people will remember in victim surveys. Incompleteness, such as unsolved burglaries, is an especially frequent kind of inaccuracy.

Sometimes an abstraction is inaccurate because good government of an activity does not require accuracy about a given matter. As outlined in chapter 3, the dimensions telling the relation between plumbing pipes or electrical conduit and the bearing structure are ordinarily left out of construction blueprints, and the thickness of the paint is always left out. This is because the relevant dimensions are better left to the craft workers. These deliberate inaccuracies are routinely taught to both architects and craft workers, so there is no lack of transparency in them. Not all formality governs all relevant aspects of the activities it governs, and the parts not formally governed therefore need not be accurate in the abstractions.

Cognitive Economy

By cognitive economy I mean the degree to which nothing unnecessary to the governing purpose is included in the abstraction, and that the abstraction is in a form that is easy to think about. Clearly all the information in a sufficient statistic of, say, the regression coefficient of grades in graduate school on Graduate Record Examination (GRE) scores was in the original data set.[1] But it is far more useful to know, for the purposes of running an arts and sciences graduate program, whether one can predict future scholarly performance from that coefficient alone, or whether instead one also needs the graduate recruitment committee's *Gestalt* about a student after having read the whole file. One does not want to read all the data points in order to estimate the impact, so if one wants the regression coefficient one wants a sufficient statistic. But one wants to know whether the *Gestalt* is better than the test alone, since it is expensive to read enough to get the *Gestalt*.

If one can dispense with the expensive information of faculty judgment, then the regression of performance on test scores is both sufficient in the statistical sense and also cognitively economical. If however the *Gestalt* has a significant coefficient in predicting future scholarly performance (for example, in a regression equation that also contains the test scores), then the economy of a regression is a false economy. If, for example, grades in graduate school are not a good measure of scholarly creativity, and if faculty *Gestalt* does pick up signs of creativity, then a suf-

---

1. A statistic is sufficient for estimating a given parameter if there is no information about the parameter in the data that is not used in to improve the estimate. A statistic that is a sufficient estimate of a misspecified model is not sufficient in our sense, because there is unused information that could be used to estimate the coefficient of the right model.

ficient statistic of the regression of graduate school grades on GRE scores is a coefficient in the wrong model; it is not in fact sufficient for graduate admissions, so its economy is false. Cognitive economy then is abstraction of only that information that is factually sufficient. Surprisingly often, the impression people have of knowing more because they have spent time reading the file is wrong, and a crude quantitative predictor works as well or better (Saks and Hastie 1978, 59–60).[2]

Cognitive economy pays off especially well when the additional information is itself biased and actually adds error. If the *Gestalt* has a good deal of sexism in it, while course grades plus test scores have less, and if gender has no impact on scholarly contributions (the difference, if any, is nowadays so minute that it is not useful in policy), then having the "full context" is positively destructive. There is much evidence to suggest that informal social life is very often more bigoted than formal social life, that, for example, college friendships are more segregated by gender and race than college classrooms. In such cases formal abstraction may be getting rid of systematic informal bias.

Conversely one of the reasons for the right to "confront" the witnesses in a trial (rather than just taking depositions) in American legal proceedings is that the court and the jury can see body language that may indicate witness uncertainty or deception, or see thoroughgoing competence and objectivity of an expert witness on minor matters so that his or her testimony on a major matter is more believable. It is especially the response of the witness to cross-examination that is indicative. Thus in particular situations the right to the *Gestalt* may be formalized; the judicial wisdom of including body language in the evidence, by protecting the right of confrontation, has not been very well studied.

The point here is that the whole criminal justice system incorporates aspects of the informality of everyday life so that any wisdom of jurors or judges in bench trials about when a person is lying is to the benefit of the accused. Not having the credibility of witnesses built into the formal legal part of the system (as, in early English law, government documents were considered authoritative on their face, and oral testimony inferior to them) therefore may improve the system.

In chapter 6, however, I analyze a case in which the highest degree of cognitive adequacy is sacrificed to economy. The basic argument there is that in immigration matters, the right to have one's case dealt with in a cognitively adequate way, or indeed to have it dealt with at all, is strictly

2. Specifically they say, "When the same information is available to both a human decision maker and a mathematical model, almost without exception the mathematical model makes more reliable and accurate predictions. In sixty studies comparing clinical and statistical prediction, the humans beat the computer only once. . . ."

limited. This is not because justice is unimportant in immigration matters but rather that, as understood by the Immigration and Naturalization Service and by the federal courts, justice is to be dispensed only to those who are moderately likely to have a good case. The economy that makes cognition "adequate" then dominates all other criteria of adequacy, except for those people who have a moderately good chance of having a case for being admitted to the United States.

Sufficiency

By sufficiency[3] I mean the degree to which everything essential to the governing purposes for a given situation is extracted from the relevant reality. (It is distinct from "scope," analyzed below, which refers to how many situations a system of abstractions is sufficient for; sufficiency generally has to do with having abstracted all the relevant causes and effects that work in a given situation.) Thus a crime has a number of components. The components of rape, for example, are the intention, the act (e.g., penetration), the identity of the person who did the act, mental and other competence of that alleged criminal, and the lack of consent by the victim. The prosecuting attorney's abstractions form the components of a prosecution "case," that is, the attempted proofs of each component of the formal crime. These are arguments that the facts in evidence can be abstracted to substantiate intention, penetration, identity, competence, and lack of consent, and so abstracted to be the crime of rape. Together with any corrections to that evidence the defense can offer, such abstractions from testimony and other evidence are "sufficient" to the degree that they establish all those components. Insufficiency is then simplified into "not guilty" (and not indictable for the same offense in the future),[4] while sufficiency becomes "guilty." The abstraction that results—a finding of guilty or not guilty—does not have to be retried by the prison system before it takes the appropriate action.

3. Much of this discussion of sufficiency is derived from Heimer 1985. She distinguishes between technically sufficient conditions written into a marine insurance contract (that is, those sufficient to estimate the risk correctly and to control it) from those socially sufficient (that is, accepted in the secondary insurance market which splits the risks internationally). Her discussion is more subtle than is needed here, but is needed to understand the formalization of some kinds of contracts. This kind of subtlety is more relevant in chapter 5 when we turn to the problem of formalizing transactions so that they can enter into secondary financial markets.

4. The definition of "same" is tricky sometimes. The legal theory of *res judicata* is that neither the government nor an individual can insist that a case already tried can be tried again, unless there are grounds for appeal, or jurisdiction on a related matter in a different court. It is perhaps the best example of our concept that formalities ordinarily make going back to the substance of the matter unnecessary, or in this case not permitted.

Similarly the axioms necessary for the logical derivation of a mathematical proposition, combined with that derivation, are sufficient to the proof unless another mathematician finds an error or a contrary case. It is central to the logic of mathematics that a contrary case only proves the insufficiency of the axioms used to prove the theorem, as discussed in chapter 7 on science; if one postulates that the axioms are sufficient, then of course it disproves at least that postulate of sufficiency.

Sufficiency then depends on whose behavior one wants to govern, for what purpose, in what situation. Convincing prison officials to put and keep someone in jail for a crime has different requirements than those for convincing other mathematicians of a theorem in a given axiomatic system. For example, showing that the evidence for a rape could have been produced without the intention to rape would have a very different impact (failure to convict) than showing that the conclusion of a theorem did not require the axiom that the function be everywhere continuous. The first would make the evidence insufficient. The second would make the axioms in the proof more than sufficient, because the result followed from a weaker condition: deriving a proposition from fewer, or weaker, axioms makes the proposition more "robust," an important mathematical virtue.

Particularly important subcases of sufficiency are that (a) in a perfect market, all information known by market participants bearing on the present and future value of a commodity is incorporated in its price; (b) a reliable technology for a given purpose is sufficient if the same skills and machinery produce the same quantity and quality of output under widely varying conditions; (c) a person's test score is sufficient for hiring if no other information about competence is useful or required to predict job performance; (d) a statistic is sufficient if it leaves no information in the data unincorporated in the parameter (left instead in the "residuals") that could improve the parameter estimate. Thus a price is insufficient information if the market is not perfect, a technology is insufficient if not reliable, a test score is insufficient if experience predicts performance better, and a parameter estimate is insufficient if information about its value can be extracted from the residuals. It is important to realize that many formal systems require people to act on insufficient information, and they sometimes take that explicitly into account. For example, the amount of evidence required for an arrest is normally much less, and is subjected to much less test and presentation of contrary evidence, than is the information required for conviction; arrests then are systematically made on the basis of what is considered elsewhere in the criminal law system to be insufficient evidence.

In general, if the abstraction in a formality is sufficient, there is no reason for the governing process based on the formality to review the reality behind the abstraction; for instance, the required majorities of a legislative vote are sufficient information, for most purposes, about the preferences and reasoning of all the legislators, and one need not delve into those preferences to execute the law. Note that in the case of an arrest, however, it is explicitly provided that the court trial go behind the evidence that convinced a policeman.

Scope

By the scope of an abstraction system I mean the degree to which all the reality that is supposed to be governed by that abstraction is effectively covered by it. Sometimes this is spoken of as the "power" or "depth" of an abstraction system. Thus a "standard" (say for steel pipe) promulgated by a professional society or by government inspection authorities, and then incorporated into specifications for contracts or purchase orders, has a larger scope than the quality control procedures of a particular factory. One purpose of having such standards with wide scope, as Bruce Carruthers and I discuss in chapter 5, is so that price competition between comparable products can be created, markets may be extended in space and over time, and options on comparable products in the future may be created. Governing activities on a large scale depends on increasing the scope of the relevant abstractions to correspond to the scope of the government. Of course it often is wise to go behind the formal standard and to contract with a supplier who regularly exceeds the quality requirements of the standard, rather than limiting oneself to the letter of the regulation.

Cognitive Adequacy and Types of Informality

The first type of informality identified in chapter 1, informally embedded formality—like the informal embedding of electrical standards in a blueprint by showing an electrical connection draped over structural details without connection—gives an inaccurate, very economical, and insufficient picture of what is going to happen in the government of activity. This is because it does not portray the abstraction *system* including the electrical standards, the training of the electrician, and so on, that will fill the gap. In the case of the embedding of the standards of an appeals court into the lower court, it is at the discretion of the higher court (and before that, of the appealing attorney) whether the higher court will govern a particular bit of action in the lower court.

What is going on here is that economy in the abstraction system is being gained at the expense of accuracy, sufficiency, and scope of the abstraction represented, respectively, in the blueprint or in the lower court procedure. The whole system with the appeals court's abstractions and the abstract electrical standards, together with the discretionary and informal incorporation of them into the governing system, has higher accuracy, sufficiency, and scope *because of its informal elements formalized elsewhere*. In particular, one does not incorporate appeals courts or cosmopolitan electrical standards into lower court procedure or general building contracts *unless* one thinks they are sufficiently formalized elsewhere to bear up under the reliance that will be put upon them.

Appeals are rare, because the assumption is that past appeals decisions will be incorporated into the lower courts. Such incorporation of past appeals decisions makes the lower courts more nearly sufficient in the future. Turning over the electrical standards to the electrical contractor and the building inspector is essentially universal in the United States, because they are reliable parts of an overall abstraction system governing the construction of buildings. It is the system, not the blueprint, that ensures that safe electrical systems are installed in practically all buildings, of very different designs. The system does that job better and more cheaply than architects' specifications could do.

When the overall government of activity is informal in the sense of "formality being constructed," it is likely to produce efforts to make the abstraction system more accurate, economical, sufficient, and of wider scope. When, for example, gypsum board replaced gypsum plaster as the material for the interior walls of most houses, different trades were then involved in placing the interior walls (in the United States, carpenters replaced plasterers) and producing a smooth finish on the seams to be painted or wallpapered (painters or carpenters replaced plasterers).

The formalities that specified the fire protection qualities of plastered walls, and the contractual formalities of who was to do the skilled work and so whose standards would reign, also had to change. In some very abstract sense, gypsum is equally hard and equally fire resistant in both forms, but that is not a sufficient abstraction to get the walls built properly. It was clear what the end result for fire regulation had to be, and after the unions fought it out it was clear who the contracts had to rely on to install them. But the abstractions had to be brought into conformity with the new situation. Fire regulations, for example, had to be stated in terms of the standard manufactured thicknesses of gypsum wallboard (to ensure accuracy); subcontracts had to be written with the contractors of the crafts with new jurisdiction (to get scope). Only then could the overall specifications govern the new situation.

More difficult problems of new situations requiring new formalities, and what they had to be cognitively adequate for, are described in chapter 4 (large flows of documents in financial markets in the late nineteenth and early twentieth century) and chapter 5 (the transformation by Fannie Mae of claims on particular houses by particular homeowners into standardized bonds in the secondary mortgage market, to produce a liquid investment market).

Classical informality has been mainly important for analyzing cognitive adequacy in the sociology of work. Many of the bugs in engineering plans are worked out by the workers, and workers quite regularly eventually bring the productivity of their machines to above the "design capacity" specified by the designers. Management would, in general, like to appropriate that learning by skilled and expensive workers and teach it to lower paid workers.

But it has turned out to be very hard for management to find out what it was that the workers (eventually) came to know about running the machines that the engineers did not, and to incorporate it into abstract formal teaching and job descriptions for new workers (Thomas 1994). Eliciting the cooperation of those workers turns out to be a delicate matter, and it is more delicate if management does not want to let them get part of the benefits to be realized by the skills they have developed, for example by higher wages. This is a situation in which the formal system is not, perhaps cannot be, sufficient to govern the cognitive adequacy that workers supply. That is a problem about whose interests are represented in the formalities the management would like to introduce; when unions or cooperatives introduce them, technical change is easier but more expensive. Sometimes this has severe structural implications, as when Cornish immigrant hardrock miners *would* not teach Mexican immigrant laborers to be miners in the Southwest, and management *could* not teach them (Boswell and Brueggemann 2000).

It is important to realize that many systems of formality do not satisfy the high standards I have just specified. For example, Meyer and Rowan (1977) argue that many of the things we want adults to be able to do as a result of schooling, we do not in fact know how to teach. This means, then, that the standards of schooling are substitutes for cognitively adequate standards; they show that students can do algebra tests rather than that they can, for example, formulate the equations relating the quality of raw materials to the temperatures at which they have to be processed. Meyer and Rowan argue that in such circumstances, the standards are pure products of socially instituted belief *about what* is rational rather than *by what* is in fact rational—that they are empty formality. The example I gave earlier of estimating how good the GRE scores are at predicting scholarly eminence, by estimating how well they predict graduate school grades, is another example of formality that may be empty.

COMMUNICABILITY

The basic idea of this section is that cognition has to be social—that is, effectively communicated—before putting authority behind it makes it effective in governing of social activity. Formality, then, is a discourse and, as in all discourse, the relation between what a statement means to its issuer and its receiver is problematic. For example, authority does no good if the person who is supposed to obey does not get, or does not understand, the order. This means that the abstraction system has to produce abstractions that can be transmitted to, understood by, and believed in by a receiver of the abstraction. Surely part of the reason Max Weber maintained that teaching was central to rationalization, for example of theologies, is that it is a requirement of a teacher (and so of the teachers' processing of the abstraction) that he or she communicate its meaning to the students.

But further, for an abstraction to be socially effective it has to both resist corruption by the interests and ideologies of intervening people and organizations in a transmission network, and resist degredation from random errors, misunderstandings, failures to check the message against the original, and the like. That is, an abstraction needs to be transmissible (in which we will include understandablility and believability), transparent (or incorruptible by interests and ideologies), and durable (resisting degredation by noise and confusion).

Transmissibility

By transmissibility I mean that those who will use the abstraction can receive it, understand it in the way appropriate to its abstraction process, and believe that it is a valid transmission from a source that is using it correctly. Transmissibility is central to most social uses of formality. One makes statutes transmissible to courts and lawyers by writing them in language that has a determinate legal meaning, established by precedent if possible. Transmission of payments by checks depends on reliable validation of the identity of the transmitter ("signature authority") and receiver, as well as the careful keeping of accounts by banks; in particular, accuracy is crucially ensured by sending the accounts and canceled checks back to the interested parties.

Messages are more transmissible through multiple links if they are written, if the communications media have low ambiguity and low error rates, if they are checked with the original before retransmission, if attention is called to the differences between the correct message and the one the receiver might expect (that is, if unusual or new provisions are "flagged"), if the receiver is not required to remember more than five or six digits, and so on. (For example, the all-number telephone address system was known to be inefficient for orally communicating one's telephone number when it was introduced.) The extensive set of norms and techniques for copy reading and fact checking of manuscripts are a good example of structures that increase transmissibility. Similarly the standardization of the names of various stocks on the stock page, the standardization of prices by giving a number for opening price, high, low, and close, and doing the subtraction for the change of stock prices are oriented toward transmissiblity of market information. Organizations sometimes forbid employees to talk among themselves in other languages, because this undermines the formal system's monopoly over what is to be transmitted and what is not.

Transparency

By transparency I mean the degree to which every aspect of the abstraction process is known, or could be examined, by everyone the formality touches. Since it is the relation of abstractions to reality that makes it wise for abstractions to govern, trust in the abstracting process is central to the legitimacy of formality. Sometimes only the fairness of the abstracting process is required, so that no one be especially advantaged, as when "insider trading" based on privileged information is effectively controlled in the stock market. The future of the value of a stock may be poorly known, but as long as no one knows it any better than another, the price is "fair."

But sometimes one insists that the abstraction be carried out in a way that produces truth rather than "mere" consensus, as in mathematical proofs. In either case, what is crucial is that one knows whether an abstraction was produced in a way that makes it worthy to govern a given activity.

Transparency is especially important in markets. The ideal of a transparent or "incorruptible" market is a continuous open auction of a standard commodity, such as shares of stock or a standard quantity of graded wheat, in a place where multiple buyers meet multiple sellers and no potential buyers or sellers are excluded. That is, the highly transmissible set of stock prices mentioned above are also transparent insofar as the prices represent multiple sales of shares in the presence of many alternative bidders on both sides of the market, managed by a market maker who maintains a continuous auction in that stock. When a market is "thin," meaning that a price does not represent many trades or there are not many alternative buyers and sellers, then the price is not as transparent, though it may be highly transmissible.

But clearly the transparency variable pervades communications. Ideology, for example, has much less to do with whether a mathematics teacher and the student believe a proof than with whether a theology teacher, and then the student, believe a proof that Christ is the Son of God rather than a very distinguished monk and preacher in what was then an obscure Jewish sect. That is, the transmission of theology is less transparent than the transmission of mathematical proofs.

Transparency is particularly likely to be undermined by fraud and its near relatives, which always must be organized informally because, if fraud is formally and publicly known, it does not work. Insider trading based on informal communication among corporate insiders and their agents, for example, does not give advantage if the bid and its originators enter immediately into the formal information system. Obviously insider trading is most profitable if the market looks transparent but is not, and much ingenuity has gone into various schemes for producing that situation (Shapiro 1984).

Durability

By durability I mean the degree to which the quality of a message involving an abstraction does not decay over time, and particularly does not decay with multiple retransmissions. Information may decay by the transmission's being imperfect, by the failing memory of an individual or organization, by being difficult to find again, by having been explicitly ephemeral in the first place, by changes in the world making it inaccurate, by water damage or passing through a magnetic field, by book burning, by becoming irrelevant to social life.[5] Durability is especially important for extending the government of a line of activity in time and space, and for correctability. A correction that is not preserved until it would be useful is effectively not a correction. An activity that takes place after an abstraction is corrupted is not effectively governed by it. Durability of an abstraction is the opposite of *ad hoc* reasoning. No doubt writing is the central social institution that increases durability of abstractions, and qualifying examinations, in schools and in the professions, that check the understanding of words and subject matter by future transmitters (especially when the examinations are written) are probably second in importance.

Communicability and the Types of Informality

Very often the raw materials to produce transparency have to be embedded in the larger system rather than in the system of formality that actu-

---

5. On irrelevancies being forgotten, see Mary Douglas's account of the work of Edward Evans-Pritchard (1986; 1981 [1980], 75–90). When treasures take physical form, moth and rust do corrupt, and thieves break in and steal; when they take verbal form in accounts or certificates of ownership of shares, entropy is enough to lose the lot.

ally governs action, because transparency requires impartiality. The reason the accounts of corporations have to be audited by outsiders is that insiders have motives to corrupt information about their own managerial performance. The practice of writing some things down, and leaving other things oral, is often a way of demarcating what is to be formally preserved and what informally renegotiated in the future. Of course conversely this means that communications that do not have third-party auditing, such as most advertising, are quite likely to be either information free or fraudulent, and oral contracts often do not hold up in court because they were not intended to hold up.

The central point here is that the cognitive adequacy of an abstraction makes no social difference unless it can reach the point of application in uncorrupted form. The social arrangements that increase the probability of arrival and reduce the probability of corruption are therefore central to formal government. The fact that the best single indicator of the variation from formality to informality is whether or not it is written shows the importance of this criterion.

Informally embedded formality deals with the problem of communicability by breaking it into two parts: a simple language that does the embedding, and a more complicated specialist language for the actual government of the activity. The assembler of a computer need not be able to read the design information about a chip, as long as that design information is well transmitted within the chip supplier. This in its turn is enabled by the sophisticated teaching and learning of communications within the specialist community, and a certification or quality control process that guarantees that the specialist standards will be used.

Thus a scientist using a measuring instrument is required to "calibrate" it so as to show in a research paper that it does indeed measure what it is supposed to, in the units it is supposed to use. Specifying the concentration of a solution in "parts per million," for example, certifies that the relevant measurements that went into the report were made with standard instruments calibrated in a standard way, in keeping with the standards of the specialist community.

This concentration may actually be measured by a "subcontract" with the supplier of reagents, who does the actual calibrations. Thus the use of the formalities of standardization of measurement may have a double formal embedding, first by the scientist informally embedding the measurement in the paper, then by the supplier of reagents incorporating his calibrations in the (often implicit) "quality control contract" with scientists. It might even be the case occasionally that the scientist would not know, without looking it up and then fooling with it until he gets it right, how to produce the concentration and how to calibrate its measurement.

The scientist certifies with his education and reputation that he or she will be responsible to the formalities embedded in the paper, and the supplying company by its reputation and skilled staff that the concentration was indeed produced to the standard.

In the following quotation from a catalog of anchors used to fasten things to steel or masonry structures, the requirement for certification is made explicit: "As in all application, the load capacity and other criteria used should be reviewed and verified by the design professional responsible for the actual product installation." (Powers Rawl 1998, 30 ff). Here the supplier certifies the strength of the fastener for standard conditions, and the "design professional" is required to certify that the standard conditions are met in a particular building situation.

For our special purposes here, a "certificate" is an assurance that, behind the informality of, say, an electrician's competence, there lies a complex system of abstractions governing his or her activity. It is an assurance that one can let a gap in one's own abstractions be filled by other competent formal government, without having to go behind the certificate. The supplier of reagents to a chemist has similar certificates of the quality control system, so that the scientist can (usually) trust them without poking through the factory. The notion that a certificate is merely a renaming of a position of privilege is incompatible with the fact that knowledgeable men and women often do not go behind it, even when they are competent to do so.

Bruce Carruthers and I, in chapter 5, go into some detail about the complex formal network that turns a house and its new owner into security for a debt to the mortgage bank, of sufficient solidity that it can be sold, eventually, as a security in the secondary mortgage market. From the point of view of that secondary market, the house and the new owner are a gap in their financial knowledge. Title insurers, fire insurers, credit rating agencies, real estate appraisers, issuing banks, and federal market-making agencies like Fannie Mae, turn mortgages into pools by filling the gap in the certified information about the market value of the house, the legality of the title, and the creditworthiness of the new owner. Fannie Mae then certifies that the gap has been filled, that the mortgages are as good as they ought to be. They certify that the appraiser's activity, for example, is informally embedded formality in the transformation of a house into a mortgage-backed security, by requiring that they be independent of both the house buyer and the loan-issuing bank.

We can often see "formality being constructed" for communicability in the acknowledgements pages of textbooks, where the authors thank many classrooms of students for putting up with preliminary versions of the book, for making suggestions, and presumably for getting questions on obscure passages wrong on the examinations in ways that showed the authors where there were problems in transmissibility. The informality of formality being constructed often includes periods of intense "supervision" of the formalities being introduced, because the designers of the formality cannot tell what needs fixing without seeing what goes wrong.[6]

Social relations outside the system of formal, usually written, communications very often carry guesses about what the real meaning of an ambiguous formality might be. Very often speculations about the motives of those who have created or are in charge of implementing a formality pass through channels of gossip, as do speculations about how serious the government by the formality is likely to be. Formalities are usually cloaked in a penumbra of seriousness and impersonality, with the punishments and rewards for actually governing activity by the formality often deliberately vague. In particular, what resources will be devoted to the new formalities are often not specified. Educational reforms are especially likely to require that teacher and student time be spent on something new, without specifying any other use of time that can be cut back to make room for it. Teachers therefore have to sort out informally what of the new, and what of the old, are most easily sacrificed. They may, of course, supply their own ideology about what can be most easily sacrificed, and may exchange ideological talk on that question with the other teachers they trust. But such informal challenges to formally certified abstractions are often measures of the bad quality of the formality: an educational reform that requires time without specifying where it is to come from is a toy reform, richly deserving the contemptuous gossip that surrounds it.

TRAJECTORY OF IMPROVEMENT

The portrait of abstraction thus far painted is rigid and static. Of course if a static abstraction cannot govern, the government of activities cannot be improved without drastically improving the abstraction. But if formalizing immediately killed human creativity, it could only have a short-run advantage over informality. There is, of course, something to that. Almost everyone has been subjected to formal authority determined to forbid every sensible action. One railroad magnate offered the generalization: "You can't build a railroad within the law." And the scientist who never thought that his problem was to tell lies to the National Science Foundation (NSF) probably did not get the grant. Our argument here is

6. Gouldner 1954a and 1954b are early studies of this process, and among the features of the informal period while a new formality was being constructed, partly produced by this intense supervision, was a wildcat strike.

hat if abstraction systems do not improve, more and more of the legal, electrical, and scientific formal organization will become nothing but fraud and ritual. Sociologists have a tendency to think that most formality is of that sort—fraud and ritual. One of the best ways to check whether it is likely to be fraud and ritual is to ask whether there is an effective set of devices to improve the abstractions in the system.

Our basic argument, then, is that no system of formality can last unless it can improve its abstraction of reality; at the very least, changed realities have to be incorporated as they develop. For example, part of the purpose of peer review in the NSF system of approving grants for scientific research is to improve the standards for the judgment of projects over time, so that they track the frontiers of science. Of course such "peers" can improve the system of standards only up to the standard of what they know, or can guess, about those frontiers. This embeds formalized scientific discourse as a whole (the science's "paradigm" for finding new knowledge) into the bureaucracy of NSF, just as electricians' formalized competencies are embedded in blueprints. Both such embedded formalities in particular embed the updating of, respectively, paradigms and of electrical standards.

Correctability

It is a feature of all discourse that people and organizations abstract, and the abstraction sometimes ends up being a false description, or people do not know what abstraction should be transmitted, or make mistakes, or misspeak, or send the right message to the wrong people. Receivers may misunderstand the message even if it is right, especially if the words or sentences carry a penumbra of meaning that was not intended. Changes in the situation can make correct messages, even if correctly understood in the past, no longer adequate grounds for governing action.

Abstraction systems usually have various kinds of abstraction-correcting mechanisms built into them. Science in particular has a whole series of correction routines, including refereeing, repeating experiments with more foolproof methods, deriving new results and testing them, improving the calibration procedure for measuring instruments, and so on. Legal systems have appeals courts, reinterpretation of contracts according to business practice, extensive restatements of bodies of law by bar associations, passing new statutes, and developing administrative regulations (and having hearings on them) to achieve the purposes of the law. In addition, business people routinely use the rigidities of contract law to write new provisions into contracts; in operation, contract law is very different today from that in the oldest precedents still used, because the contracts are different.

The correctability of a particular abstraction, then, is the degree that it is on an expectable trajectory of correction, so that it will be better in the future just as it is better now than in the past. If today's abstraction is on average better than yesterday's, but worse than tomorrow's, it is highly correctable. If an abstraction system tracks changes in the world, so that, for example, safety seats for children are exempted from the luxury tax on automobile accessories when they come to be required by law, then the system is correctable.

Robustness

By robustness I mean developing abstractions that abstract correctly, for the purposes at hand, in more different situations. For example, the obvious way for a department of a department store to measure the overall success of a product line's design and marketing is total sales. A more robust way is to measure the rate of growth or decline of total sales, because very large sales do not mean the same thing if last year's sales were very large too; it may in fact be that sales have declined. A still more robust way is to measure the rate of growth or decline of the store's market share for the category of products that are near substitutes for a firm's product. A decline in sales does not mean the same thing if everyone in the market has lost sales, perhaps because of a general recession, and if one's own market share has actually increased.

Similarly the quality control of steel beams is more robust when acoustic or x-ray imaging can find faults that are internal to the beam, and such inspections are substituted for inspecting the surface of the beam only. A decision on an academic promotion is more robust if the departmental committee waits until two books by the candidate have been reviewed by peers, rather than deciding after only one. All these more robust abstracting processes give adequate cognition under changing circumstances.

Clearly one can improve abstraction systems by improving robustness. But in some sense robust measures built in from the beginning ensure that one is more likely to get good analyses out of one's formality farther into a changing future. If one's abstraction system uses control groups, large samples, and other devices that make abstractions more robust it will respond more flexibly to change.

The main feature of institutional structures and organizations that indicates robustness of the abstraction system is flexibility. In chapter 5, Bruce Carruthers and I analyze the main market institutions that arrange for flexibility, namely, those that make markets "liquid." Liquid resources can be devoted quickly to new purposes, so that economically rational reactions can be worked out to changing conditions. I extend the mechanisms identified in that analysis to the arrangements in formal organizations that make them flexible in response to changes in their environment. Carruthers and I argue that formality of particular kinds is essential to socially organized flexibility, or robustness.

Algorithms and Reasoning Devices

One of the main uses of formality is to bring activities within the purview of reasoning devices—algorithms—that relate abstractions to each other. Blueprints properly constructed make sure that the planned sum of the room dimensions and wall thickness dimensions add up to the planned outside dimensions of the building. A weight-bearing algorithm supplements the blueprint's graphic algorithm to give sizes for foundations sufficiently strong to bear the weight of the building above them (and the weight of the books in the building, if it is to be a library), to be then entered into the relevant part of the blueprint.

Accounting is a system of algorithms for various purposes (Stinchcombe 1990, 84–87), which require, for example, that all causes of the value of commodities appear as costs. Any supervisor who ignored causes of good performance that were free would, of course, be fired for ineffectiveness, so cost accounts are clearly not sufficient for industrial management. They are however very useful algorithms for some purposes, for example for pricing decisions.

While technical drawings and calculations based on them, and accounts, are central to the formality of formal organizations, not all the formality involves algorithmic processing of the abstracted symbols. Standard operating procedures, background provisions ("boilerplate") in contracts, organization charts, legal maxims such as old regime French, "*Nulle terre sans seigneur*" (roughly: "No jurisdiction can be without a judge"), sequences of review for purchase orders, and the like are usually nonalgorithmic. They are abstractions, but one cannot calculate with them. In general, quantification is for the purpose of using algorithms, hoping that the addition and subtraction of numbers corresponds to a relevant addition or subtraction of real things. Algorithms generally cannot make use of "contextual" information unless it is extremely regular, as for instance the sum of small random causes producing a normal distribution of "errors" is a manageable "context" for statistics.[7] Most bureaucracies do not use the information on the probable sizes of errors in their governing processes, and it is very difficult to get information about such sizes of average errors into legal proceedings (Lempert 1997).

7. See Stinchcombe 1978, 5–7, for what is required in the way of abstraction for items to be counted.

This of course implies that both the abstraction of the units that make up the quantities, and the algorithms for extracting from the quantities those abstractions that should govern, can be improved. Algorithms can become more accurate, more robust, more flexible in the sense that there are more options among the alternative calculations that can be done. But the original quantities can be improved as well. Inventories can be evaluated, rather than at historical cost, at values nearer to what they can be sold for (net of costs of selling), or nearer to what they could be replaced for (gross price of bought goods in inventory, including costs within the organization of getting them into the inventory), depending on how the inventory values are to be used. The quantity that then goes into the account, to be fed into the relevant algorithms for capital evaluation, taxation purposes, and so on, can itself be improved by making more accurate abstractions before calculation.

Informality and Trajectories of Improvement

Informally embedded formalities from elsewhere can be improved either by improving the abstractions elsewhere (as when seed is improved in agricultural experiment stations and seed companies rather than on the farm), or by improving the embedding (as by the diffusion of seed appropriate for the ecological situation of particular farms). Thus the formal research and development of the experiment stations and seed companies can be updated in its own scientific system, and the informality of diffusion from experiment stations then will update the farms with close contacts to the station quickly, those farther away more slowly. If one could improve the embedding—for example by recruiting leading local farmers as planters of experimental varieties on one plot, traditional varieties on another—so that they were actively involved in the local testing and development of cultivation techniques, then the trajectory of improvement would move faster as well.

In some sense our second type of informality, comprising the development phase of formality, is simply the first stage of a trajectory of improvement. It could be collapsed into this section as merely the type of informality one has when one is on a trajectory of improvement of replacing informality. But this loses the delicacy of the relations between informality and creativity in formal systems. So it is wise to go into creativity here as a special kind of informality (this problem is considered at length in chapter 7.) For present purposes, such creativity broadens the reach of an abstraction system or improves its grasp of reality by forging improvements in the system that have permanent value.

Thus creativity is measured with respect to the abstraction system it improves. Relativity in physics, for example, improved the theory of gravitation by making it consistent with the developing theory of electromagnetic radiation, and specifically with the fact that electromagnetic energy transmits causes across space faster than any other known relation between causes and effects. It unified the abstractions developed by Maxwell and Newton. The mathematics developed by Lorenz, motivated by the fact that the speed of light was the same when measured in the direction of the earth's movement and perpendicular to that movement, modified Maxwell's equations to be compatible with that fact. But these were then incompatible with the Newtonian formulation of space and distance, and it was that incompatibility that Einstein's proposed theory solved. It could fit as an addition to physics because both Maxwell's and Newton's abstractions had a solid existence in the activities of many physicists. It explained why Newton was just about right, and Maxwell was just about right, and showed that Lorenz had been on the right track. This is, of course, an extreme example of a very coherent formalization and a well-documented creative innovation using all three of the achievements of great physicists, which clearly would have been impossible without these previous formalizers, but which improved the formalization decisively (much of this is outlined in Kuhn 1978).

The frequent conferences of leading European physicists, often focusing on this problem, were informal organizations explicitly oriented to improving the formalities involved. It clearly would have been a disaster if Einstein's formal superior in the Swiss patent office, and his informal superiors in the conferences, had used formal authority to tell him what answer he had to come to. The refereeing process that accepted the Einstein paper for publication formalized (tentatively) the proposition that this was an innovation that people ought to pay attention to. That is, the fact that the previously existing formality had to be improved was formalized in the refereeing process, in the agendas for the conferences, and in the publications of Maxwell, Newton, and Lorenz, showing that the formal system itself formalized an improving trajectory. The fact that Einstein's resolution was an improvement in the formal system that amounted to a creative innovation is shown by the detail with which the previous innovations were explicitly incorporated into it. The importance of the informal conferences to the innovation in the formal system is reflected in the anecdote that when Lorenz was talking (about something else) at a conference meeting and said something that struck Einstein strongly, he turned to his neighbor and said, "I love that man." I presume it was *agape* rather than *eros*, but in either case it was not formalized.

The impact of informality, in the sense of everyday life in formal organizations, is further illustrated by my meeting in a bar with a patient in the open ward of an army mental hospital, about whom there had been a "grand rounds" case analysis earlier in the day during which he was interviewed. I had attended as a corpsman, but knew him from occasionally working as a substitute on that ward. After the meeting, the patient had heard laughter in the room. He talked to me in the bar, with tears, presuming we had been laughing at him (we hadn't been). I did my best to straighten out the facts and to reassure him, and later told his psychiatrist about the problem. Without the meeting in the bar, the communication between the patient and his psychiatrist might have been distorted for weeks.

The point here is twofold. First, personal relations may, of course, interfere with formal communications, but they may also straighten them out; to a responsible person, a mental patient who trusts you crying in public is a crisis. Second, people in rooms presume that doors are effective barriers to accidental perception; this is true of words, but not of collective laughter. And because the words give context to the laughter, outside the door the laughter is without context. The transmission of the laughter without the words is a special kind of distortion of organizational communication, which requires the sociology of everyday life to analyze. Many jokes that release tension in formal interaction take place behind closed doors, but jokes and laughter are hardly ever formalized, so there are no rules for looking outside the door before one laughs.

Informal social life happening in the same place as formal social life is perhaps generally orthogonal to formal social life. Sometimes it provides alternative networks for working out subversion of formalities. Sometimes it corrects mistakes in formalities. Sometime it makes life livable even though there are formalities. And sometimes it is the most miserable part of life, from which formalities are a cool and sheltered retreat. But the transmission of communications involving formal abstractions is always subject to correction or misperception engendered in the social life outside its governance.

FORMALITY AS ABSTRACTION PLUS GOVERNMENT

Formality in social life is a particular arrangement of discourse. Discourse is always characterized by many variables: by what it says about the relation between people and groups participating in it, by how it abstracts, by how it is transformed by transmission, by how its transmission limits and changes the actions of the transmitter and the receiver (its "authority"), by what error-checks and correctives are built in, by media of transmission and their omissions and biases and static, and so on. Causes bearing on the arrangement of discourse can shape it through any of these channels.

Discourse is also ordinarily a product of human minds[8] and transforms them. Much of human conscious thought is made up of discourse, real and imagined. Many sentences that enter real or imagined discourse, but very few mathematical proofs, have never been heard or read by the transmitter before; discourse is "creative" or "generative," but it is harder to create new mathematical discourse than verbal discourse. The kind of conversation one has in one's mind to translate a mathematical intuition into a proof is very different from the one that produces a sentence.

A mathematical proof is much more abstract: its symbols have minimal (but crucial) semantic content and fewer operations in the legitimate grammar than an ordinary sentence has. The discourse in the mind that produces such a proof must therefore have those same features, as will, usually, the discourse by which it is communicated. It therefore requires that the mind reach what Inhelder and Piaget (1958) called the "formal" stage of psychological development, and usually formal discourse at that level has to be written to be effectively communicated (see Stinchcombe 1974, chap. 1). This is obviously intimately bound up with the kind of discourse that presenting mathematical proofs is. For example, the kind of authority a proof has, and how it might be "corrected" by a receiver, is very different from the authority and correction of a usual authoritative command.[9] Mathematical proof, both in discourse and in the mind, is an example of very "formal" discourse.

Formality is "embedded" in other sorts of discourse. For example, the mathematical basis of the rational numbers (a very formal system) is embedded in the discussion of prices, among other ways by conventions of rounding to the nearest conventional unit of currency. Those conventional units are often larger in the stock market than in retail stores. We would still say that prices were like rational numbers in ignoring a great many things, *so that* the resulting abstractions can be added, subtracted, multiplied, and divided. Most sentences, even those about work in a business, have no symbols in them that can be divided or multiplied. Business is, however, more formalized than marital relations in part because more things are abstracted into discourse involving multiplication and division. But the conventions of rounding to the nearest unit of currency em-

8. The exceptions are mainly when body language or other unconscious features of discourse, which may not be "in the mind" in some senses of that phrase, nevertheless communicate to others. These communications sometimes communicate unintended meanings. Usually more formal discourse is marked by a higher level of conscious control of all the meanings communicated; when it is not so controlled, it is often considered a "mistake" in that discourse (see Smith 1990).

9. A deep analysis of the authority of mathematical proofs is Koetsier 1991.

bed prices in a retail store differently than the same operations are embedded in discourse of a mathematics class.[10]

This book is devoted to discussing the various ways that more formal discourse is related to its "context." By its context we will ordinarily mean two main things. The first is how the cognitive part of formality is *abstracted* from the blooming, buzzing confusion by what is ignored and how it comes to be ignored. The second is how the abstractions come to have *authority* to govern further social action, more or less regardless of what they have left out. My basic definition of formality, then, is "abstractions that govern."

Obviously mathematical proofs "govern" other mathematicians in a different way than contractual provisions in fine print govern the relationships of business people, and of course proofs govern other mathematicians differently than mathematicians themselves govern students in a mathematics class. But this is just the beginning of the variety of formalizations we will discuss. I start in the following section by describing some of the variables that distinguish abstractions that are important for how they govern further social activity, and then some of the variables that distinguish the ways abstractions govern, to become socially as well as cognitively significant.

CONCRETE FORMS OF GOVERNING WITH ABSTRACTIONS

The effectiveness of abstractions in governing activity is partly determined by the quality of the abstractions. Dimensions of quality that are relevant in determining whether effective "formal" government can go on are summarized by our variables cognitive adequacy, communicability, and trajectory of improvement. We cannot understand what kind of formality we find in a given social setting without understanding what sort of grasp the abstractions in it give of the relevant reality.

---

10. Lave (1988) shows that people who have trouble with story problems have no trouble solving those that are mathematically the same in retail stores. Paige and Simon (1966) show that young people learning algebra who learn it fast do so by using the physical imagery of the problem, while those who are well trained in mathematics use algorithms that are more purely algebraic. Thus, for convenience of use, one may want to develop "the same" abstractions in several different intuitive contexts, so that people with different ways of thinking about things can use them easily. Computer software often translates algorithms that are easy for humans to understand into algorithms that computers can understand. Sometimes software developers have to hire special nonprogramming humans to write the manuals, or to shape the screens and menus of options, so they can be grasped quickly. Thus "algorithm" is not, in practice, a precisely clear concept, because an algorithm has to be communicable as explained above.

There can be many things wrong with an abstraction system from the point of view of how well it can serve to govern activity. The earlier sections of this chapter anaylze the variables that describe the adequacy of abstractions for government. One has to remember that all these variables have high values and low values. We are interested in the high values because they give the conditions under which formality is useful. Low values tell us that the formality embodying them is very likely cant and ritual.

But to examine the whole system of formality, we need to specify also the variation in the incorporation of abstractions into authoritative systems. I have already suggested that the authority of mathematical theorems over mathematicians is quite different from the authority of commands over subordinates, for example. To unpack such variations in government, we need a typology of *authorization processes* that give abstractions authority.

A large set of socially established governing devices are used to turn abstractions into core elements of formal government of action. By this I mean that governing systems arrange that after an abstraction has been turned into a formality, action governed by it does not routinely have to go behind the abstraction, back into the reality from which it was abstracted. The risk of making a mistake about the reality is "assumed" by the agency or social process that "validates" the abstraction.

I classify these validation devices into four major categories: (1) formal validations, such as signatures or sequences of initials, academic degrees, votes in authorized bodies or by electorates, trials, audits, "listing" on a stock exchange, refereeing for publication, and the like; (2) risk assumption, such as title insurance, performance bonding, and other forms of insurance, minting of currencies and similar processes for other bills of exchange, underwriting of bond or stock issues, market making in stock exchanges generating reportable prices for securities (for example, when a stock market maker offers a price, the security can indeed be sold for that price whether or not the market maker has buyers at the moment, and the market maker assumes the risk of a difference; this is rather like the function of an insurer); (3) attention directing systems such as negotiation, debate, adversary procedures in courts, auctions, teaching, publishing appellate opinions, and that background formality (for example, "fine print" in contracts) that, so to speak, attends to things that are not in the focus of attention at the moment; all of these are meant to ensure that things that *ought* to be attended to can get into the focus of attention where the decision is being made; and (4) standards, routines, and protocols, which ensure quality by making certain that activities for creating quality have taken place.

Thus, for example, a criminal conviction does not have to be looked into in order to execute the decision because it has passed through a trial that formally certifies it, after an adversary procedure (in Anglo-American law) has directed attention to everything that can be offered on the two sides of the decision. And the risk that the judge was wrong is assumed by the government as a whole, and particularly the appellate bench, rather than by the prison officials that have to do the dirty work of putting the convict in jail.

Formal Validations

Formal validations are processes themselves governed by abstractions about authority and about procedures for creating authority. Such processes are supposed then to produce valid abstractions so that others need not go behind them. Very often in the modern world the authority of abstractions is established by committees, boards of directors, legislatures, trial courts and appellate courts, editorial boards with multiple referees for each submitted paper, and the like. The doctrine of legitimacy is often that such committees or collegia—commonly composed of "peers" (that is, equals of each other)—are supposed to collect and discuss all the relevant evidence, resolve any disagreements, and modify the abstractions or vote down the minority. Once that committee or legislature or court sitting *en banc* validates the abstraction, it is often then expected to govern further activity without further debate, except perhaps about fitting cases into the categories.

Sometimes the collegial body is a constitutional fiction, so that, for example, in American universities many degrees are in fact awarded by registrars. The registrars are indeed following rules set up by collegial bodies of faculty, but assembling the separate grades given the student by individual faculty members into credits necessary for graduation, fulfilling the requirements of the separate and collegially governed departments where students have taken their "majors," is not done by a meeting of any collegial body, but by a registrar. A somewhat similar structure often characterizes the refereeing of scientific papers: referees are asked for written opinions, which are "composed" into a complex decision (with reasoning and advice for revisions) by the editor or his or her deputies.[11]

11. Zuckerman and Merton (1971) have treated one aspect of that composition of a decision, namely, an editor's judging which referees' opinions to trust. Referees do not actually turn out to be each others' peers; some are more equal than others. Writing a competent referee report is one of those good deeds that does not go unpunished, because then one gets more papers to referee; but each writing of a referee's report is taking a chance of being humiliated in front of the editor.

Often responsible plenary collegial bodies create subordinate collegial bodies to collect and codify the evidence and opinions, to formulate a possible decision with attendant reasons, and to report back to the plenum. Departments and schools in American universities create subcommittees to report on the merits of particular candidates, to consult with their disciplinary peers elsewhere on those merits, and to recommend a decision on hiring and promotion to the department as a plenary body. The houses of the American Congress likewise turn bills over to committees for hearings, modifications, and recommendations before the house as a whole votes, and similarly the two houses create subordinate joint conference committees to resolve differences between bills (see Polsby 1968).

These complicated collegial structures are more likely to be called on for the creation and validation of abstractions by which we will be governed than for actual administration. Appellate courts are often collegial, but they are not called in unless there is some dispute over the abstractions that should have governed the lower court. If further, or cleaner, evidence is required, a lower court usually has to collect it. Lower courts usually actually enforce the procedure to generate courtroom evidence (and arguments for and against the evidence), listen to arguments about the applicable law, and make the decision. Lower courts are not ordinarily collegial bodies, but arrangements of official unequals. The prosecutor's office or the plaintiff is ordinarily distinguished from, and not equal to, prosecuting or plaintiff attorneys appearing in the court procedure. Defense attorneys are distinct in court from their clients. The judge is often trained as an attorney, but his or her authority is not equal to that of an "attorney" in its original meaning of an agent of a party in a dispute. The judge officially cannot take one side or the other, but is superior to both in organizing the discourse and bringing that discourse to a decision on law; the judge often has less authority than a jury in deciding the facts.

Such a complicated arrangement of discourse also characterizes the usual deliberations of legislatures, where participants have a formal role in the debates, a formal role in turning debate and investigation into amendments, and then into a final decision, all according to parliamentary procedure. Then there are often further formalities that certify that the decision is indeed the law, before it is administered. These last can be very complicated in somewhat federal systems, in which local authorities may have to "register" the law before it becomes valid within the local jurisdiction.

The general point is that these formal procedures (unlike many of the actual applications of the formality so created) are arrangements of discourse so as to "compose" an abstraction. For most normal purposes, even those of us who generate contributions to the information used in giving degrees by grading term papers do not go behind the formality (in graduate admissions, for example, we do not read the term papers on which the applicants' grades were based, though grading them is work that we routinely do). To use the language of the sociology of education, we admit on the basis of certificates, and expect most employers of our graduates to do the same (Collins 1979). But the pattern of not looking behind the abstractions is true for statutes produced by legislative processes in almost all courts; it is true of the stock market for auditors' reports on corporate capital and earnings; it is true for 90-odd percent of the readers of scientific papers in refereed journals that they do not recalculate the quantitative analysis.

Looked at from the outside, many of these processes that require a particular person's signature or seal look authoritarian. Sometimes they are indeed authoritarian, and the official in charge actually makes the decision alone, consulting whomever he or she thinks appropriate. But very often behind an authoritarian treasurer's signature there is a series of procedures required within the organization before a check can be issued with a signature machine: a purchase order has to be given, an invoice to be checked against the shipment received, and accounts payable to calculate to take full advantage of the discount for early payment but not pay before the discount term runs out. That is, there is a collegium of unequals that has in fact approved the payment in its several components before the authoritarian signature is affixed.

A similar procedure may be modified in a board of editors by the editor being "first among equals," who is always the one to summarize the sense of the meeting in a letter to an author. Deans in American universities often have a similar relation to the school or college privilege and tenure committee, which may vote and then have its vote overturned by a dean. Chief executive officers, kings, and presidents have often had that relation to a "cabinet" or "executive committee." It is usually wise, for the sake of long-run legitimacy of the chief, for that authoritarian power to be used sparingly; the first among equals is in a position as ambiguous as the phrase describing it.

Like other abstract systems, authorizing bodies often do not do the work required of them to see that the authorized abstraction represents the reality in a communicable and transparent way. The tanks reported as full of cooking oil may in fact be empty and so the business in fact bankrupt; the master's degree thesis may in fact have been written by a research service, and the student may be unable to state the main argument of his or her thesis; the budget bill may have riders attached that have not passed committee scrutiny nor really been debated by the full house. The authorization to act without thinking, which is the core of authorization processes, may mean that nobody thinks.

The general point here is that the abstraction process often requires a specially structured arrangement of discourse, itself governed by an abstraction that tells what kind of a process will, in its turn, produce a valid abstraction to govern still other action. That second order procedural abstraction in the legislature may include committee hearings and reports, debate in the full chamber, formal voting, and the like. In a court hearing the abstractions include, in Anglo-American courts, an extensive law of evidence, contending counsel, a judge appointed by a government or by an arbitration agreement, perhaps votes (with different majorities for different kinds of cases) by juries, and the like. For a signature by a corporation, it takes authorization by a board of directors saying who is an agent of the corporation with authority to sign checks or contracts, and what sort of prior authorizations are required for that treasurer to sign.

Such authoritative procedures for producing authoritative decisions are often talked about in common parlance as "management" or "authority of office," but they are rarely that simple. For bureaucratic authority the files must be consulted; for legal authority the legislatures and courts must have been, directly or ultimately, consulted; for elections the electors must have been consulted. One checks whether an abstraction gets its authority by authorization by checking whether there is an authorization practice that is itself authorized, that seems to have arrangements to make its abstractions valid before authorizing them. The central hypothesis of this book is that such processes will tend to pay attention to the criteria of good abstractions for governing action, laid out above. And when they do not, a subsidiary hypothesis is that there will be other symptoms of the purely ritual character of the formality, such as voting that gender discrimination is illegal with much specificity, but providing inadequate means of enforcement.

Assumption of Risk

A key aspect of formal authority is that the receiver of an abstract authoritative communication takes little risk in following it, because the issuing authorities have assumed that risk. "Do this at your own risk," is a way of telling people not to do it. Thus a common precursor of formalization is formal risk taking. This is especially evident in American practices in transferring title to real estate, where the crucial document is not a title document, which is often delivered a year or more after the sale or perhaps never, but an insurance document from a title insurance company. Further the trail of paper that transfers title is supervised in detail by employees of the title insurance company, so as to make sure that nothing fails to happen that must happen and that nothing happens to cloud the title; before the mortgagee bank will lend on a house, the title insurance company has to be satisfied and the title insured. Performance bonding of contractors in construction contracts, fidelity bonding of responsible financial officers, certification and rating by marine insurance classification societies for ship delivery, and many other insurance contracts serve to formalize the contracts whose components they insure (Heimer 1985).

Sometimes the relevant risk assumption is done by financial institutions other than insurance companies. Thus, as we discuss in chapter 5, discount houses in the exporting country validate notes from importers so they can circulate. In the United States Fannie Mae and Fannie Mac, government agencies backing residential mortgages, form the mortgages from issuing banks into pools, as security for secondary mortgage bonds. Market makers in stock markets maintain continuous sell and buy prices as the "official" price by taking the risk that, after selling or buying, they cannot find buyers or sellers at those prices.

These are quite often backed by "minting work" like that of the title insurance company, which then makes it possible for the document so minted to serve as "currency" in the relevant market. Considerable detail about seaworthiness is in the documentation by marine insurance classification societies, and the inspection fees are a moderately substantial (and increasing) percentage of the cost of a ship: a ship is certified as seaworthy to a given degree by the "class" awarded by a classification society, which may have spent as much as 2 percent of the cost of the ship in the "minting work" involved. Just as mints had to certify purity and weight of coins, so discount houses that turn individualized export contracts into notes that function as currency must check the creditworthiness of the importer's bank, market makers must keep track of anything that could disturb the continuity of the price of a stock, and insurance companies have to certify the insurability that is required for the formalization of many contracts. But the care in abstraction that is being certified is rendered believable by the willingness of the certifier to take the risk involved in guaranteeing that the abstraction is valid.

Organization of Attention

The key patterning of discourse in many of the social devices described above is the exchange of views and evidence. The law of evidence is more about how to arrange courtroom discourse than about epistemology. Congressional hearings and debate are generally organized so that all views may be stated and supported by relevant evidence, and when they

are not the interested parties complain. Negotiation of contracts is sometimes differentiated by courts from "contracts of adhesion" where one of
the parties refuses to negotiate the terms of the contract, and even then
the "boiler plate" or "fine print" that people do not ordinarily read often
has a weaker legal force than the truly negotiated terms. Generalizations
in scientific papers that are not argued with evidence, or with theoretical
derivations from solid theory, tend to be rejected by referees and editors.[12]

Appellate courts forwarding an interpretation of law in ambiguous
circumstances are generally required to give their reasoning, sometimes
under circumstances in which minority opinions are legitimately made
public by dissenting justices. Many organizations that are formally autonomous regard it as betrayal if people publicly report their disagreement. But such lack of publicity for contrary evidence and argument usually means that others outside the organization are allowed to regard such
decisions as "selfish" or otherwise "none of our business," and do not re-
gard them as legitimately governing their own outside activity. In general, then, evidence of conscious attention by multiple interested parties,
where it is permitted that the parties disagree, is central to much validation of formality.[13]

People can of course believe simultaneously that unanimity is essential for authority to work properly, and that open debate over disagreements is a sign of seriousness of the authority. These disagreements
about how authority should work are often structurally located in different places. People simultaneously believe there should be a board of directors at the top of a corporation, and that there should be a single chief
executive officer responsible for everything. *Coups d'etat* are often justified by the military on the grounds of the inability to agree on policy in a
democratic congress, and then they often promptly create a *junta* governing body to work out their own disagreements.

To put it another way, consensus tends to become formally valid only

12. Sometimes one can see clearly that these standards are "formal." For example, Einstein's early contributions to quantum mechanics showed that Planck's black body results
required discontinuous energy. Therefore, for example, Maxwell's equations could not
apply; at least high frequency radiation therefore had to be made up of discrete photons,
and specific heats of materials had to approach very near zero at temperatures near absolute zero. Almost all physicists thought they must be wrong somehow; for instance, the results seemed to be incompatible with interference patterns. They were published because no
one could find anything formally wrong with them. See Kuhn 1978, 170–87. Einstein was
very young at the time and had trouble getting an academic job, so publication was not due
to his fame. Frauds as well as great discoveries have passed such formal validations.

13. In the early Marshall Court era, there were no public reports of disagreement in the
U.S. Supreme Court. One could argue that this resulted in Marshall's having many enemies
in the other branches of government, who did not believe his opinions were superior to
their own.

when it is established in the face of opposition, or at least potential opposition. If there is evidence that the opposition was cowed rather than won over, it is often presumed that there is no consensus. Thus, in associational life, "Roberts Rules of Order" or their equivalent—ensuring that people in opposition have had the right to speak, to offer amendments, and to provide evidence—make the decisions more legitimate. A 6-3 vote by the U.S. Supreme Court, with no written dissent, would be very unsettling.

A line of cases concerning environmental impact statements (EISs), required of builders or land developers by the federal Environmental Protection Act, establishes that the EISs and the way they are processed must show that alternative projects were taken seriously, that evidence was really collected, that the alternatives with which the proposal was contrasted were ones that might be implemented, and that the reasoning in the comparisons had to be shown. That is, the procedure had to show that attention had been paid to the comparison, and to reasoning about the comparison, before the procedure would be considered as producing a valid decision (Espeland 1998, 135–81; Taylor 1984, 72–90). Thus the adversarial structure of debate may be shown by confrontation among alternative decisions, rather than confrontation among people.

The basic proposition behind the legitimating function of debate (or related structures of discourse) is that debate makes abstractions better, both in the sense of representing reality better and in the sense of making better evaluative judgments about that reality and policies to deal with it. Debate on technical matters to deal with reality may be organized in a more hierarchical and specialized way than debate on values or on the division of the benefits of an enterprise, because technical problems can often be organized into specialized separable parts, while debate about trade-offs usually has to range over the whole field of interests and values being traded off.

Standards, Routines, and Protocols

Abstract versions of procedures or technologies may be formulated in terms of their outcomes (by "standards" they must meet), or by the sequences of actions that are thought to reliably produce the best results one can expect ("routines," "protocols," or "standard operating procedures"). Or, to put it another way, quality may be ensured by inspections and selection at the end of a technical process, or by ensuring that the core of each component act in a sequence is done in such a way as to produce quality.

Very often emergency procedures are set up with abstract protocols, which then have to be practiced by emergency teams—for example in "fire drills"—to work the bugs out of them. Software programs are often set up as a sequence of decisions and operations contingent on the decisions, sometimes represented by a flow diagram that gives an abstract form to the needed concrete computer operations. The flow diagram then governs the creation of computer code. Such flow diagram protocols will be modified if they produce a bug when translated into machine operations.

There are usually abstract conditions that "trigger" a protocol, such as an order to ship (and invoice) a given product, or specified signals of an emergency, or an overall software "architecture" for a given application, which specifies a frequent sequence of operations.[14] Standards are relatively easy to understand, so I concentrate here on protocols: abstract sequences of actions that govern the overall action.

Protocols, procedures, agendas, sequences of initials of reviewers okaying a decision—all arrange abstractions in the form of a description of an idealized sequence of action. I use "protocols" for all such abstractions of sequences of decision making that go to make up a complete line of action for a given purpose. We have already touched on these above in the special case of sequences of approvals as an organization of attention.[15]

These protocols ordinarily have different sets of considerations that are supposed to be taken into account at each point of the sequence, and the actions that follow that point may branch depending on the outcome. A protocol, then, is a flow diagram connecting decision points so as to generate a sequence of actions. One of the branches may be lead to exiting the protocol. If an arrest is not followed by an indictment, then the abstract sequence that might end with a prison sentence is aborted at that point and the person is set free. Similarly, the sequence of medical diagnostic procedures for persons suspected to have multiple sclerosis (MS) used to be to eliminate all the other known possibilities until being left with symptoms that could not be explained in any way other than a diagnosis of MS. Each test that produced a different explanation to account for the symptoms aborted that particular branch of the sequence leading to a diagnosis of MS (see Lopez and Heimer 1996). Each alternative branch in such a sequence may, in its turn, have a separate protocol prescribing a separate line of action, such as diagnostic tests and therapy when rheumatoid arthritis seems to be the alternative to MS. Giving a single name to such residual diagnoses is a hypothesis that a single cause

14. A frequently used protocol is often called a "subroutine" or an "object" in computer programming.

15. I heavily rely here on an unpublished paper on medical protocols by Carol A. Heimer. See the comments on protocols in Heimer and Stinchcombe 1999.

explains all the inexplicable. When a positive test for MS is found, the whole protocol may be replaced.

Sometimes the connections between items of a sequence are loose, as is typically true of agendas for legislative meetings or committee meetings. These agendas may have subparts, the "items" of the agenda, that are more protocol-like (for example, "Vote on amendments before voting on the bill as a whole").

I argue here that the movement from a general list of topics or proposals like the usual agenda to a more theorized series of sequential actions or decisions is a movement to increase the government of action by abstractions specified in advance. For example, the justice system is required to observe increasingly strict standards of the "presumption of innocence" as one moves from arrest to indictment to conviction. A police officer may arrest if he or she has probable cause to believe that a crime has been committed and that the person arrested has committed the crime. An indictment requires evidence of both of these and of such a character that it could be offered to and perhaps examined by a court. A conviction requires that this evidence be able to be attacked and possibly refuted by evidence brought on his or her own behalf by the suspect, and that after such a presentation of evidence guilt be established beyond reasonable doubt. This protocol of arrest–indictment–conviction, then, is theoretically unified and essentially always goes in the correct order. This sequence is, then, more of a protocol than the agenda of an average legislature.

REDEFINITION AND THEORY

The purpose of this redefinition of what is meant by formality, describing it as made up of a score or more of variables, is first of all to argue that these variables are unified by their theoretical function. They describe what I allege is necessary for formality to be serious, to be better than informal life could manage for a given purpose. I have given frequent evidence to that effect by pointing to examples of the kinds of failures created by formal systems not satisfying the alleged requirements. I do not claim that most formality indeed satisfies the requirements—only that when they do, they may do so because they work. These variables fall into two great categories: what it takes for a system of abstractions to be fit to govern a line of social conduct, and what it takes to make only "good" abstraction systems be validated as governing of that line of conduct. The first set describes what is needed in a cognitive system, a system of conscious abstractions, for it to be better at grasping an area of substance than everyday informal life is. The second set describes what sorts of social processes are required to make such abstractions governing, that turns thoughts into government.

Although I get a good deal of joy out of abstracting, my purpose here is not to make abstractions about abstractions more complicated than they need be. My purpose is to build a conceptual system that will tell us what sort of systems of formality will be useful in different circumstances, and yet to recognize what holds together the fit between blueprints and construction contracts, and between citations and refereeing as forms of authority and scientific papers presenting new knowledge, and ties both of them together with "bureaucracy." We need to have such a conceptual scheme in order to avoid the pitfalls that led Max Weber in the direction of identifying rationalization with Prussian autocratic bureaucracy.

Formalities of the most various kinds can be described by the degree to which they are cognitively adequate to the situations they govern, are communicable to the people who must act in those situations, and are improvable and in fact improving. They can also be described by the role of formal validation of the abstractions: risk bearing by people or organizations who have validated the abstractions and have organized discourse before formalizing them so that all sides have been heard and the relevant evidence assessed, and then translating the abstractions into standards and sequences of action. The overall argument of this book is that the more all these things are true, the more substantively rational the formality is. And when substantively rational formality governs action, that action is more likely to work for the purpose than is love, charity, and hopefulness.

CHAPTER THREE

LEGAL FORMALITY AND GRAPHICAL PLANNING LANGUAGES

THE PROBLEM: AN INDICATOR OF THE EFFECTS OF FORMALISM

One feature of "formalism" in the law is the assumption that there is one "plain meaning" of a group of words and other documents in a contract (say, describing the required performances of the parties) or other legal text, and that that plain meaning should be enforced in court. Further in order to make "formalism" possible, the document or text itself has to be formalized, perhaps with the aid of past cases, so that there is only one plain meaning. I argue that plain meaning is the extreme value (namely, zero) of a variable that describes the variance of meanings in a linguistic community, given a text. A community language, say the graphical language in which a future building is described for bidding for construction contracts, will then be said to be formalized to the degree to which there exist institutions and understandings that reduce the residual semantic variance (say, about client wants or about construction labor and materials required), given the text.

In other words, a formalized linguistic community has institutions that reduce the remaining ambiguity of certain kinds of documents. Some communities are more formalized than others, and some kinds of texts within a given community are more formalized than others, and this variation in semantic institutions is the indicator of formalism I use in this chapter. It flows directly from the argument in chapter 2, that when formalism is of the sort that ought to work properly, the variance in understanding what is meant by the formalities will be relatively small—otherwise people would have always to go behind the formalities to figure out what was meant. The lower the variance of meanings possible, given the contract or other text, the higher the level of formalization of that contract or text in that community. This emphasizes the criterion of "accuracy" among criteria of cognitive adequacy, and "transmissibility" among the criteria of communicability. My purpose here is to show by illustration that the reduction of the variance of meanings in contracts by blueprints requires attention to many of the criteria developed in the preceding chapters. A central kind of informality in the whole system in which construction blueprints are found is informally embedded craftsmanship, good workmanship, which is in turn, to a considerable degree, formalized elsewhere—that is, governed by abstractions distinctive to a craft or a profession. But this chapter is written without constant reference back to that formal introduction, so that the reader can see that introduction live and breathe.

Blueprints are planning documents for buildings, machines, or other structures that translate purposes, and design solutions for reaching those purposes, into "formal" documents.[1] The blueprints (which are no longer blue—at one time the accurate reproduction of drawings was in blue and white) are abstractions that describe (approximately) some important features of a building that is expected to be built or a machine that a company plans to manufacture. They involve producing graphical presentations of overall plans, to which then are attached further graphical plans for details, and further "specifications" about performance requirements, materials, suppliers of parts, methods of construction, and the like. When a blueprint does not exist, and a contractor consults with the client and the architect about what they want as the work proceeds, the contract is usually "time and materials" based *post hoc* on what has in fact happened, rather than a contract about future specified activities. It does not have the formality of a contract for well-described construction performances (compare Macaulay 1996).

Such blueprints and specifications of planned structures are ordinarily produced by technical experts who have been trained specifically to make such "drawings," or "designs." They are invariably much more abstract than the actual plan as it will be enacted on the ground, much as maps are much more abstract than the land, site surveys more abstract than the real estate lot, scientific illustrations more abstract than the actual field of view of the microscope, or statistical graphs more abstract

1. Much of the information in this chapter was obtained by taking a course on how to read blueprints. The field notes were often jottings in the margins of the textbook or the returned examination. I have used "it" as the pronoun for all the actors in the construction process that are usually corporate, and otherwise I have pretended that there are more craftswomen than there really are.

than the original data they summarize.[2] One needs to learn the graphical language in which things are represented (and to make additions to that language in a key or legend) in order to "write" or "read" the graphical texts so produced. I write mainly about building construction in what follows, because the blueprint class I took studied construction blueprints.

Typically the finished structure will be redescribed in several ways after construction to facilitate maintenance rather than construction, or operation rather than maintenance. Thus, for example, the design drawings for an automobile spawn several sets of drawings, each very different from one another—"shop drawings" for manufacturing, repair guides for auto mechanics, and much simplified sketches for operational advice for the car owner. Sometimes parts of these documents are drawn in something quite like the original "blueprint" graphical language used for planning the project in the first place, as is usual in the "as built" drawings for a building or other large and relatively unique structures. But often the postconstruction or postmanufacturing graphical language will be quite different, with a new key or a more transparent and more "lay" symbolization than is used for "technical" purposes.

In some ways, then, blueprints are a very good place to study formalization if that is to be conceived as turning out a set of abstractions that will then govern activity, because there is a special subdiscipline for learning to draw and read in this particular language of abstraction. The fact that one has to learn this language shows that it is a distinct semantic system: for example, one has to know how a notation of "Finished Floor Elevation 1919.00'," is turned into practical measurements on the ground for building forms to pour concrete into. This means in turn that what pertains to that set of abstractions in the actual activity system is easy to identify, by tracing the use of blueprints that are written in those abstractions. It also means that the respects in which what appears in the documents is an abstraction has to be explicitly taught and learned.

Whatever is said that is out of the standard graphical language is supposed to be provided by a "key" supplied in the document (the omission of the key in a set of documents, selected from the complete set for instructional purposes, can create a near-revolution in a blueprint-reading class). Thus, by noting what is in the key, one can tell to some degree what is sufficiently distinctive of a particular project so that a special language is required to communicate it. Furthermore there will often be ex-

2. Gilbert and Mulkay 1984, 141–71; Tufte 1983, 1990; MacEachern 1994. The Gilbert and Mulkay chapter is entitled "Working Conceptual Hallucinations," which represents the general attitude toward abstractions throughout the sociological literature. I wish I had thought of it. Gilbert and Mulkay do acknowledge that they work.

plicit provisions about where other formal aspects of the plan for the building will come from, such as a note that welding will be done according to standards of the American Welding Society.

My general theoretical purpose here is to analyze the *semantic system* that translates client purposes into blueprints and related documents, and then those documents into a building that, more or less, represents client purposes, traded off in a sensible way against building costs. That semantic system is what reduces the variance about what kind of building people might have in mind, and what kind of construction activities will be the "performance" in the contract. Thus one measure of "informality" is the residual variance in what is meant by a client's wish about what should be built, given the documents. Another measure is the "variance explained" by the documents in what the construction craftspeople will do (as a transmission of the intentions of the client). The latter measures the formalization of the construction process by the abstractions of the documents.

I do not try to estimate this "variance explained," partly because I don't know how to estimate what the variance in meaning would be without the documents.[3] I try instead to outline the semantic systems that restrict the meanings of blueprints and related documents that might otherwise make contractors fail to bid, clients fail to authorize construction to proceed, or architects to leave the profession for an artist's studio, where ambiguity is more legitimate. I discuss the relation of a text to a semantic system that restricts its meaning as "embedding." Note that the informal embedding of things formalized elsewhere in chapter 2 restricts the meanings that can fill in the gap in a given system of formality, the meaning in the gap being restricted by the formalization that exists elsewhere.

THE EMBEDDING OF ABSTRACTIONS IN CRAFT LORE

The central purpose of the drawings for a building is to communicate to a particular craft contractor what it needs to know about the rest of the building, not what it needs to know to do their own jobs. That is, the embedding must transmit how craft skills are to be embedded in the overall plan for the building. The formalization of those skills is only rarely left

3. In some ways the central methodology of postmodern analysis is to take some particular piece of text and to explore all the other things that might have been said in that place in the text. Each of those alternatives suggests a possible variance of meaning, and so lets us interpret the actual text as a restriction of those alternatives. Sometimes, for example, the other things that could have been there would communicate that a different context was assumed, and so tells us what context is being assumed in the text at hand. For example, the positivist style of a scientific paper can be compared with the style in which the same experiment is talked about in the laboratory, which tells us something about the implicit context of the positivist style. See Gilbert and Mulkay 1984.

to the architect.[4] For example, the size and location of foundations (foundation walls, piers, footings, and piles) need to be calculated from the loads of the building they will have to bear and from the qualities of the soil and subsoil on which the building will rest. The results of these calculations are designed into the drawings of foundations and the reinforcing steel specifications for those foundations. The concrete contractor needs to know also how much space to excavate so that its workers can build forms, how to support and brace the forms, how much concrete it will take to fill the space, which parts have to be vibrated so as not to leave unfilled spaces, what lifting and pumping capacities will be needed to place the concrete, and so on. None of the latter will be in the drawings, though occasionally, for very crucial aspects of the structure, the contractor may be required to supply its own drawings for how it expects to achieve the purposes built into the abstractions.

Similarly the pipes for plumbing have to be put into the walls and floors after the walls are framed but before they are finished, but the plumbing fixtures have to be fitted to the walls and floors as built, not as the blueprints describe them. The actual floor may be easily an eighth of an inch off; a plumbing connection between a toilet and a waste line that is an eighth off can put a lot of sewage on the floor. Neither the exact location of the plumbing in the walls nor the exact location of the fixtures is described in the blueprints, and both are designed with adjustable connectors (in the old days often made with packing and molten lead) so that they can be adapted to the building as built.

Sometimes specific allowances of adaptability are specified, such as a frame that must be within 1/4″ for each 10′ from plumb. But this means that all further building depending on that frame has to be adapted to that much variation. Otherwise a door may "naturally" swing open rather than naturally staying put.

Thus just as a cookbook recipe for a bread relies on one knowing what "smooth and elastic" bread dough feels like (though if designed for beginners, the cookbook may include an extended essay on the craft of bread making at the beginning of the series of recipes), the blueprint re-

4. That can occasionally be a real mistake. For example, under most conditions, adding more reinforcing steel makes concrete stronger. But in cantilevered construction the fact that steel is about three times as heavy as ordinary concrete, and is a good deal more flexible, means that extra reinforcement can make the overhang in a cantilevered slab sag more. A craft contractor in a building designed by Frank Lloyd Wright—Edgar Kaufman House, "Fallingwater"—added more reinforcing steel, which caused a cantilevered slab to have recurrent cracking. (McCarter 1999 [1997], 210). Because most slabs in those days rested on the ground, the extra steel helped, so the craft knowledge "added" by the contractor was "usually right." It is very rare for an architect to be able to outguess a craft contractor (and in this case the contractor's structural engineer as well) on structural matters.

lies on a plumber knowing how to fit a 1 percent grade of a waste pipe into a wall as that wall has been actually built (up to 0.2 percent out of plumb). The semantics of the abstractions in the first instance are given by craft knowledge, quite often craft knowledge that the architects or engineers themselves do not have. They also rely on the knowledge built into manufacturers' product descriptions. Just as in a recipe "all purpose flour" is defined semantically by General Mills' processes, in a blueprint a double-hung window is defined semantically by a manufacturer's product number (often supplemented by "or approved equivalent").

Thus embedded in the abstractions are meanings derived from work systems, crafts, or factories, outside the building as such. The boundaries between what is included and what excluded from the drawing or specifications are somewhat variable. It is partly determined by the architect's experience of the sorts of craft deviance one has to worry about—such as how curing concrete or mortar in freezing weather is more of a problem in Minnesota than in Florida.

Often along the boundaries between crafts, the drawings giving abstract communications about one craft's interdependencies with another's activities or systems will be supplied by the subcontractor or manufacturer rather than by the architects or engineers hired by the clients. There can be a good many different "dialects" among these suppliers and subcontractors. What exactly will be described by a German elevator constructor, and which part of that will be in German words and which part in German drafting conventions, may be quite different from the graphical conventions and supporting text Otis would use for an American-built elevator. Obvious problems of coordination can result.

Local dialects of, say, heating, ventilation, and air conditioning (HVAC) subcontractors have to have enough in common that the abstract connections of ducts with the products of more cosmopolitan furnace and compressor manufacturers can be made in each locality. The "local traditions" have to connect to the same "great tradition" of manufacturers for the abstraction system as a whole to work. Of course sometimes they do not work, and the HVAC contractor has to come back to reroute the ducts.

Some of the notations in the great tradition seem to be specifically designed to provide fit to a variety of local craft traditions. For example, "Weep holes each 20 feet maximum" (weep holes get rid of water condensation between brick veneer and the wood frame) leaves the exact location to the aesthetic taste of the mason, perhaps in consultation with the client. But some great traditions are very rigid, as when a gas company, moving the meter outside, regards their meter as statuary for the decoration of a front garden, whatever the householder's taste.

This implies, of course, that the abstractions for coordination may change as the craft tradition changes. As plaster disappears and gypsum wall board takes its place, the specifications of variations between walls in thickness for fire protection purposes in fire codes and blueprints has to change to reflect the standard manufacturing thicknesses of wall board. The switch from masonry (especially brick) bearing walls to wood frame bearing walls with brick veneer likewise resulted in a set of standard ways of representing the new kinds of walls—for example, one now specifies the dimensions for locating window openings from the outside corner of the wooden frame, rather than the outside corner of the house, which will not nowadays be there when the opening is built.

A divorced or abandoned wife used to be described as a "grass widow" because widows were often as young as divorced people tended to be. Now that "widow" much more uniformly means a woman in old age, divorced and abandoned women are not "naturally" like widows, and the slang has gone out of use. So also "outside corner" no longer means outside in the sense of in contact with the weather, but instead where the carpenter building the window opening can measure from when the window opening has to be built (which is before the brick is laid). The conventions of abstraction have to change as the activities system being abstracted changes. This fact shows that the craft activities are the semantics of the abstractions; the abstractions have to change as their semantics changes.

The main point of this section is that, far from being contrasted to the formality of blueprints, the informal competence of craftspeople is part of the semantic system that tells us what the blueprints mean. An excavator can produce forms that will provide a foundation footing of the appropriate dimensions to bear the load of a concrete foundation wall. The forms are actually built by form carpenters, and provided with reinforcement by ironworkers. It is by these activities that the foundation dimensions in the drawing, the specifications and drawings for reinforcement, and the quality control procedures for the concrete ("slump," curing temperatures, vibration to avoid cavities, and so on), are indeed added to the abstraction. If they are not added accurately, the wall will not stand up.

This set of formal and informal traditions in the various relevant trades, then, are means by which the blueprint abstractions are given meaning. The formality would have no purpose if that system of craft knowledge did not tell us (or at least tell the people who do the activities) what it meant. The informal system is the semantics of the formal system, which is why the formal system works.

EMBEDDING IN OTHER FORMAL LANGUAGES: BUILDING CODES, STANDARDS, MEASURING SYSTEMS, AND ESTIMATING MANUALS

American architects draw floor plans using feet and inches, while American civil engineers designing foundations use feet with decimal fractions, I suppose because it is difficult in solving triangles to find the sine with the ratio of two quantities of feet and inches in order to use surveying instruments. This difference in the measuring systems in which numbers are interpreted and computed is a trivial example of the embedding of blueprint abstractions in different semantic systems. The steel structure specifications will nearly always include the American Welding Society's standards for welds by reference. The rate of air turnover in commercial buildings will often be specified by the building code, and the units of both the numerator (cubic feet [air flow] per minute) and the denominator (air volumes of rooms in cubic feet) of this rate are understood to be the units of those regulations.

Quite often building codes will be in the form of minimum standards, so that there will be a maximum distance between electrical outlets in residences, a minimum slope for gravity waste lines, and a maximum run between attachments of electrical conduit to the frame. The standards may be in the form of a list of standard sizes, for example, of reinforcing steel. Implicit in what was drawn are standard formulas for load bearing (in various directions) of various mixes of concrete with various sizes of reinforcing steel.

Specialized field measuring systems also become standard, varying from the rough measurement for quality control purposes of the amount of water in delivered concrete by the "slump" (how far a pyramid of mixed concrete of a given size spreads out in a standard time, measured by the decline in height of the peak), to laser leveling systems for super-flat concrete slabs that will be used for precise materials handling machinery. These are described in standard terms recognized in the trade, often in the first instance by the manufacturer of the measuring system, later perhaps incorporated into construction industry standards.

Architectural drawings are ordinarily drawn to scale in a standard way: the scale is routinely given and architects' rulers make conversions to measured distances on the building easy. Many plumbing drawings are not drawn to scale, because the exact dimensions are determined by the plumber only at the end. Since the architectural drawings are largely about the interdependencies of the building as a system, and those interdependencies depend in crucial ways on the interrelations of distances, being able to take the dimensions off by scaling (that is, by measuring relevant distances on the drawing and multiplying, perhaps with the ruler itself) is often useful. Thus we can tell which dimensions in the building are architecturally important by whether one can measure them from the drawing.

In contrast to the interdependency within the system, no part of the system other than plumbing depends for its functioning on the plumbing's exact scale, so no one but a plumber needs to know that exactness. However, the broad structure of the plumbing system is needed so that, for example, the walls will be big enough. Specifications may have to be written so that in fitting a plumbing system into a completed construction, the plumbers avoid weakening the reinforced concrete beams and instead drill through the floor slabs (perhaps to be concealed then by soffits) from one level to another. But once the purpose of avoiding drilling through the beams is in the specifications, it is better to leave it to the plumber to design the offsets required.

An absolutely crucial aspect of the coordination is that from the plan of the building, contractors and subcontractors have to "take the quantities off." Before a plumbing contractor can bid on the plumbing subcontract, it has to know quantities like total feet of 4″ heavy plastic waste pipe, or the quantities of plumbing labor to install seven water closets and four urinals in a men's toilet once the walls and floors have been constructed over and around the rough plumbing.

In the English system, the blueprints go from client-approved architectural drawings to a "quantity surveyor," who does the translation of the drawings and specifications into quantities of materials and work for all the bidders and contractors. For example, a quantity of concrete poured eighty feet high in a building is a quite different amount of work than the same quantity poured in foundations, so those quantities have to be calculated separately. In the American system, each contractor or subcontractor itself has to take the quantities off the drawings and specifications directly. This makes making each bid more expensive to the potential contractor, and locates the liability for a mistake in the contractor system rather than in the architect-client-quantity-surveyor system. But the quantity surveyor *or* the bidding contractors have to take the quantities off in order for tenders to be bid.

The point is that the drawings, specifications, schedules of doors and windows, and the like have to be sufficient for the contractor to extract the quantities of materials that are required to use the estimator's manual or the millwork manufacturer's catalog. Those quantities have to be such that, when combined with the standards and building codes, the amount of work estimated and materials taken off will indeed be sufficient to produce the effects ("performances") described in the prints and specifications. The general experience with such contracts seems to be that the standard deviation of actual costs, given the winning bid and hence the amount of the contract, is about 10 percent of the bid price. The whole system is then fairly full of error.

But note that the 10 percent standard deviation of actual costs, given a contract based on what the contractor estimated as costs, is a measure of how large the remaining ambiguity of the performance description is (the ambiguity includes straightforward errors like forgetting a floor, as my father, a painting contractor, once did—he said he got the contract because he made the biggest error). At best the bidding contractor can estimate the costs to it of the performance required, while being aware that the actual cost is fairly likely to be up to 10 percent higher or lower. But it is not very likely to be more than 10 percent off. If the client's formal description of the planned building is so ambiguous as to make it impossible to communicate at this level of definiteness of meaning, it will have difficulty getting contractors to bid on it.

As compared with industry standards for welds incorporated into the contract, or minimum slopes for gravity waste pipes in the building code, estimators' manuals are themselves estimates of industry average performance standards, rather than formally enforceable abstractions. From a legal point of view they are reports of "industry practice." But in order for contractors to bid rationally, drawings and specifications from which the quantities have to be abstracted have to be closely coordinated with the quantities that industry practice, as represented in an estimator's manual, is going to have to take off.

As new materials or new prefabricated units come on the market, those industry estimating standards have to be reformulated, and the description of quantities worked out so that the bid with those new materials can be rational. For technologies where the quantities cannot yet be taken off in such a way as to make costs predictable, most contractors will require the cost risk to be transferred to the client, and computed on a time plus materials plus percent gross profit (overhead plus true profit) basis. Common experience as well as economic theory suggests that, if bidding and a fixed-price contract are possible, the work is done more efficiently and cheaply than on a cost-plus contract. Thus having a well-described drawing and specification with more or less conventional technology often produces a more efficient and cheaper building process. A set of drawings and specifications coordinated with estimators' manuals, then, ordinarily produces a cheaper building. An architect who always changes its mind produces an expensive building.[5]

These formalized systems that help translate drawings into realities are partly there for regulatory purposes, for instance so that a plumber will not build a waste stack without a vent even if the architect forgot to put it in. This also means that plumbers, then, will be building to common and continuing standards in a given area, and so can use their past experience directly in making the estimates, and will know that they are competing with contractors that do likewise. Partly formalized translation systems have to do with simplifying the production of documents. Specific standards can be imported into the contract that have been worked out by, say, electricians. This produces an implicit contract that is both up to standard and as unambiguous to other electricians as possible. But part of the formalized embedding is for the purpose of rationalizing bidding practice, and to make architects and other producers of documents provide sufficient standard information so that bidders can bid rationally.

DRAWINGS EMBEDDING IN EVERYDAY LANGUAGE

In my blueprint reading textbook, one of the review questions asked about a "mechanical pit" in a given section of a building. I first thought of the sort of pits used in small garages for the mechanic to get under the automobile or truck, so I looked for drawings of driveways and the like. But in construction talk "mechanical" means mainly plumbing, heating, air conditioning, and electrical installations. Some of these are likely to be taller than the whole basement needs to be. One can make a particular part of the basement fit taller machines by excavating a mechanical pit and pouring the slab (usually a thicker slab) under that part so it has a lower floor elevation than the rest. But that meant that I should have looked for quite different things in the blueprints than driveways (for example, heating duct plenums) to find it.

Most of the everyday language of construction refers directly or indirectly to the purposes of a given part of the structure. For example, a beam has the purpose of carrying loads horizontally to a vertical structural load carrier (for example, a column or a bearing wall). When one pours a monolithic reinforced concrete floor in a "waffle" pattern, the view looking up to the ceiling from the floor below will show thinner

5. See Macaulay 1996 for why a contract with an architect who is an artist is cost plus, and a rough estimate of what that costs the client that wants a classic building.

parts as hollows (that are the slab floor of the next floor up), and thicker parts whose main purpose is to transfer the load of that floor horizontally to vertical bearing structures. These thicker parts are called "beams" because that is their purpose, even though they are of a piece with the floor above.[6] The mechanical pit likewise has the purpose of creating a location for the mechanical installations in the building; the "access panel" and "access space" near a large restroom in a commercial building has the purpose of allowing one to get to the water shutoff valves when replacing or repairing urinals, sinks, or water closets.

This language allows discussion of many purposes that are distinctive to the construction industry. It is of course necessary to the everyday life of a homeowner or a teacher in a classroom that the beams continue to redistribute loads horizontally, but that it does so is not a routine problem nor a matter requiring householder or teacher action. It is therefore not something one needs routinely to discuss. When an exposed ceiling in a classroom building corridor shows concrete in a waffle pattern, ordinary users of the building need not know the purpose of the thick parts, or that they are called beams, because they do not have to do anything with beams. Only when a new computer system requires craftspeople to put communicating cables through the floors does anyone have to tell anyone else to avoid drilling through the beams.

Similarly a "chamfer" (a bevel) on the outside corners of an exposed concrete finish need not make any sense to people using the building. It is created by putting inserts into the corners of the forms into which exposed concrete is poured, so as to make the corners beveled. This avoids the sharp, and therefore weak, corners that can be chipped every time someone moves a file cabinet around that corner. Since ordinary users do not have the purpose of preserving corners for posterity, they need not know the word *chamfer* nor how it is described on a detailed drawing that gives its dimensions.

Similarly a plumbing system's descriptions uses such words and phrases as "traps," "vents," and "clean outs to floor level"; heating systems speak of "plenums," "air handlers," "supply and return ducts," and "mixer boxes" for "dual duct systems"; the language of brick masonry includes "soldier courses," "weep holes," and "control joints." Electrical service is not like any other kind of service, and the capacities of wires or cables are stated in amps rather than the kilowatt hours that appear on one's elec-

---

6. In a real waffle pan the shape is to bring the heat to all parts of the batter equally, and after cooking the purpose of the "beams" is to hold the syrup while it soaks in, so we would never call them beams.

trical bill.[7] Thus the drawings and documents are tied together by their embedding in a language of the purposes of building, much of it distinctive of the different trades and describing particular purposes best pursued with that trade's technologies.

The point is that the competencies of the building crafts are organized into groups of techniques to achieve various building purposes. For example, nearly all the building trades at some point or other need to use shims, which are thin pieces of some material to adjust something that is slightly out of line. But the use of shims are built into the set of techniques of *carpenters* for making door frames plumb and doors balanced so they swing freely. For *ironworkers* shims are part of a set of techniques to make angle irons welded onto one structural member meet those welded to another member so that bolts or welds will produce a solid corner connection. The specifications may specify a maximum size for such shims so they do not undermine the quality of the welded connection. That set of techniques also includes temporary or permanent bracing, or stringers, or a bit of temporary extra torque on bolts. Thus the building plan's description in terms of purposes to be achieved will prompt the various trades to supply and use shims when they help achieve those purposes, without shims ever being included in the drawings. This explains the necessity of intuitive translation in drawings in terms of purposes, and consequently the necessity of embedding the drawings in understood purposive language.

THE REALITY OF EMBEDDING VERSUS THE REALITY OF BLUEPRINTS

Translating what the client wants into purposes to be carried out by various craftspeople and their supervisors is, by and large, the job of the architect, if there is one. Clients may not consciously know that they did not want fragile sharp corners on their exposed concrete, or even that they wanted exposed concrete. If they were to think about it, they would not want sharp corners broken by dollies or fork lifts, or splitting the

7. In this case the actions of the householder are coordinated with the capacities built into the circuits by the electrician's installing different sorts of receptacles depending on the capacities and voltages wired to them, and the appliance manufacturers' using matching plugs on appliances that operate on that type of circuit. That the householder need not be concerned about safety when receptacle and plug "fit" is an achievement of the electrical standards industry, especially in the United States of Underwriters Laboratories. These standards come from the firms that take (underwrite) fire risks in the insurance industry, as explained in chapter 2.

scalp of a child who fell against it. But clients would not know in advance that they wanted their form carpenters or cement finishers to satisfy that desire. Not having fragile corners, they might never discover that they had wanted them.

Architectural activity, and the detail of architectural drawings, tends to be most intense in those parts of the total building process that deals with space and relationships among spaces (for example, corridors, how many steps in the stairway between floors, and finishes). Space is so deeply tied up with structural integrity that architectural drawings have a good deal to do with the load bearing aspect of the building.

Because architects and structural engineers are so central to the system of interdependencies of crafts, they usually have to have close communication with each other, and write in a graphical language that everyone can understand. In particular, some of their drawings (the elevations) have to accurately depict what the finished building would look like, so the client can see whether that is the building it wants and the finishing crafts can make it look right.

The dialects unique to those crafts on which other building systems do not depend so much can be much more hermetic. Nothing is suspended or supported by an electrical conduit other than insulated wires, and the whole purpose of the conduit is that the insulation of the wires *not* be interdependent with anything else, because interdependence would easily damage them. Consequently the language for reporting conduit need not be learned by other crafts, and the route of the conduit (as distinguished from its origin and destination) is hardly ever specified on drawings. The drawings often look as if the wire were draped across the room from the switch to the fixture. The only notations specify how many conductors (sometimes of what size) need to be inside the conduit. HVAC ductwork drawings are sometimes nearly impenetrable to outsiders, showing that others need not usually penetrate them. They sometimes conceal much of the more important machinery of those systems that are inside the ducts, showing that only the parts interdependent with the spaces need be shown. The crucial drawings for the elevators are those supplied by the elevator manufacturer, except that the vertical spaces to run the machines through have to be drawn into the structural plans. The interpretations of those drawings can be in German, as long as one of the elevator constructors knows German.

Especially the mechanical trades and the final finishing trades (for example, painting, landscape architecture, suspended acoustic tile ceilings) tend to have a special language. The plans for those trades are generally separated from the architectural drawings, and they usually have a separate key with symbols appropriate only to each. The electrical and plumbing and HVAC systems each have to be interated integrated within itself so that, for example, there are not more loads on a circuit than the circuit can carry, and the waste is not mixed with rainwater. For aesthetic reasons the landscape architecture needs to be integrated, and particularly it has to be satisfactory to the client. This is also sometimes achieved by drawings. All these various drawings produced by the different crafts may indicate that they are not involved in building system interdependencies by not including, for example, any of the crucial spatial dimensions of the building or of its rooms.

Nothing a painter does in one room needs to be integrated with what he or she does in another room, so no special drawings are needed to integrate painting work. Nothing has to be measured to fit, and the paint is easily adaptable to the as-built situation and need not be planned far in advance. A similar detachment from interdependencies characterizes carpeting, flexible floor tiles, and the like.

My immediate point here is to show that the language of the graphical system for describing a building is specialized into dialects oriented to different sorts of interdependencies of the real activities. The way electrical cords are draped in drawings, but put through conduits in the walls in real life, indicates that no one else has to know where they actually go. This is somewhat less true of plumbing, because some of the pipes are big enough that the walls have to be bigger to accommodate them.

But the general point is that the system of abstraction and the corresponding semantic system for translating it into a building is nicely adapted to what needs to be communicated. Nothing about the path of conduit through the walls needs to be said, so the electrical symbols and drafting conventions have no way to say it. That is left to the electrician. The beams and rafters that transmit loads to the concrete foundation and the bearing walls are interdependent with the whole structure, so everyone has to know where they are and know not to mess with them. If a concrete column on one floor is offset with respect to the column on the floor below, one might as well not have columns. The graphical language is carefully developed to deal with the agonizing fact of gravity creating downward loads, and of the low strength against twisting and bending (low tensile strength) of concrete.

To put all this specifically in terms of the subtheory of formalization of this chapter, the formalization is carefully adapted to the semantic requirements of different systems of the building. Because nothing has to be said semantically in order to make things work—about where the electrical conduit is, for example, or how exactly an adjustable connection of a toilet to its waste drain has to be adapted to where the floor is actually built—there is no graphical abstraction to describe it. It will not do to say that more is left to informality in the electrical system. There is nothing at all informal about the standards that specify what size wire a convenience outlet requires, what sort of receptacle can go on that size wire with its voltage, or what size conductor and voltage connection a motor of a given size requires. These are all very interdependent with fire hazard standards, but not at all interdependent with the planned measurements of the walls.

My argument is that the abstractions of the system have to be such that the semantic system can translate them reliably into reality, so that the excavating contractor or the electrical contractor can take its quantities off. The first requires a lot of carefully measured dimensions (excavators have to relate civil engineering survey dimensions and building load dimensions); the second hardly any. Practical knowledge that is passed from one generation of craftspeople to the next has to mesh with their part of the abstraction system. A painter's abstraction system has to know total wall area and the number of lines between different kinds or colors of paint, in a rough kind of way (a count of the number of windows and doors is usually good enough), but its relation to the building's structure is so remote that it is unlikely to be mentioned in the drawings.

Thus in a certain sense the abstract and formal system in the blueprint *has the same knowledge* as other parts of the formal system (such as building codes) and other parts of the informal system (such as what a plumber will swear about). Knowing the interdependence that is supposed to be represented in the blueprints, an excavating contractor is likely to notice whether the footings as drawn will be adequate to support a new part of a building whose walls and roof are supposed to meet those of the old part.[8] The informally embedded formality here could correct a mistake of the specialized drawers of the formal design, because they were informally talking the same semantics as the formal part. That part was only informal by architectural mistake. A painting contractor would never notice if the roof did not fit together properly, and would paint it all the same color if that's what it had been told to do.

That informal craft knowledge and the embedding of formal drawings in a system of building codes and standards are part of the same system is shown by the fact that, when the real-world interdependencies require that things be related or distinguished, the formal system enables them

---

8. This happened on a job in which Kirk Stinchcombe worked as a laborer for the excavating contractor. Part way through the project, the designer had fired many of his personnel and replaced them with cheaper, recently graduated design students, or so the excavating contractor was told as an explanation of why the foundation was drawn in the wrong place.

to be so. The formal blueprint system is most integrated with the project as a whole, through the architect and the engineers that work with it, when the building subsystem it deals with is highly structurally interdependent with the other subsystems, or with client aesthetic or functional demands.

The formal system has to pass the test of lack of ambiguity—namely, the estimate for the building made by the architect must reasonably approximate the bids made by the contractors based on the same set of documents. If the two estimates do not estimate near the same cost, none of the alternatives will be cheap enough. Thus the formal system has to pass a semantic standard that approximately (say within 10 percent) the same amount of work is derived from the drawings by the architect as is derived by the contractors. It often also has to pass the semantic standard equivalent to an excavating contractor being able to correct the drawings because it knows that what it was told to dig would not, when filled with reinforced concrete, support the walls as drawn. That is, the informal system has to correct the formal system by talking the same language. And of course it is supposed to pass the semantic test that if the excavating contractor sees no reason to correct the formal drawing, the footings will indeed hold up the wall as drawn.

The formal system must also pass tests of internal consistency, so that if all the rooms to the left and right of a corridor are built to the size dimensioned, the corridor will have the width drawn into the drawings.

This formalization, of course, quite often does not work so well. But it very often comes within 10 percent. And that is half as much error as the relation between what we teach in our classes and what the students learn, where an average of 80 percent of the test answered by the student correctly is pretty good. So construction formality probably does at least as well as the formalities of textbooks and classrooms.

CONCLUSION

A blueprint is clearly an abstraction of a building (after all, the building does not exist when the first set of blueprints are produced) because it has to communicate with a large number of people, because it is a crucial element of the legal meaning of a construction contract, because the error of the projected meaning has a convenient measure in the standard deviation of costs as a percentage of the bids. For all these reasons, it is a very good place to start studying formality. In addition it has the convenient property that there are formal classes that teach how to deal with that formality. And in those classes, the difference between a grade of A and C is a preliminary measure of how transmissible the formality is. Finally, it is wonderfully methodologically convenient, because the blueprint is clearly not ordinary English, so we can tell quite exactly when a person with a ruler is trying to translate the abstraction into the thickness of a real wall. When we see that person with a ruler, we know that we cannot follow Derrida's advice to stay within the text; staying within the "text" of the blueprint when the foundation is drawn in the wrong place makes the wall and roof fall down, which undermines the value of the formality.[9]

By "accuracy" in the chapter 2, we meant agreement with reality. A building is real, and is often created to conform with an abstract drawing. That abstract drawing has been used to create an estimate for the client about how much the building will cost, so the client could choose another if it could not afford this one. The client is buying the spaces and surfaces and maintainability, while the contractors build the walls and foundations, so the relation between the spaces, surfaces, and maintainability and the structure are central to the meaning of the drawings. All this is difficult to achieve, and a building of any complexity cannot be done without planning in advance.

Planning in advance cannot go on without abstractions, but if they are not accurately rendered in the reality, such planning cannot do much good. Of course, sometimes planning in advance really does not do much good anyway—if the abstractions are bad, or if the purposes or wealth of the client change, or if the contractors do not build what the drawings show, from ignorance or bad faith. So accuracy in the sense of agreement among the intentions of the client, the drawings of the architect, and the completed building is central to the whole business, though not of course perfectly achieved.

But intentions about spaces and surfaces and weights of contents have to be translated into strengths of foundations and beams, inside dimensions that add up to outside dimensions, corridors and doors that lead to rooms, and the like. Unless the communications from the client through the architect to the craftspeople ultimately mean the same thing to all parties, and result in a building corresponding to that common interpretation, it all will not work.

The principal source of technical change in building is the improve-

9. I believe this problem with drawings is not uncommon. In the class I took one of the exemplary blueprints given to us to interpret had one foundation drawn as two different sizes in two different sheets of the blueprints. Presumably the author of the textbook and accompanying blueprints had reviewed them, probably used them in his own classes, and had had faith enough in them to ask a printed homework question asking for the dimensions, so quite a few people had not noticed the error. It's similar to not knowing how many places in one's software one has made the mistake of putting in a two-digit year rather than a four-digit year. This is one of the reasons to double all the important safety parameters, so the mistakenly small foundation actually is strong enough.

ment of components, rather than the redesign of buildings. Building have always been built to purpose, always redesigned for the next building. But they are redesigned in standard modules: foundations, structural members, walls, windows, doors, interior partitions, heating, plumbing, and so on. Technical change in the construction industry is not counted by increases in the efficiency with which space is used, as in redesign of chemical-processing machinery, or putting computer cable connections in the space under the office building floors before putting in the floors. Nor is it measured by whether the new toilets flush using half the water, or the air conditioning uses half the energy of older units, or windows nearly opaque from outside are clear from inside. It looks then as if there is no substantial advance in the efficiency of the construction industry, because that industry is basically organized by informally incorporating rationality being improved "elsewhere." The plumber does not walk more efficiently from one restroom to another in a new building, though the restroom lasts longer with less plumbing maintenance, flushes with less water, and is easier to clean, all because of new materials.

Different construction contractors and different craftspeople are more or less efficient in incorporating rationality from elsewhere. The careful selection of a general contractor by the client and architect, or of subcontractors by the general contractor, and the more efficient coordination of all of them can make the construction process more efficient. But there are sharp limits on the variability of that process, in part because of the intractable rationalization of the separate parts: for example, an incompetent architect finds it impossible to build a waste stack without a vent to the roof, because plumbing standards are, rationally, intractable.

For very large projects, though, it is a good idea to have subcontractors in on the design, so they can provide specialized ideas about how money can be saved or performance increased on their part of the project. Sometimes that works better if such subcontractors are given equity in the outcome, so they will maximize more enthusiastically. But there are limits. That is, if the intractability of the subcontracting standards actually results in important irrationality, one hires a subcontractor who is specialized to develop new, more rational, standards. But a safe rule of thumb is that one should not accept welding on the steel structure that does not satisfy standards unless one really knows what he or she is doing.

The limits of rationality tend to be transcended in the separate parts. In beams being welded, stresses can be created because the temperature for melting the bead of welding material is so different from the temperature of the beam. Stress damage can be minimized by heating the beam before welding. Standards for how hot to heat the beam are not likely to be developed well by a client, an architect, a general contractor, or even the structural steel contractor. That development is probably best done in a university, with specialized stress-measuring instruments and computer simulations of heat distribution over time. Similarly the required strength of the welds in earthquake zones, or in zones subject to tornado- or hurricane-force winds, is probably not best left to amateurs, even if they have a lot of construction experience.

We can see that the system is, to a large degree, a serious one by the fact that the blueprints reflect in quite a direct way the things that must be coordinated between crafts, especially those having to do with the structural integrity of the building. These are clearly differentiated from things that other people are responsible for being rational about. The ones dealt with in the prints could not be coordinated without the formality, but also not without the correctability of the formality. The people who can correct it are those like the plumber finding no vent or the foundations contractor discovering the foundation not properly placed under the structural members it was supposed to support. They act informally, but usually either by following formalized standards such as the building code or the welding standards, or by calling to the attention of the architect that the foundation has been drawn wrong. And everyone knows that they are supposed to act informally to improve the formality as drawn.

I have made a detailed functional argument in this chapter that variations in how well a blueprint abstracts and governs varies with how good the alternative formalizations in the crafts are, with how interdependent the crafts are, with how important coordination is for the weight-bearing function of the structure. I have shown how improvements of the abstraction system are required by technical developments such as the replacement of plaster with gypsum board, or understanding the implications of substituting welds for gigantic rivets for heat stresses, or weep holes and different measurements for window openings with veneer brick and wood frame housing construction. The capacity of the formalization system to change has been central to technical progress in building. I have shown how technical features of the abstraction system, such as drawing rooms and walls to scale to make sure by geometry that they add up right, are clearly related to the functional requirements of craftspeople distant in the communication system being able to build a building with the spaces the client wants properly enclosed.

The central empirical support of functional theories is that the more a function is required, the more the structure being analyzed ought to be designed to fulfill that function. So far this is conventional sociology. But the central point of this book as a whole is that the abstraction and governing systems that are represented by functional arrangements are likely to have to satisfy the requirements of cognitive adequacy, communicability, and a trajectory of improvement. So I have tried to show that the relations between the kinds of informality found in the construction industry, largely of the "informally embedded formality from elsewhere" variety, and the formality represented so starkly by blueprints are nicely adjusted to produce cognitive adequacy, communicability, and a trajectory of improvement.

However, by repeatedly showing people in the construction industry and among its regulators changing the formalities to serve a function, I have given the impression that everything is okay with the construction industry. But to show otherwise it would only take an earthquake in a city where walls are not reinforced with steel or where their size makes them resonate with the most destructive earthquake waves. Buildings three to five stories tall have the most resonance—I live in a house with three stories with unreinforced masonry walls, within the range of the very severe but rare mid–North American earthquakes. My irrationality has not yet caught up with me and my town's backward building code.

CHAPTER FOUR

CERTAINTY OF THE LAW: REASONS, SITUATION-TYPES, ANALOGY, AND EQUILIBRIUM

From a legal point of view, chapter 3 was about formalizing the performances in construction contracts. The primary function of such abstraction of performances is to guide the construction activity, but of course there is a reason that it is called a contract rather than "guidelines and suggestions." The reason the blueprint with specifications is embedded in a contract, rather than in an essay on construction with illustrative diagrams, is that if things do not go well, the contract may have to be enforced. The law that, in the United States, determines what it means that the blueprint is part of a contract has been developed in what is called the common law. This is a practice of authoritative interpretation of contracts, so as to determine the damages of nonperformance.

As Lisa Bernstein (1996) has pointed out, the legal enforcement of the contract is part of the "endgame" of a business relationship that has not worked out. We do not think of the divorce settlement as a good description of the marriage it brings to an end, so we should not think of the settlement of a dispute about a contract in court as a good picture of business practice—of what gets buildings built, for example. But as we learn from game theory, the endgame and the practice of the game influence each other. A dominant strain in the common law tradition is that the endgame in courts of law should facilitate commerce, should encourage people to form and have faith in contracts that will allow them to conduct business rationally. When a construction contract gets into court, for example, it is supposed to recognize the responsibility built into the building code that plumbers are obliged to put vents in waste lines, even if the architect left them out. Otherwise plumbing contractors may engage in a destructive practice of putting the responsibility for plumbing on an architect who is not trained as a good plumber, taking advantage of every architect mistake to cut corners. Common experience with plumbers suggests that having a strict endgame may facilitate capitalism. But that should not be taken to mean that we always will be committed to using molten lead with packing for connections in waste lines.

When commercial practice changes, the way the law reads contracts must also change if formal contract law is to accurately recognize the agreements business people make. But in order to write agreements so they will stand up in court, so that the possible endgame of the relationship does not undermine what is rational for them to do as a business practice, the parties need to know what the law will do in that endgame. Capitalism, then, depends on "certainty of the law." In this chapter I contrast two theories of how to make commercial law adequate for capitalism: that of Max Weber, which is conventionally called "formalist," and that of Karl Llewellyn, which is generally recognized to be less formalist. I argue that Llewellyn is much closer to my argument in chapter 2 about what a formal system has to look like in order to track changes in reality. I also argue that Weber himself probably really knew that case law worked, and let his theory get away from him.

THE SOCIOLOGY OF LEGAL CERTAINTY

When Max Weber (1954 [1924]) argued that legal certainty was essential to capitalism, he meant two main things: (1) a sufficient lawful control of the use of government (and other) coercion so that property and the value of money was secure, and so that coercion was reliably supplied when necessary to enforce civil law, and (2) interpretation and enforcement of contracts, of charters of firms, of bankruptcy judgments, of wills or other rules of inheritance, that could be understood in advance of court decisions. That is, legal certainty involved control over the use of the coercion of the state (and of legitimated actors other than the state) by predictable laws. And it required an apparatus to interpret "private" economic matters, especially in commerce but also in family life, so that the discourse that controlled state coercion and its use in private life could be understood and manipulated by firms and households.

Both of these, Weber argued, required the substitution of reason for magic in the law, and the rationalization of tradition. That is, unless the discourse controlling the application of law is rationalized, it cannot be reliably used to construct social relations for economic ends. A tradition that says only, "Do whatever is necessary to achieve one's traditional ends," is not predictable in Weber's sense, especially when the ends are household welfare, sacred observance, arbitrary princely power, or victory in warfare. Reason in law can make court decisions or government action predictable, but does not make the substantive outcome of such decisions (for example, the welfare outcome, or whether the prince is happy) predictable.

But since the purpose of the certainty and predictability of legal decisions and their enforcement is the capacity of governments and contracting parties to pursue substantive ends, such legal certainty is inherently precarious. Warfare, civil disturbance, and gangsterism always disrupt the certainty of application of coercion. The change of contractual devices to pursue new enterprises by agreement also threatens to undermine legal certainty.

For example, much of the law of contracts assumes a stable currency, so a dollar in one place and time is a dollar in another place or time. When there are two currencies in such a contract, or when the value of a dollar is an outcome of policy that may change, people must invent new contracts so that future moneys enforced by future courts in two or more countries are still predictable.

To solve the problem of where certainty of the law came from, Weber adopted the legitimating fiction of Continental law that a science of law existed that constituted a complete conceptual system for all issues that could be brought to court under that law. That is, he defined rationalization by one of its variants, the Euclidean view of reason, that reasoning from true axioms by valid methods leads to true results, so one should start by giving the true axioms. The alternative is often called "empiricist" or "inductive," but that is misleading.[1] Everyday reasoning by judges (or juries, but juries were suspicious for Weber (1968 [1924], vol. 2, 767–68) was then sufficient to bring all evidence adequately under such concepts. Rules for the production of decisions and remedies under such concepts could be (and often had been) sufficiently developed as to make all such decisions predictable. Weber's own formulation of this hypothesis is (borrowing from Rheinstein's introduction to Weber's chapter on law [1954 (1924), li]):

(1) that every decision of a concrete case consists in the "application" of an abstract rule of law to a concrete fact situation;

(2) that by means of legal logic the abstract rules of the positive law can be made to yield the decision for every concrete fact situation;

---

1. This is true even for mathematics, where except for a deductively organized mathematical induction, induction is not generally legitimate. But mathematicians do not in fact throw out useful theorems when they have consequences that turn out not to be true, but instead change the axioms to preserve as much as they can. See Lakatos 1976a (1961). So some of the axioms come, in the long run, from adaptations to disproof of their own previous versions, "induction" of a sort. But there is no empiricist step in it.

(3) that, consequently, the positive law constitutes a "gapless" system of rules, which are at least latently contained in it, or that the law is at least to be treated for purposes of legal practice as if it were such a gapless system;

(4) that every instance of social conduct can and must be conceived as constituting either obedience to, or violation of, or application of rules of law.

Thus certainty of the law, by Weber's hypothesis, depended on the science of law, and in particular on its abstraction, its gaplessness, and the devices for embedding all social facts and corresponding enforcement in its terms. Only thus could all people, and in particular all capitalists, calculate their futures.

The intellectual tendencies that Llewellyn attacked in his *Common Law Tradition* (1960; see also the general background article, Krygier 1998) have a similar structure to Weber's ideal type of the Continental production of legal certainty. He is usually understood to have shown that appellate judges do not in fact decide and reason in the way they are modeled in this formalist tradition. My argument here is that Llewellyn had a much stronger argument—namely, that formalism is a bad way to produce legal certainty in capitalist commerce, because the facts about commerce to be enforced by rules of law soon escape preset legal category systems. That is, they do not produce a rationalization that can render the law predictable, because they have in them the wrong categories for new facts. Such categories then represent capitalist agreements (and state regulation of them) badly, and the content of the contract or regulation is therefore no longer correctly represented in legal remedies.

But to make this argument, I have to show how Llewellyn thought that greater legal certainty was produced by appellate courts filling gaps in the law as they arise in business practice and government regulation of it. I discuss this as if it were Llewellyn's answer to Weber's "problem of England."[2] Weber noted that the principle of *stare decisis* (roughly, "Let the precedent stand") looked like a traditional rather than a rational principle, and so *ought not* be able to produce legal certainty sufficient for capitalism. But in fact England's common law system apparently worked well enough to produce the world's most vigorous capitalist system, with *stare decisis* and craftlike apprenticeship of lawyers (for example, in the Inns of Court); so it must have, in fact, produced enough certainty to make capitalism possible.

Llewellyn can be seen as having argued that *only* craft rationalization

2. See Rheinstein's introduction to Weber 1954 (1924) lviii–lx, where he actually improves Weber's formulation; relevant comments by Weber are at id., 74–75, 198–204, 266–68, 315–18.

of specific cases can make the law sufficiently rational to be certain in developing capitalism. It does so by being able to abstract the details exactly, and so to fit both abstract rules and remedies to what the contracting parties (or government regulators) understand themselves to have agreed to. We can tell when that has been achieved when there are sufficient precedents that fit the cases so that litigation about a new area declines to a normal level. When the appeals courts, which deal with issues sufficiently uncertain that a writ of error calling for appellate litigation makes sense, are no longer seeing hard cases in an area, then legal certainty has been achieved.

Llewellyn's clearest expression of how one recognizes legal certainty is perhaps this:

> Nor can any series of cases pass muster if they fail to move with care and slowly grasp into a rule which can guide and which so can decrease the flow of litigation or turn it into those channels natural to new developments out of a point now settled—for a while at least—with moderate clarity. (1960, 223)[3]

For Weber, one might have a general set of rules about the transfer of chattels, a general subtype of chattels like money or circulating notes that represent claims on a fiduciary or governmental agency, and a different subtype for certificates that gave property rights in an enterprise, such as a stock or a charter party. There may then be rules to protect a firm that has passed on a document forged by someone else, but no protection for passing on counterfeit money. There might be general rules for how to handle the risk of fraud in each kind of transaction where the property is not thought to inhere in the paper, and so the transfer involves a sale separable from the transfer of the documents. But the system provides specific protection for those who paid for a stock that was fraudulent, and a different protection for those accepting a document transferring real estate when the fraud was several generations back.

These general categories with their attached rules, according to Weber (and other formalists who were Llewellyn's primary targets), provide legal certainty by their strict application to people by all authorities, including in particular judges. Weber thought that this rigidity of a gapless system of rules, with authoritative backing for officials' interpretations of the rules, provided the legal certainty required for commerce, and especially for manufacturing for a distant market (Weber 1954 [1924]).

---

3. Llewellyn also uses an aesthetic criterion: that one knows when there is certainty one can rely on when there is a "singing reason" for a type-situation. This is another field in which I am nonmusical, so I cannot tell, but see below for an analysis of when it might obtain.

Llewellyn argued that such a system cannot in fact be gapless and still be certain in all its parts, because special situations and especially new economic practices come to depend on "arbitrary" definitions of which side of the rigid line they fall on. Llewellyn's certain system has to develop methods for filling gaps that, as it turns out, the system in fact has, and that is what keeps the system "nearly everywhere gapless"—except for a finite number of hard cases.

LLEWELLYN'S CONCEPT OF PIECEWISE EQUILIBRIUM

Llewellyn (1960) used an image of certainty that is logically equivalent to that of equilibrium. In an economic equilibrium, for example, different forces (for example, supply and demand) push in different directions. Equilibrium is then defined as a point of stability where the forces balance. If Weber's model of stability is a bridge standing firmly on both banks, Llewellyn's is of a suspension bridge with tension cables balancing each other. Llewellyn loved to study all the processes of change of the law through judges adapting reasons for decisions into rules, and so he defined certainty as the point where the change stops. In much of the literature, people have noticed that Llewellyn had a theory of what changed case law, but not that he also had a theory of what happened when it stopped changing, and what stopped it.

My basic argument here is that piecewise equilibration of law within situation-types as described by Llewellyn solves capitalism's problem of legal certainty better than Weber's model of "rationalization" of law. But we need to specify the functioning of reasons and analogies in Llewellyn's thought to see how the equilibrating process works to produce certainty.[4] We do not want to imagine that the certainty of the use of abstraction after equilibration had to be built into the law's principles in the beginning; what had to be built in is the formation of adequate analogies to produce

4. I select the aspects of Llewellyn's argument essential for me here. While I believe that all of what I say is in Llewellyn's argument, he himself was most interested in what appellate judges had to do to lead to a satisfactory and certain equilibrium, what "legal craftsmanship" consisted in. He spent (1960, 430–45), for example, many pages to analyze when Justice Cardozo was headed toward legal certainty, or when he was bouncing off in the wrong direction. I myself do not have the competence to outthink great judges in their own business, and I am not therefore perfectly confident that Llewellyn had it. His analysis of legal craftsmanship is, however, an essential logical requirement for his equilibrium concept to be effective "almost everywhere," which in turn is necessary for his praise of the common law tradition to hold water. He convinces me that he is right about the generality of the process, if not that Cardozo was sometimes headed in the wrong direction. Weber's own originality in closing gaps in the sociological conceptual system by looking at hard historical cases should have made him more sympathetic to common law judges; in his main business he was comparable to Cardozo.

situation-types, and adequate reasons of justice and legality to produce a
rule for each.

Frederick Schauer (1991, 167–233, esp. 229–33) constructs a scheme
that he calls "presumptive positivism," which can be used to understand
the role of Llewellyn's concept of equilibrium in his analysis of appellate
decisions.[5] The basic idea is that a rule is *entrenched* insofar as appeals from
it to deeper justifications are rare and expensive, and that the authority or
person who upholds the rule is held immune for that upholding. Using
the language of chapter 2, a rule is entrenched when judges, almost always,
do not have to go behind it. Having to show reasonable grounds for an appeal in a writ of error makes appeals rare. Having to pay in various ways
to prepare and try the appeal makes appeals expensive. The worst punishment for a lower court that has followed a rule is usually simply trying
the case over. Thus "presumptive positivism" means that the rule is entrenched most of the time, and one won't go far wrong trusting it.

The usual ground of such appeals is a proposal to distinguish the case
at hand from some precedent or other source of authority (Levy 1949, 2;
for the argument that follows, see the brief summary id. at 101–2). Levy
argues that, for example, many of the distinctions in the nineteenth-
century cases under the commerce clause rested on a general acceptance
that some parts of the economy were "entirely local." The rule defined
the jurisdiction of federal law as, for example, excluding manufacturing
and therefore manufacturing labor relations. By the middle of the twentieth century it was hard to imagine that, say, coal miners' wages for coal
sold to railroads were radically local to West Virginia (or any other locality), and so that West Virginia coal labor relations were a local matter.
The same applied to the supply of prostitutes for local services in another
state under the law against white slavery, or to liquor for smuggling into
dry states; no one believed those were only local matters, and so the
courts, eventually, did not either.

The growing public appreciation of the "interstateness" of all commerce resulted in a long series of cases where the traditional empirical
distinction between interstate and local was attacked, resulting in different rules becoming entrenched. But the cases were rare, so Levy could reconstruct their essence in a short book; were appealed only with care and
expense; and were always decided over the objections of opposing attorneys and often of dissenting judges. In the meantime, manufacturing labor relations and prostitution labor relations were decided by local law,
according to previously entrenched rules for determining jurisdiction.

---

5. Schauer's brief summary (1991, 191–92) of Llewellyn's argument is not, I believe, accurate.

In short, Schauer (with Levy providing an example) in these pages turns the variable of entrenchment of rules, that he treats as a dichotomy in most of his book, into a continuous variable. This is because when he turns from philosophy to the law, the only sensible way to talk about whether one can go behind the rule to its justification is as a matter of degree, because that is the way courts treat it. Llewellyn provided an indicator of that degree of entrenchment (the degree of presumption in presumptive positivism in Schauer, the degree of certainty of the rule in our analysis above) in the amount of appeals litigation it creates. High amounts of appeals litigation about a rule in the law indicates a low degree of presumptive positivism of that rule.

The rhetorical trouble I am in is that rigidity seems the natural definition of legal certainty, *and* where Llewellyn's legal certainty is in fact found, it is perfectly all right for the application of the rule to be rigid, to be entrenched. What is not all right is to get to legal certainty *by being* rigid, even though it is better to be rigid when one can. The key is to locate the lack of rigidity in the development of the concepts of the law. I argue that this is where Llewellyn located it.[6] He was as gratified as Weber was when rigidity worked, but for him the gratification was in the exact fit of the abstract law, the singing reason, to the situation. But though the law's calling was to develop toward rigid certainty, his own calling was to analyze how one could provide leeway in the law so that one could get to the place where rigidity would not hurt certainty more than it helped. Llewellyn was not a romantic objecting to abstraction and praising the looseness of informal social life; he wanted to grasp informal life exactly in legal abstraction so as to make informal life work better, by formalizing it correctly.

The stopping place for the process of change, then, is an equilibrium in which the rule and its reasons fit perfectly and yield the norm required to give justice in a situation-type. We recognize that it is an equilibrium when the signs of uncertainty (litigation, especially appellate litigation, and uncertainty about how to handle new [business] developments) disappear. In particular, continuing appeals litigation is a symptom of uncertainty about the law in the lower courts. Not knowing how to handle

6. Weber mostly located the creation of a gapless system of categories in academic systematization, often commissioned by a prince as part of the process of creating a governing bureaucracy. He often thought of these creative processes as responding to forces outside the rational–legal order of the state bureaucracy, for example, to the traditional authority of princes, or to the functional requirement of systematization for teaching purposes in universities, or to the routinization of charisma into rules to make succession to charismatic authority predictable. Llewellyn located rationalization mainly in the practice of legal craftsmanship by officers in appellate courts, and in the legal training and experience of those who draft statutes.

new developments creates pressures for new uses of precedent, going behind the formal precedent (the "holding") to its broad reasons or behind the "facts" to distinguish situation-types. Such processes then subdivide or extend a precedent, or provide definitions for vague statutory words or purposes, or even, in the cases analyzed by Levy, destroy distinctions among situations that were there previously. The equilibrium involves an adequate set of distinctions among situation-types, and a reason for decisions that repeatedly fits its particular situation-type, producing a different equilibrium (a different rule) for each distinct situation-type.

The key operation to bring about this piecewise equilibrium, and thus eventually to produce legal certainty, is the analysis of the legal facts of a situation so as to see whether it is analogous to the situation in the precedent. The new situation is analogous whenever the reason for the previous decision "applies neatly" to it. That is, the reasons for a decision in a precedent are the central concepts for distinguishing among factual situations, and so conversely for deciding that an analogy between situations is sufficiently clear (Llewellyn liked the word "clean" better here) to create a "situation-type." A situation-type is a sufficient description of the analogy among factual situations to see what reason, and eventually by developing the reasons what rule, applies to produce the right decision.

Thus the situation-type and the reason co-evolve into the rule adequate for legal certainty, because they jointly no longer create an undue amount of litigation and easily handle the evolution of life outside the law that otherwise might require new situation-types and new reasons. Llewellyn himself (1960, 120) calls this "coral style creation," which wonderfully captures the idea of growth in the niches still available for growth, rigidity in the spaces already adequately filled with limestone.

After trying to explain legal certainty from the rigidity and authority of abstract law, formal law, Weber had to have been mystified why it was England and the Rhine valley that developed industrial capitalism without the certainty of Prussian authoritative abstract law.[7] He had come up against the problem earlier in his studies of medieval shipping law (1924 [1889]) and later in his essay on cities in *Economy and Society* (1968 [1924],

---

7. One suspects Weber never had the "problem of England" until he had treated legal certainty as coming into being by way of a Prussian academy working under a Prussian bureaucracy. The Prussian bureaucracy grew out of a more or less typical status-group society with a powerful royal house, and Weber should not have been surprised that the sort of law and the bureaucratic discipline produced in such a structure were not very well fitted to capitalism. His own experience in bringing a deep understanding of stock markets to the development of the German statute law regulating such markets may be a case when academic study did what Llewellyn demanded of great commercial judges, by way of academic advice to a bureaucracy; Weber thought the Hamburg stock market, with a more customary law regulatory system, worked better than the one in Berlin that was under direct Prussian regulation.

vol. 3, 1212–1372): capitalism grew where authoritative rigid bureaucratic administration of abstract law was thin on the ground.

REASONS AND ANALOGIES

Llewellyn reports (1960, 102) that 9 percent of a sample of appellate opinions use in their own holding the *dicta* (the other reasons given), not the *ratio decidendi* (the reason for the decision) of the precedent's (narrower)
holding. The *dicta* of the precedent become the *ratio decidendi* of the sitting
court. That is, when there is no strain in making analogies between fact situations, so that the appellate court need only cite the earlier case as precedent, the cited case's holding is sufficient. But when cases are apparently
distinct, one can see the deep analogy between them only by examining
both situations in relation to the wider reasoning of the earlier one, and so
"extending" the precedent. Conversely where the reasons, the *dicta*, do not
reasonably apply, the facts must be distinguished on the basis why the reasons did not fit; thus the distinguished situation-type requires a new deciding reason, so a new decision in the case. The instant case—that is, the
case at hand—being decided is a good analogy to a precedent when the
reason for deciding the precedent (in its holding) again gives the right answer for the facts as described in the instant case. The reason for distinguishing the instant case's fact situation from that of the precedent is that
the reason does not apply, so does not give a just outcome. When a case is
distinguished, then, it is in general because the reasons for deciding the
precedent do not apply. That is why the most frequent kind of departure
from merely citing a case is citing its reason or reasons, its *obiter dicta*.

It is important to notice, however, that appealing attorneys and appeals court judges do not ordinarily go all the way back to first principles
and ultimate justifications; one does not revise all jurisprudence to distinguish cases. That is why the reasons that seemed relevant to the court
in the precedent, though not decisive but rather *dicta*, are the most frequent recourse for the appellate court in modifying a precedent. Not all
appellate decisions that do not affirm the precedent "overturn" the
precedent, for they do not say that the precedent does not apply to the
factual situation it decided before. And the reasons for the difference are
"nearby" enough to occur often as dicta in the precedent. This limited
revision is central to legal craftsmanship, as understood by Llewellyn; legal craftsmanship is not *Khadi* justice appealing to first principles.[8] The

---

8. Weber constructed an ideal type out of his understanding of how religious judges in
the Muslim tradition, the *Khadi*, decided cases—by deciding what outcome seemed "just"
by high and sacred principles, and by following "substantive justice." I deal with this idea
below.

appeals court needs a little elbow room, not a revolution. Or to put it another way, the fact there are gaps in the conceptual scheme did not mean
to Llewellyn that the law is all gap, through which one can see all social
life directly.

The purpose of this section of the chapter is to lay the basis for the logical equivalence of Llewellyn's case method for filling gaps and Weber's
complete legal conceptual scheme method for producing a gapless system. That is, when both work perfectly, they logically come to the same
result: a conceptual scheme with boundaries around types of cases and an
attachment of legal remedies to those types. There is a logical equivalence between the construction of concepts of types of cases by analogies
and distinctions between cases, and the construction of types out of legal
concepts with an understood method of classifying concrete situations
into types of cases.

The Continental legal system's classification of cases into types describes an implicit analogy among each pair of cases within each type,
and (usually explicit) distinctions between cases of different types. The
common law set of judgments of analogies and distinctions between
cases, extended to all cases, creates an implicit typology of cases, such
that all cases analogous to each other (and to a precedent) but distinct
from other cases constitute one type, perhaps leaving the distinct cases
standing alone until enough development of reasoning about such cases
creates a new type.

This means that insofar as the dynamic of Weber's argument about legal academic formality creating legal certainty is a theory of how *rationalization* comes about and is formalized, Llewellyn can give an equally
good argument about how formalized rationalization can, logically, be
produced in a common law system. Then the difference between them is
only whether appellate judges, deciding whether a given instant case is or
is not analogous to the precedent, or writers of legal codes, saying what
generally distinguishes cases to which we want a given remedy to apply,
are more likely to draw boundaries in the right places.

For example, when a new statute excludes loans to corporations from
laws defining usury—as in *Jenkins v. Moyse*, 254 N.Y. 319 (1930), a case
Llewellyn treated and that I discuss below—the exact definition of "corporation," how one determines who or what a loan is to, and the correct
way to calculate the interest rate when, for example, a person signs on for
a debt of a given quantity but is actually delivered a different quantity, all
have to be worked out.

A Continental legal academic can define corporations conceptually—
the debtor for a loan by abstract features of the contract, and the amount
of the debt as whatever was recorded in that contract (rather than what

was actually paid)—if that is the way the conceptual scheme is organized. The formal law then might leave it to the legislature to redefine, by revising the conceptual scheme, the payment by the lender to the debtor that is less than the debt as raising the interest rate. In most real estate deals in the United States, the bank taking a mortgage as security for a loan to buy a house must go through that calculation whenever the buyer has to pay "points" to obtain the mortgage, and so in fact is lent less than the amount of the debt; the calculation is specified as required by legislation, as Weber might demand; it was not routine before the legislation.

Llewellyn treated this as a case in which arguments are made about whether a one-person corporation, taking out a loan then with limited liability, after having tried to get the loan for the expansion of his business without corporate form, is actually a corporation. He claimed that in general this is a better way to figure out what is really essential about being a corporation, why the legislature might have wanted exemptions for limited liability corporations from usury laws, and what business practice requires in this case. But my point at the moment is that if a gap shows up in the system requiring us to determine whether a new corporation created only to receive a business loan and consisting of only one person is really a corporation, then it can be solved by conceptual innovation in either system—either by "deduction" from new legislation in a Continental system or by "induction" in a common law system. The same innovation can be made either way.

Or to come back to the problem of England, if "rationalization of the law" is all that is required for legal certainty for capitalism, then logically speaking specifying analogies and distinctions between cases is as good as describing categories well enough so that judges can classify all cases into the right type. There is no difference in logic between a complete set of analogies and distinctions, and a complete set of categories. The only distinction is how one gets to them, and which path is a faster and better way to a good set of categories.

To understand this better, it is important to analyze the logical relationship between analogies and abstract concepts. This is easier to see if we think of a concept as a class (for example, a class of situations, such as what Llewellyn called a "situation-type") with a definite boundary, in which class membership is determined by the criterion that describes the class. When a class is defined by a criterion, by an attribute (or a conjunction of attributes) that all members of the class have, we usually call the criterion an "intensional" definition of the class (or of the concept). For example, at one time the class of all wives was defined as those who had gone through a marriage ceremony with a man who was still alive.

We can also define the class by enumerating its members, the "extension" of the class. But if it is the same class, then, with respect to the attribute(s) in the intensional definition, each of the members is analogous to all the other members. That is, each wife resembles any arbitrary other wife by having been married to a man and not divorced or widowed.[9]

If it is not clear which intensional criterion will work best, a strategic way to determine it is to specify what we want to follow from the class's definition. For example, we used to want to know whether a child of the wife could inherit if there were no will, and therefore whether illegitimate birth disqualified the child. Then as one went (perhaps) through a series of situations (wives whose children claimed part of the estate) in which one of the cases serves as a satisfactory precedent (for example, married in the usual way), the instant case (for example, a child of a couple who lived together and presented themselves as man and wife but never had the marriage solemnized) may or may not fit.

One then looks to see whether the reason fits—whether, for example, the child may have married someone whose parents expected that the child would inherit a competence, relying on the parents' presentation as man and wife. If it does fit, it justifies *so defining* the analogy between cases so that it extends to that case, as in the tradition of a "common law marriage." The concept is now usually called "*de facto*" marriage, and is usually defined in regulations by the same criteria as were used to define common law marriage.[10] The reason it used to be called a common law marriage (even after it was recognized by statute) is that, except for the certificate or the church ceremony, it was lived analogously and presented analogously to a marriage. So a judge might decide that it was a marriage within the realm of the law of property, and that the community, whose law of property it was, would want it treated as a marriage.

If such a case did not seem analogous, as a child of a prostitute might not have seemed to be in like situation to the child of a common law marriage, it would justify so redefining the analogy between *de facto* wives and wives solemnly wed as to exclude prostitution relations from marriages. Similarly in immigration regulations nowadays, prostitutes cannot claim *de facto* marriage on the ground that they have frequently slept with a citizen or a resident alien. The set of cases to which the reason applies, of being a marriage on which the couple and the community has relied and expects to rely in the future, includes those included by the intensional definition and then further those recognized by a close analogy. The con-

9. A more extended development of this equivalence, with a concentration on developing scientific theories, is the appendix to chapter 1 in my *Theoretical Methods in Social History* (1978), 25–29.

10. See Joel 1984, 15–116, for suggested documentation of *de facto* marriages for Australian immigration purposes.

dition of living together for a number of years and presenting themselves as man and wife distinguishes a common law wife from a prostitute.

As more information is added about the empirical content of the cases to which the reasons for a given decision apply, we are more ready to give a satisfactory intensional definition of the class, to identify more precisely the situation-type to which the reason applies. It is the logical identity of an intensional definition of a class with the set of analogies between cases that enables us to learn the adequate defining criteria of a situation-type by studying the analogies between cases that fit the reason and the distinctions from these of cases that do not. So to speak, we learned that we intended to include, in the original definition of marriage, couples who live together, have children, and present themselves as a family by studying the injustices and litigation that arose over which bastards were really bastards, in the sense of noninheriting.

What Llewellyn basically said is that the purpose of doing justice in individual cases, and giving reasons for the decisions so that in the future lawyers, judges, and the lay public may know what is authoritative justice, makes case law a good way of writing law. It is especially good when new business practices produce new situations that give rise to new injustices under the old law. In such cases "the written law" produces what judges (and attorneys and businessmen) see as injustice.

To return to Llewellyn's specific analysis of corporations and usury, he described (1960, 227–29, esp. 228) the *Jenkins v. Moyse* case, cited above, that involved an old law against usury, depriving the usurer of the security in case of default. A later statute (recent at the time) exempted corporations from the usury law. What happens for a corporation specifically formed at the request of the usurer so as to make the usury possible, when the borrower repudiates the loan as usurious? The exception of corporations was presumably designed to take account of the developing capital market for claims on corporations, where the price of risky claims might be assumed to be set by the market, that is to say, not to be really "usury." It presumably was also relevant that the limited liability of corporation owners helped prevent individuals from being "ruined" by usury; stockholders could only be ruined to the extent of their stockholdings. The question before the court, then, was whether the borrower was analogous to a person (as he claimed by repudiating the loan) or to a corporation (as the lender had insisted that he become to qualify for the loan). The criteria for distinguishing this person-corporation had to be the justification for the legislation exempting corporations from the law against usury, not the deep philosophical question of whether a person and a corporation are the same sort of thing.

Another case analyzed by Llewellyn (1960, 228–29), *Shaw v. Railroad,*

101 U.S. 557 (1879), involved two lenders' being fraudulently offered the
same bill of lading (a railroad document showing that a shipment had
been accepted by the railroad to be shipped to the buyer). One was a discounting bank paying a distant seller's claim, on the security of what
turned out to be a copy of the bill fraudulently supplied by the intermediate buyer. The other was in a commercial relation between the ultimate
local buyer and the intermediate buyer. The ultimate buyer gave an advance on the goods represented by the bill, which had been "sold" to him
by the intermediate buyer. If (as was true) the discounting bank was held
not to have been negligent, and the ultimate buyer was held to have obtained the bill of lading as security for the advance, then both "lenders"
who had been provided the same bill as a security were "equally blame-
less." Statutes had recently made bills of lading negotiable "in like manner as bills of exchange," which had been thrown out because they redis-
tributed the risks of the loss of the paper versus the loss of the goods for
which the commercial relation had paid an advance. The ultimate question was who owned the security each had been promised.

Both *Jenkins* and *Shaw*, then, were gaps created during attempts to legitimate new business practices (Llewellyn noted, for example, that older
port cities on the Atlantic did not accept bills of lading as negotiable). For
the bill of lading as security gap, Llewellyn suggested that the one might,
in such uncertainty, divide the losses between equally innocent "lenders."
Elsewhere he commented (1960, 394), that, even with such a decision, it
is a very useful increase in certainty to know where such gaps creating uncertainty are, so that a lawyer acting as a counselor can advise a client to
avoid them.

Llewellyn's point here was to show how two "coral niche" gaps arise
out of developing business practice. The difficulty they posed for both
the appellate judges and Llewellyn himself have suggests that general
concepts would not have helped here.

SITUATION-TYPES AND EQUILIBRIA

It is characteristic of Llewellyn's mode of thinking that the degree of certainty applies to situation-types rather than to the legal system as a
whole. Llewellyn thought of a series of cases in a newly distinguished situation-type as a "gap being filled," because no one knew the gap was there
before cases arose to fill it. This in turn meant for Llewellyn that although the system repeatedly approaches the state of gaplessness, the exact number and nature of the gaps that remain are determined as the cases
arise. A temporary filling by a first case in a gap will only eventually be
replaced with a gold crown, exactly fitted to the gap, as the cases specify

more and more about the nature and shape of the gap. A lawyer as appellate judge is a craftsman as a dentist is, filling unique gaps in the system as he or she determines their exact shape.

The concrete activity that ensures growth of the law into the gap is the giving of an opinion that will "give guidance" in the situation-type to future courts. Equilibration depends, then, on the consciousness that a case decision and its reason, tied together in the opinion, ought to live up to its responsibility to be a precedent. Only on the basis of the cognitive work of responsible opinion giving can a precedent provide certainty to a previously uncertain situation-type. Such an opinion makes the system aim for equilibrium in a piecewise fashion, as the successful coral organism adds to the reef.

The work of an appellate opinion thus starts with a more or less "frozen" record of the facts, a somewhat less frozen posing of the legal issue in the grounds of appeal (in the writ of error), and a clear, and small, set of alternative decisions possible. The combined set of facts, issues, and the lower court decision must have persuaded the appeals court that there was some uncertainty. Most appeals do not have sufficient uncertainty in the eyes of the appeals court to generate an opinion. Thus appellate opinions are restricted to those few legal cases that seem to the appeals court sufficiently uncertain as to be worth discussion. This indicates a possible gap, sufficiently defined by the conjunction of facts and legal issues as to require at least a temporary filling. Llewellyn was nearly unique in presenting and analyzing opinions that failed to fill the gap, illustrations of the lawyers' adage that "hard cases make bad law." But a series of hard cases with an occasional great opinion can fill the gap, producing certainty even for those hard cases.

The situation-types that dominated the gaps in the law Llewellyn analyzed had to do with large flows of payments attached to large flows of property. Many of the cases dealt with financial intermediaries that handled large flows of documents representing claims on property: banks, participants in foreign exchange markets, discount houses, and commodity or stockbrokers commonly appeared as one of the parties. Sometimes these flow managers appeared instead as offenders whose malfeasance or insolvency created a dispute about which property claimant took the loss.

Llewellyn found that the commercial devices for creating enough certainty to trade routinely and rapidly were, in his period (roughly 1850–1950), not well understood by judges. The filigree of guarantees and securities multiplied the complexity of competing claims on any particular property, and it was certainty of these claims that backed the flow of documents. To transfer a claim to thousands of dollars in a daily flow of millions, without stopping to evaluate the certainty of all the claims on each, is the essence of financial markets.

Exactly why a claim on a corporation was so different from a title deed to a piece of real estate, and why the corporate stock or bond could be traded in a large flow on a securities market, was hard to communicate in the language of early-nineteenth-century precedents or statutes. Llewellyn and his heroes[11] are portrayed as receiving information about the practices that accomplished such large flows to define the required situation-types for disputes arising from them.

The reasons that were developed to distinguish such situation-types are those that legitimate the devices of certainty that such dealers in large flows rely on. The large flow cannot be created if large claims routinely have to be litigated whenever the guarantors of the values of the claims and of the security backing those claims default. If titles to the things in action in those flows are routinely complex and have many sources of uncertainty, the flow will slow. The judges, then, were creating the legal bases of the liquidity of financial markets, and so of the certainty of claims in large flows of goods and capital.

For example, to transfer many remittances at current market prices through a currency exchange, the traders must make many contracts per hour about claims on, say, drafts on various American banks and drafts on various Italian banks, and those contracts are invariably oral (or electronic) for much of their existence. Thus, to understand what the promises and securities in the contracts are all about, a judge must understand the situation of the American bank, of the Italian bank, and of the elements that make up the flow through the market. It is quite a different situation than a ship captain carrying a bunch of gold coins across the ocean in 1800 to pay a commercial debt, and requires a different "situation-sense." The point is that one does not understand the words of contracts and guarantees, especially the oral part, unless one understands the situation as a whole, in which the semantics of the words are embedded. Often the situation-sense is brought to the court by appellate counsel experienced in the industry, who has learned what people had to mean in order to make the system run.

But out of that holistic grasp, the appellate judges must generate the legal grasp of the situation-type in the case, the exact nature of the generation of the competing claims. Who has unfulfilled obligations to whom, whose fault is the failure to perform them, and what remedies are available to the court to do the best justice possible? The answer to this set of

---

11. Especially Holt, Mansfield, Scrutton, Cowen, Hough, Hand, and Cardozo. See Llewellyn 1960, 235, 244, 401–45, and the index under these names.

questions is the reason for the holding, and the set of *obiter dicta* sufficient to translate the understanding of the situation-type into that holding.

When the situation-type is exactly grasped, and when the reasoning about that situation-type (especially if it clearly differentiates and rationalizes conflicting precedents so as to project the situation-type into the legal tradition) generates the holding, then a "rule" is formed. If this complex yields decisions that keep the large flows flowing without much appellate litigation, that gap is closed with a local equilibrium. Another coral organism is turned into lasting limestone. Legal certainty is reestablished, not by a once-and-for-all rationalization of ship captains entrusted with gold coins, but by creeping steps taken in a series of cases to produce a rule that does not require new appellate litigation.

LEGALISM

Lawrence Friedman's argument on legalism (1966; see also Shklar 1964) seeks to undermine Llewellyn's argument as restated above. Using the language of "gaps" that I have borrowed from Weber to illuminate Llewellyn's thinking, Friedman argues that requiring gaps to be filled with legal reasoning tends to produce specious legal reasoning, namely, "legalism." The core criterion of legalism is adding specious generality to particular decisions. It is specious because it does not in fact grasp the situation, or does not generate a just outcome, or misrepresents the legal materials in the course of justifying the decision, or mechanically applies a concept when the reason underlying the concept does not apply. Friedman argues that there are many gaps that cannot be well filled within the legal canon and, provided that canon is highly limited, especially to sacred texts, that legalism contaminates the whole with specious gap filler. His conditions for that to happen include that judges must decide, that they must give reasons, and that they "are expected to give reasons only from a closed system of rules or concepts" (1966, 150). Friedman says specifically that appellate judges tend to be subject to those constraints (150–51).

If we look at the cases Llewellyn chose to exemplify legal craftsmanship by appellate judges, we find that the gap is often filled by materials supplied by the parties, or perhaps better, by other people or corporate bodies in similar roles to the plaintiff and defendant. Because the contracting parties in large flows of financial claims are almost all full-time professional market participants, they depend on knowing what the contracts "really mean." Aside from knowing their own intentions, they have enough daily experience to learn what the contracts mean to others. Because the law of contracts gets its primary content from the contracting parties, there is something substantive for legal craftsmanship to work on. A "singing reason" in Llewellyn's concept of craftsmanship can after all sing because the market professionals implicitly know the tune. Thus we should expect that Friedman's kind of legalism should come about when the parties (and their peers) do not produce the materials for true legal craftsmanship to work with.

Friedman observes that legalism has drifted into regulatory law rather than the law that routinely comes into court. For example, the U.S. agency responsible for defining which deferred tax retirement invest-ment instruments (individual retirement accounts [IRAs] and pension funds) can be "rolled over" to other deferred retirement savings schemes is the Internal Revenue Service (IRS). It certifies only retirement plans that can give and receive rollovers in the United States. The substantive similarity (due to imitation) of Australian superannuation funds to eli-gible American plans does not, therefore, make rollovers possible.

There is no place in the IRS retirement exemption system to argue that Australian and American retirement plans are substantively the same thing. Therefore transfers either way across the international boundaries require the payment of income taxes on employer contributions and ac-cumulated earnings. This is not going behind the formality of certifica-tion to the substantive similarity of purpose, and so reduces the liquidity of transfers in the capital market across international boundaries; in short it is legalism in the IRS regulations, and cannot come into court. Fried-man argues that this may relieve courts from some of the pressure of the efficiency that comes from having hard and fast rules, because hard and fast rules can come from regulations. This relocates the legalism that Friedman predicts, so the reduction of specious reasoning ("legal fic-tions," for example) that we observe in the courts is not in fact a refuta-tion of Friedman's generalization.

Vilhelm Aubert (1963) argues that the spread of such false grasping of the situation tends to be limited by the structure of legal thought to the narrowest possible ground on which a case may be decided. One can re-gard this as an immune system to ward off infection from specious gen-erality. Inappropriate reasons do less damage if they are very narrow in the first place, and then if each extension of them to another case must be justified unless it is "obvious."

Thus when Friedman gives the example of whether agreement to a contract comes into effect when it is mailed or when the agreement is re-ceived, the scope of a precedent on the topic is very narrow. To decide it on some deep philosophical ground—for example, that it begins with the intention to form an agreement—would be destructive. Similarly when an apartment on the coronation route is rented for a few hours on coronation day at a very high price by people who want to view the procession, and then the coronation is postponed, one can argue that the value of the one-day lease was destroyed and the contract frustrated through no fault of the lessee, who should therefore be relieved of the contract, or that the apartment is still there and serviceable and the lessee was not guaranteed a coronation procession, and the lessee therefore obliged to pay. However the court comes down, one wants its decision to be confined to risks very similar to coronation postponement, and surely not to risks in the commodity futures market. Friedman would suggest in the pension funds and coronation day rentals contracts that any reason offered for the decision was a specious gap filler. But the precedent would, at any rate, not reach very far.

Leaving the scope of a precedent unclear is one of the ways Friedman suggests that judges get through such problems. As he suggests, if the reason for the decision in the precedent does not apply to the instant case, *stare decisis* is simply a gap filler, giving destructive generality to the reason for the decision in the precedent. If the reason in the precedent also did not apply to the precedent itself (if it was "bad law"), the gap is filled with mud without even straw in it.

Obviously Friedman has made a very powerful argument against Llewellyn's optimism about appeals courts. The argument is basically that Llewellyn was too ready to postulate "singing reasons," reasons that neatly fit the situation-type to the remedy in a way that satisfied our "aesthetic of justice." Friedman can be read as saying that Llewellyn's postulate that legal craftsmanship was not very rare in appeals courts is normally wrong. I leave this for Friedman and Llewellyn to fight out, when they meet again. For my purpose here, I argue that Llewellyn is right about what is required to justify optimism about commercial common law. Friedman is right that if any gap filler approved by a judge, fitting or not, is routinely taken as authoritative, it will not satisfy the criteria of effective formality, which I laid out in chapter 2. My own bet in the end is on Llewellyn, because I believe that eventually Friedman's postulate of arbitrary gap fillers leads judges to build houses of cards—that eventually fall down.

Such careful restriction of legal thought does not necessarily apply in a legislature.[12] If all the members of the House of Representatives had to produce an "opinion" of what the law means, it would undermine the for-

---

12. Sometimes legislatures do pay attention to precedents, and refuse to pass bills because they don't want to create them. This was true of bills for emergency relief in disasters (Landis 1998), which the early American Congress treated as "cases" of disasters, carefully limiting the definition of disaster so it would not generalize to the many common causes of poverty, which they did not want to provide relief for.

mality of the vote. A few do speak, and those speeches may be used occasionally to discern legislative intent (especially when the same intent is mentioned by both opponents and proponents). But the courts do not want to penetrate too far into the legislative machinery and its reasons. Very often this shows up in purposeful generality, even vagueness, in legislation, so that many parts of the legislation may become the reason for a decision in various kinds of cases arising under the statute.

American courts in particular usually do not want to delve too deeply into the reasons for legislative decisions, and especially not into the reasons the legislative minority dissented. Part of the function of a legislature is to defeat the reasons of the minority. The path back from a court decision to ultimate values through the legislature is more straightforward than the tortuous path, traveled only one small step at a time, back to ultimate values through the precedents. Aubert's argument (1963) is that this is the way the body of knowledge of legal thought, reasoning through precedent on narrow grounds, is supposed to be. And Friedman agrees with the reverse proposition, that legislatures are rarely the source of the specious generality of reasons in the legal system; if legislatures are overly general, it is because they are not required to write an opinion. One would, for example, expect that testimony by social scientists on general causal connections would be received in a different way in the committees of Congress than in court, according to the habits of mind of the two institutions.

CONCLUSION: WEBER'S PROBLEMS OF ENGLAND AND NORTH ITALIAN CITIES

What Weber thought he saw in English common law was traditional authority, and he thought tradition was inflexible.[13] He did not read the decisions of Lord Mansfield with as close an eye as he turned on German scholars' systematizing of Roman law. In his dissertation, Weber (1924 [1889]) tended to attribute the resulting system to the ancients, as continued in ecclesiastical law, and appearing in the Latin words in the case law of North Italian and Catalonian shipping. But the "marine partnership" (*societas maris*) he had focused on was, by that time, interpreted in a system of courts in city states in Italy and Catalonia, and as far as I can tell from his references was only systematized into a *Lex Mercatoria* in Catalonia. And that case law was one of the main bases of the commer-

---

13. I think he was wrong about that, too. "Traditional" astrology nowadays advises on questions my grandparents would think immoral ever to ask. And the astrology of the wise men from the East at the birth of Christ is hardly recognizable as kin to the astrology column in today's newspapers.

cial part of English common law. The coral bank of the law merchant was also applied to English ships and Dutch ships.

But this suggests that Weber was himself a precursor of Llewellyn, but applying common law reasoning to the sacks of gold coins on a North Italian or Catalan ship. Like Llewellyn's formalists, he mistook the coral reef for a monument whose architecture was of classical principles, not noticing[14] the thin film of new growth of the same sort that had laid it all down, shaping it so as to stabilize commercial flows during the growth of capitalism. The rationalization by German law professors did not generate enough Mansfields filling gaps with singing reasons, so not as much legal certainty of large flows of capitalist trade. To be sure, by the time capitalist principles were applied to manufacturing that Weber took to be central to modern development, they were pretty well formalized, looking fairly Germanic even in England.

So perhaps there never was a problem of England's industrial revolution; rather the problem was Weber's forgetting that the laws of commerce with Roman roots, systematized by German professors, were developed by autonomous unbureaucratic cities in case law courts in medieval Europe. They were applied to the detailed problem of creating industrial firms, industrial labor relations, and industrial sales of commodities after being preserved by many generations of appellate judges.

The danger Weber saw in the case method is perhaps most strongly formulated by Friedman in his essay on legalism (1966); it might be called the danger of "casuistry." Casuistry is the theologians' doctrine developed around the proposition that "circumstances alter cases," as the Oxford English Dictionary puts it in its article on casuistry. Presumably Moses, who brought down the tablet with "Thou shalt not kill" engraved on it, needed casuistry to justify his genocides.[15] The contortions that give "casuistry" a bad name also make "legalism" as Friedman discusses it a worry for the law. If the rule is overly general and cannot easily be changed with the circumstances, the social conditions for casuistry and legalism are laid down. Llewellyn thinks his great judges are craftsmanlike rather than casuistic or legalistic. What makes the difference?

The appeals court in the first place is dealing with an isolated part of the lower court case—the case has already been abstracted from the tes-

14. Of course Weber noticed a lot of changes, even "development" of concepts, in the law of Mediterranean commerce. He did not take his early observations seriously enough when sketching out his sociology of law. If he had finished looking it over and producing a finished draft before he died, he might have remembered what he had once known. For the history of the manuscript, see Rheinstein's introduction to Weber 1954 [1924].

15. Numbers 21:34–35, 31:7, 15–18; Deuteronomy 2:34, 3:2 and 3:6 (repeating Numbers).

timony creating authenticated "facts"; the legal issues have been described, and some one or more of them made the basis of the writ of error. Thus the task of the appeals court is not to decide what, taken as a whole, is justice in the real world. Some specific aspects of the case have been specified as possibly unjust in the writ of error. And of those, those reasons have been argued that might imply that the classifications of cases, implicit in the precedents, which gave the reason for the lower court decision, had led to the wrong reason for its decision.

This selection out of all the justice and injustice in the original situation that gave rise to the dispute in court is validated by being reasoned out in the writ of error, and its narrowness is validated by the acceptance of the appeal in the higher court. This reasoning and validation then approves the posing of an abstract issue for the appeals court, not the whole set of issues dealt with in the lower court. If the issue posed is that the whole procedure in the lower court was tainted by the error, the appeals court returns the case for retrial to them, rather than trying the whole themselves. Together this means that, as far as procedure can manage it, only a well-posed, isolated, abstract legal issue results in a change of precedent.

The posing of this abstract legal issue and its bearing on the justice of the case then requires that the reasons for distinguishing the case must be in the reasons that bear on such cases. Those are likely to be found in the reasoning that surrounded the specific reasons in the case that formed the precedent. That is, Llewellyn emphasizes the finding that most of the reasons for the new precedent are in the *obiter dicta* mentioned in the precedent, but not the deciding reason in that case.

Finally, legal craftsmanship of appeals courts requires of itself that, as far as possible, no casuistry or legalism not now embedded in the new precedent will be needed in the future. If it is well enough reasoned for this purpose, then any new precedents will be very likely to use the *obiter dicta*. In appeals court casuistry in the future, one will again not confront the whole of contract law but merely the narrow issue of whether, for example, the property claim constituted by a bill of lading resides in the contractual situation as a whole or in the formal document: Is it more like the writing of a contract where the contract exists only because of an agreement in the world, or more like a dollar bill where the value exists in the document itself, as far as the exchange is concerned.

The casuistry required to get Moses out of the apparent conflict between the commandment and the genocide he ordered presumably would come under the military exception to that commandment, now governed by the Geneva convention on prisoners of war, by the constitutional protection of free speech for Quakers to argue against that exception, by the grand difference between a *Lebensraum* argument in a herding society where, without water and grass the herd and people die, and that same *Lebensraum* argument in industrial Germany. But aside from the argument not having been posed abstractly in a court in Old Testament times, the reasoning involved in the casuistry is very hard to isolate from deep political and religious questions. Casuistry thus cannot be a mere chink in a well-developed legal system, with only a few relevant reasons on each specific issue creating a gap.[16]

The theoretical point here is that the negative meanings attached to legalism and casuistry do not apply to Llewellyn if his description of legal craftsmanship is accurate. It is not a way of dodging formality by manufacturing a ritual formality to get particularistic justice, but instead a way of improving formality by distinguishing cases in such a way as to create a class of cases that fit the new precedent, and to make that new class of cases and its distinction from the older analogous cases as accurate as possible. It is carefully designed to produce a trajectory of improvement, as I described in chapter 2, in the common law. Llewellyn as I have interpreted him contrasts clearly and testably with Friedman's argument that the trajectory is instead toward legalism. The test would consist in applying two criteria: whether the new situation-type and reason for the remedy results in a decline of appeals litigation, and whether the opinions that filled the gap constitute a "singing reason."

16. I myself would have taken Moses to the War Crimes Tribunal, or its nearest equivalent at the time.

CHAPTER FIVE

THE SOCIAL STRUCTURE OF LIQUIDITY: FLEXIBILITY IN MARKETS, STATES, AND ORGANIZATIONS

Bruce G. Carruthers and Arthur L. Stinchcombe

In the previous chapter we saw Llewellyn's judges grappling with how contract law had to be read in order for law to cover large flows of financial transactions, as came into existence in the nineteenth century. Such large flows indicate that many buyers can meet many sellers in many transactions in organized markets on agreed standard terms. That is, they indicate liquidity. So chapter 4 and Llewellyn's monograph were arguments about the legal foundations of liquidity. The argument of this chapter is that the meanings of the items in these flows cannot be established with just the law. The reason the law can grasp the nature of these flows generally is that the items that constitute them, starting with the currency (or currencies) in which they are traded, have to be themselves highly formalized.

In order to move, then, from the case law requirements of large flows to the social requirements for liquidity reaching down to the commodities being traded, we have to analyze the concept of liquidity more deeply. This chapter does that, and elaborates the definitions by studying two cases of the origins of liquidity. One can argue for a theory about what some particular function requires by showing that when that function came into existence, it did so by establishing the requirements. That is our strategy in this chapter.

By liquidity of a market, economists mean that standardized products can be bought and sold continuously at prices that everyone in the market can know, and they are not normally sold at prices above or below their market price. The theory is that everyone can know at all times what the price of a given product is, and there is no competitive reason to go elsewhere if that same price is offered. The basic mechanisms that economists have specified for this to be achieved are continuous auctions in which a crowd of knowledgeable buyers meets a crowd of knowledgeable sellers; market makers who, for a small margin, are willing to take the risk of transferring large quantities and maintaining a continuous price; and homogenization and standardization of commodities by grading natural products, by manufacturing standard products, or by creating legal instruments with equal shares of a risky income stream. The main connection of this elegant abstract "stock market structure" with the messy complexity of real life economies is in the standardization of goods. Our central argument is that this standardization is a cognitive achievement, and that buyers, market makers, and sellers all have to have a deep conviction that the "equivalent" commodities in a large flow of, say, financial instruments are really all the same. Otherwise a competitive price for that good would not make economic sense, let alone be the outcome of routine activity by a crowd of buyers and sellers gathered around a market maker, who can give and accept a new price every few minutes.

The sociology of liquidity, then, has two aspects. First, the market of people interested in liquidity have to reach down to specify what they will accept as standard and homogeneous. We[1] show in this chapter that, for example, people in the highly liquid secondary mortgage market are not willing to accept shares of mortgages on particular assets, issued by various mortgage banks, as homogeneous goods that will always have a price. Instead they have to be turned into a flow of homogeneous goods by a government agency set up to make a market in those flows of mortgage payments by homogenizing their risk and return features. We also show that in the late seventeenth century the bonds of the sovereign of England were not accepted as standard commodities, with a continuous price, but that by the eighteenth century they could be sold to corporations that already had liquid shares, forming part of the asset and income streams of those entities and so of those shares. This resulted in indirect liquidification of the government bonds, by transforming them into claims on the flow of income of corporations that owned them as well as other claims on other income streams.

That is, the sociology is in taking the heterogeneous claims on streams

1. "We" in this chapter refers to the two authors, Bruce G. Carruthers and Arthur L. Stinchcombe, or to those authors and a reader who is invited to go along with part of an argument for the time being, so as to understand and judge the argument as a whole. I (this means Stinchcombe, in fitting the paper on which this chapter is based to this book) have omitted some material from our joint paper (Carruthers and Stinchcombe 1999) that bear mainly on the economic importance of the processes we analyze, on its relation to economic theory, and on its relation to political economy, which are not of direct relevance to our purpose here. I have also added material from our earlier draft on the flexibility of organizations, which was cut from the published paper but is relevant to our purpose here.

of income associated with different sorts of assets, and turning them into standard commodities (Berle and Means 1991 [1932], 249). But one has to take into account what the crowd of buyers and sellers and the market makers have to know about that homogeneity, in order to be willing to take the going price in an auction as all they can, and all they need to, know about a large flow of commodified claims on income streams. That determines what a U.S. government market maker taking in the mortgages from issuing banks, securitizing them, and then reselling them on the secondary mortgage market, has to do, and what it therefore has to demand of the issuing bank. It also determines what the Bank of England or the British East India Company had to know about the bonds, and what the stock market had to know about the corporate assets and income streams of those companies represented in their ownership shares, for them to be able, indirectly, to treat the bonds of the British government as homogeneous commodities.

This chapter studies these two cases of homogenization, carried out deliberately and accidentally respectively, "in order to" make a market of commodified financial claims. Our purpose is to pose the theoretical problem of explaining such homogenization by studying these cases where it worked. This makes the structure of the argument look "functional," because it studies how the functional requirements of liquid markets came about. But in the case of liquidification of the British national debt, the liquidity was derived from transforming the public debt claims into claims on corporate flows of income that were already liquidified in the stock market. The stock market was not invented in order to do that job, but instead to trade stocks that were already homogenized by the law of share corporations. Further, the British had had a sovereign that could not liquidify its debt in this way for several centuries, before it was brought off at the end of the seventeenth century, and mortgages for the middle and working classes of the United States were extremely hard to get before the innovations of Fannie Mae. Both institutions lived on in part because they "served the function" of making the debts liquid, so money could be raised more cheaply. But the fact that there was no necessity that anything would fulfill that liquidifying function is shown by the long historical period in which it was not in fact fulfilled.

Fannie Mae, the nickname for a government agency whose early official name is forgotten, set out to do the job, done by accident for British government bonds, for residential mortgages. It was given this task for public policy purposes that the government thought to be connected to increased home ownership. Clearly this shows that the functional requirements of liquidity can be produced in quite different ways. We argue that the key that links these two ways is the kind of knowledge they produce about the homogeneity of claims on risky streams of income, a "sociology of knowledge" of the homogeneity requirements of continuous auctions in financial markets.

To test our understanding, we suggest a line of research into organizational flexibility, especially flexibility of organizational budgets. Besides being a plan, a budget is a set of authorizations to spend money belonging to a corporate group. The arrangement of flexibility has to be compounded of a set of rigidities so that the group as a whole does not go bankrupt, and a set of reserves that bear the risk that the plan will not quite work out, that new opportunities would be missed if the group stuck to the budget, or that losing operations would be allowed to continue until they sank the whole corporation. We argue that the combination of rigid formalization of the homogeneity of dollar amounts budgeted and the flexibility of authorized reserves is of the same general structure as the flexibility produced by liquid financial markets.

The cognitive and legal homogeneity of commodity flows, such that continuous prices can be maintained in such a way that everyone knows what the price is and knows they cannot do better elsewhere, explains the evolution of the dominance of financial markets in the modern world. That homogeneity is produced by carefully organized abstraction, so that the few remaining determinants determine the characteristics and behavior of those abstractions. We show that very similar processes produce easy fungibility in budgets within organizations by abstracting funds committed to a particular subbudget from all the purposes and risks of other departments; that abstraction is often protected from serious error by contingency reserve budgets at higher levels of authority. Thus something like liquidity in markets can happen within organizations.

LIQUIDITY IN ACTION: WHAT IS TO BE EXPLAINED

A Definition of the Degree of Liquidity

The eight indicators of a highly "liquid" asset are generally understood as follows: it can be sold or bought (1) quickly (Tobin 1989, 42), at (2) a price near its "market consensus" price, (3) which is known with a high degree of certainty, such that its value (4) is highly predictable for some (5) known interval of time into the future, by the prediction's (6) being some known function of prices of other valuable things (including of course money) at that time, (7) with very little information available, in addition to that price or future value information common to market participants, that is of any use in pricing ("transparency of the market" with few insider trading opportunities), and (8) with either a low or a well-known degree of risk or uncertainty (see Stiglitz 1993, 265–66). Some of these indicators are causally related to each other and so are not independent measures of liquidity, but they give a notion of why, say, Treasury bond markets are more liquid than markets for industrial installations.

All these aspects of "knowledge" about an asset have to be socially established in such a way that many buyers and many sellers in a market believe the same things about that asset. If they did not, then market prices would be unstable, bid and ask prices would diverge markedly, speculative use of information or willingness to take risks would create insiders with secret information, or delays for appraisal of values and risks would slow the market. Thus the degree of liquidity of assets is a problem in the sociology of knowledge.

Obviously a market price is a social construction, and everyone who shops in two grocery stores (let alone in two hardware stores or with two real estate agents) knows of markets where knowledge of prices could not be shared by opening and closing prices of carrots, and where the extra carrots one bought by mistake could not be sold quickly near that published price. Illiquidity is not uncommon in most of the markets most of us do our buying in.

It is important to realize that the knowledge people seek that creates liquidity is not knowledge of everything that could be known, but rather everything that others in the market might know at the time. Later more will be known about the true expected value of a stock option when the option falls due. Insider trading is forbidden because it creates inequality in knowledge, not because it destroys perfect knowledge; it is inequality that can be "unfairly" exploited by insiders.

Thus the "certainty" that creates liquidity of a stock price on an exchange is the certainty that no one knows the consensus market price better than the people who are selling (or buying) at that price, because of the way the market is structured. This creates a socially established "evolutionary" epistemology. As long as one knows the selective pressures on the knowledge, one "knows" that at the present time (though with no commitments to the future) one cannot know better what the expected value of a given income stream represented by a security is.

Further, this epistemology is relative to other participants in the market, rather than relative to the *Ding an sich*, rather than relative to some ultimate reality about utilities and production costs on into the future. It is fear of game-theoretical exploitation of superior knowledge that makes markets stiff and illiquid. We need a sociology of knowledge that represents buyers' and sellers' own epistemology of the market. They hold that epistemology to be certain in the temporary evolutionary sense that it is the best knowledge available, because of the way it is created.[2]

For most of the examples in this chapter we talk about markets in which there are many professional, or at least sophisticated, traders. A somewhat related phenomenon for ordinary people is the notion of a "fixed price" in stores. Thus, for example, lumberyards and many hardware stores usually have discounts for contractors, and therefore are not fixed-price traders. But most people do not believe that they could get the contractor's price; even fewer believe they could buy directly from the wholesalers. Thus many times the fixed price clients treat as a "market" price is not actually fixed at a given time. The more professional the traders at the local hardware, the less likely they are to pay the "fixed" price. But in an ideal liquid market, except for explicit transaction fees, both professional and amateur buyers get the same price, and the price is published in the financial pages of newspapers. Thus the sociology of knowledge question is how there can be a certainty about a fixed price that is available to everybody, and no one believes that he or she could make a special deal for a better price outside the market, because the "real" price is lower.

The argument of this chapter is that there are three master social mechanisms that work together to produce such socially constructed facts that can be known quickly with a high degree of certainty: continuous auctions; market making; and homogenization of commodities (including the formalized stratification of risks). The first two are routinely studied by economists and serve mainly as background here. We describe them as variables that determine the degree of liquidity of an asset or an asset market.

The degree to which there are continuous auctions of an asset is the degree to which there are many buyers and sellers in continuous (or more exactly, small interval) bidding and offering competition against each other.[3] These buyers and sellers bid for or offer varying quantities, according to the amount of demand and supply in the market. In general the highest liquidity means that brokers physically present in the auction, or in telephone or computer contact with it, buy and sell on orders from

2. Presumably something similar is true of the paradigms that, at a particular time, reign among research scientists with the best training and the most creative minds. A paradigm is the best known at a given time, known to be the best because of the way it was created and the evolutionary pressures to which it has been subjected. But if it remains that way in the future, there would be no occupation for scientists in improving it, just as there are no wins in the options market when future prices are controlled.

3. Smith (1989, 31) shows how even discontinuous auctions can function to create prices for unique or hard-to-value commodities, but they do not create certainty that the good can be traded later.

investors. The essence of such a social structure is that in "very small" time intervals a new reading of market consensus is created.

Thus a structure is more nearly a continuous auction the shorter the time intervals between transactions and the more the competition among buyers and among sellers reflects a market consensus on the value of the asset. The interval is shorter the larger the volume of "identical" goods demanded by many buyers, and offered by many sellers, that flows though the auction. The auction reflects market consensus when the distance between "over the counter" prices (prices by contracts outside the auction) and prices "in the exchange" (where the continuous auction goes on) are very small.

At the other end of the spectrum from a continuous auction is the social process of "appraisal" of a more or less unique object as in real estate mortgage origination.[4] In appraisal there is usually at most one potential buyer and one potential seller who have agreed to a price, and the market consensus is estimated from roughly comparable real (in the "market method" of appraisal [Friedman 1968]) or imaginary (in the "cost method" or the "income method" of appraisal) sales.

Market Makers as Creators of the Eight Conditions of Liquidity

By a "market maker" we mean an individual or (more usually) an organization that takes an illiquid asset and turns it into a more liquid one.[5] Such transformation work occurs in a number of different ways, including the stratification of risks associated with an asset. The maker may itself assume the extra risks of the "subordinated" or "residual" claims, and sell the more liquid "senior claims," or may estimate the market consensus more accurately (for example, by rating bonds), or agree to buy (or sell) the asset in the future ("options") at a known price, or organize an auction or make an auction more continuous.

For example, by pooling large numbers of mortgages and guaranteeing the income stream from the pools, Fannie Mae makes them more liquid; by offering to buy a pool of mortgages of a given kind from a mortgage-issuing bank several months in advance at a given interest rate, it makes the consensual market price of such a mortgage pool predictable for the length of time required to close on them (Fabozzi and Modigliani 1992). Pooling large numbers of home mortgages also reduces the amount of information needed to understand the value of the loan: instead of compiling idiosyncratic information about each individual home

4. Or, similarly, the determination of a transfer price from one division of a corporation to another in the absence of comparable market prices. See Eccles 1985; Eccles and White 1988.
5. Telser 1981 and Telser and Higinbotham 1977 describe how organized futures exchanges create liquid markets.

and borrower, a lender need only compile aggregate information about means and variances of the pool of mortgages. Pooling renders the value of a loan more generally "knowable" and encourages those with little particular knowledge of the individual mortgagee to nevertheless lend their money.[6]

Thus Fannie Mae increases the liquidity of the mortgage market by transforming a future flow of investment funds, from the secondary mortgage market, into an instrument that governs the further flow of funds to the issuing bank, and thence to the real estate client. The instrument is a forward price of funds offered by Fannie Mae to the issuer. Fannie Mae guarantees the issuing bank will get funds from the secondary market at a given rate, or itself make up (or keep) the difference. This gives the issuing bank a short-run guaranteed resale price for mortgages they will be originating (the interest rate Fannie Mae guarantees will be the issuer's price of funds).

It increases the liquidity of mortgages so generated by transforming the flow of mortgage interest and principal payments from the client into a guaranteed income flow (or at least "rated for risk" flows) for investors in the secondary market. Fannie Mae then is a "market maker" in our sense. Market makers are paid for their work and risks by a "spread" between a higher rate of return for the more illiquid asset (here the mortgage) and that for the liquid asset (here the share of a mortgage pool or a security based on it).

Fannie Mae itself takes "subordinated risks" on both sides of this process: the risk that the cost of funds will be higher or lower by the time the issuer closes the pool and sells it to Fannie Mae, and the varying risk of default or prepayment on a pool of mortgages lowering or raising various parts of the income stream at particular times. By absorbing some sets of risks (although not all), Fannie Mae reduces the complexity of home mortgages as an asset, and renders them more liquid.

Degrees of Liquidity of the Investment Base of the Market

Of course at the bottom of the pyramid of stratification into more or less liquid and abstract claims is the use value of some thing, or some going concern that can produce real goods and services. These productive resources, people, or organizations themselves have different degrees of liquidity, in the sense of multiple practically available buyers and sellers, known values, large flows of homogeneous goods with small intervals between sales, and the like. Wholesale wheat or steel of a given grade, or

---

6. If organized futures markets encourage trade among strangers, then Fannie Mae encourages home mortgage loans among strangers.

even retail gasoline of a given mix of chemical structures, are toward the highly liquid end of commodity markets. The classification of wheat into homogeneous categories arranged by the Chicago Board of Trade helped to increase the liquidity of nineteenth-century commodity markets (Lurie 1979). Real estate plots possibly containing oil resources exploitable only with exploration and development are at the illiquid end of value, only to be combined with a long stream of organizational, financial, and labor resources in a highly uncertain future. They are therefore not easily marketable because few know what they will be worth. Making mineral rights as liquid as blue sky stocks is a formidable challenge at any time. Wheat still in the fields, or oil refined into motor fuel, are already a good basis for a liquid futures market.

Producing Liquidity as a Means of Producing Investment

In the previous discussion of liquidity, the capital market is understood to produce instruments that investors requiring high liquidity will invest in. But it is crucial to the production of liquid investments that in their origins the investments yield an original use value return substantial enough to pay the ultimate return to the investor in the liquid instrument, and to pay the administrative "origination" costs, and the credit, risk-taking, insurance, and administrative costs of market making. It is because illiquid or "invested" capital has substantive productive returns, for example to the homeowner or to the renters of space in a shopping mall, that it can pay liquidifying costs plus returns to investors demanding liquidity.

One source of illiquidity for financial assets is that real investments do not have predictable money returns for the period of years that it takes to amortize the capital invested and pay interest. But it is the social and economic fact that the substantive returns from capital come from such investments that makes governments and others want to solve the problem of liquidity. Fannie Mae and Fannie Mac were deliberately created by the government to liquidify mortgage loan banks' claims on homes, so as to increase the capacity of the society to build homes for individual homeowners. By increasing the willingness of those who demand liquid assets to invest in such mortgages, the total flow of investment into single family dwellings could be increased. The demand for money by householders to invest in illiquid houses could be supplied from the money of investors requiring quite liquid investments only if the government made mortgages liquid.

Many such institutions have been created by merchant and industrial capitalists, so as to make it possible both for potential *rentiers* to invest their money profitably without losing liquidity, and for firms to acquire capital for activities they thought would produce high returns from illiquid investments.

To reconcile the illiquidity of many investments with the liquidity preference of many investors can require considerable effort. The claim on a stream of profits constituted by a corporate common stock, for example, could find a great many more investors if it could easily be sold in a continuous auction on a stock exchange, because a continuous auction creates liquidity of the capital value. Senior claims at a lower rate of return, such as preferred stocks or corporate bonds, could reach still other investors, provided there were markets in those securities as well. Public debt likewise could find more investors if it were rendered liquid in markets, and the use of a previously established private institution like the stock market to liquidify the public debt allowed commercial countries like the Netherlands and England to conduct successful wars, especially in capital intensive arenas such as oceans and seas, against larger but unliquidified Continental powers. (We consider this more closely in a later section of this chapter.)

One device to render a financial instrument more liquid is to make it valid for repayment of all debts, or all debts to the state. Insofar as one believes in the continuity of the state and its commitments, the promise to accept legal tender for all sorts of taxes creates some of the kind of certainty of value that renders a money liquid. Situations in which those commitments are not credible make money less liquid (Zelizer 1994). For example, paper money is not ordinarily liquid during a revolution or in an occupied territory after a war.

The Mechanics of Liquidity in Markets

MARKET MAKERS

Market makers in stock markets conduct a continuous auction of a given stock. By "auction" we mean situations in which a group of physically present potential buyers meets a set of one or more sellers. "Continuous" means that sometimes for short periods the market makers must own stocks for which there are no bidders at the moment (a "long" position) or have sold stocks they have not yet bought (a "short" position). To maintain liquidity then they have to anticipate the next bid or the next offer, and must have credit or capital to cover the balances or shortages.

The more volatile the price, the larger the "spread" between buying and selling prices the market makers will demand. If there are long intervals between sales or purchases, this is essentially the same as higher unpredictability, and so has the same effect as high volatility. If we fold these two together with market volume (interval times volatility times amount of exposure) as "uncertainty" during the interval between buying and selling (or vice versa), the larger the uncertainty the larger the spread a market maker will demand. At too large a spread, sellers and buyers will seek to do business together directly, and the market will become discontinuous and illiquid. Other "securities" besides stocks have the same broad requirements for there to exist both a buying and selling price at all times.

Thus there are four basic indicators of the degree of liquidity of a market in a given security: (1) whether or not people or organizations are willing to become and remain market makers, so that there are continuous prices in the market, maintained *au courant* by a theoretically continuous auction; (2) how much use there is by market makers of the short-term money market or their own capital, with greater use indicating more market making; (3) high or low volume of exchanges so that there are a small intervals on average between offers and between bids, and many sellers and buyers in the market in each small interval of time, maintaining a close contact between market consensus and the market maker's bid or offer price; and (4) the spread between the makers' buying price and selling price, with a high spread indicating volatility or long intervals and so low liquidity, and low spread indicating high liquidity (Telser 1981, 17).

TRANSACTION LENGTH AND RETIMING AS LIQUIDITY

Bills of exchange were a financial instrument invented in the late Middle Ages to effect payments for long-distance trade. Cash was scarce and hard to ship over long distances, so bills of exchange served as an alternative source of liquidity.[7] Bills of exchange also allowed an exporter (or other seller) to make a debt owed him by the buyer liquid so it could be used to buy more materials and pay wages to manufacture something else to fill future shipments with. If the buyer did not (or could not) pay for the goods until it got them, it would instead give a bill of exchange that promised to pay when the goods were received (or thirty days afterward), let's say "collectible in London" on that date. So the timing of the substantive transaction was constrained by the fact that the importer (or other buyer) could not sell the goods until he got them, but the seller had sold the goods and shipped them and wanted to make more.

The bill of exchange then could become negotiable, and thus function as a kind of money, if, say, a bank of the importer guaranteed to pay the bill when it became due, and this guarantee became security for a loan for the intervening period. The rapid underwriting of this loan was obtained by "discounting" the bill of exchange at the exporter's bank, which in turn

---

7. For the details on how bills worked, see Neal 1990, 5–7; Fletcher 1976.

discounted it (at a lower charge) with a "discount house." In essence, then, the discount was interest on a short-term loan, in modern times usually by the discount house. The difference between the discount the exporter had to pay and what its bank had to pay to the discounting house was in part a difference in the interest rate for lending to a bank (by the discount house) and lending to an exporter on the security of the shipment and the corresponding promise of the importer's bank to pay when the shipment was received, or thirty days later (and presumably the promise of the insurer of the shipment to pay if shipment was not received).

Similarly the credit investigations and other matters involved in acquiring a mortgage create a fairly long time lapse between when the lender quotes the interest rate at which it will lend and the time the transaction is "closed." If the lender depends for funds on a secondary market, then there is a question of what rate that secondary market will be offering for mortgage obligations when the mortgage is in fact sold. What the lender "needs," then, is liquidification of its promise to sell a mortgage at a future date, by knowing what interest rate the secondary market will be offering at that date.

STRATIFICATION OF RISKS; HOMOGENIZATION OF SECURITIES

What Fannie Mae did was to guarantee to buy a block of mortgages of a given size at a given rate at the end of a specified period in order to "make a market" in mortgages still to be transacted, that is, several weeks in the future. On that assurance, the lenders could lend with their own money promising a (somewhat higher) rate determined by what they could then "borrow" on that security at a later date.

Both the exporter and the mortgage lender face the problem of liquidity because the period of the real transaction is so long. In the first case, an exporter that has sold its goods cannot afford to sit still while it waits to receive cash from the buyer. Instead, it receives a note (a bill of exchange) that it then endorses and uses as if it were cash to buy more supplies, pay wages, or satisfy whatever debts it has acquired. The bill changes hands as it is successively discounted and endorsed, and each endorser in effect guarantees the debt when it finally becomes payable. In the other case, lenders know they can sell a mortgage loan on the secondary market, given that the loan conforms to Fannie Mae standards and has satisfactory creditworthiness. The liquidity of loans encourages them to lend since they themselves will not get "locked in" to a long-term illiquid investment. This liquidity is created by the action of Fannie Mae in standardizing and pooling mortgages, and then guaranteeing them. By reducing the credit and interest rate risks to investors, Fannie Mae enlarges the set of buyers for mortgage loans and so renders them more liquid.

Liquidity in both markets requires overcoming the "friction" of real transaction times, and requires guarantors in the form of Fannie Mae, endorsers, or discount houses. Then the issuing banks or first discounting banks can in their turn guarantee credit, combined perhaps with transaction services, to the substantive transactors, and consequently render the substantive transactors' assets (for example, those of the exporters and importers) more liquid.

In investment markets, the primary differentiators of commodities are the level of risk, and how that covaries with other risks. For example, for debts the primary determinants of risks are (1) the probability of default by the going concern or person that owes the money, (2) how that covaries with the value of the security, and (3) how the probability of paying off the loan covaries with the market interest rate, so that it won't be paid off if the market interest rate is higher than the contracted interest rate and will be paid off if the market rate is lower. The standardization of these abstract features of a debt is central to the standardization of the loans as commodities in investment markets.

The stratification of risks by all these variables is the primary task of the formalities at the bottom of the market. For mortgages, as we discuss below, the credit rating and income data are central to the default risk, the appraisal and the down payment are central to the value of the security, and Fannie Mae's pooling and classification of the pool risks into "tranches" that are more or less exposed to early payment are central to market risk of interest rate variation (see Lewis 1989, 136–37, and below on stratification of risks).

The outline in this first part of the chapter, then, has given the basic provisions of the social structure of markets for which the achievement of liquidity is a specific and well-understood objective. Three features can be seen at the core of ensuring liquidity: the existence of a continuous auction; the existence of people who do the work and take the risks of the continuity of the auction (market makers and discount houses); and the stratification and homogenization of risks, and the specialized bearing of those risks, by those who provide short-term credit to ensure the continuity of the auction.

TURNING HOUSES INTO MARKETABLE BONDS IN THE SECONDARY MORTGAGE MARKET

On the Illiquidity of Real Property

There are two main sources of illiquidity that inhere in real property: the variety of consumer benefits or utilities from residential property, and the variety of risks in expected income streams from residential rental, commercial, or industrial property. Both types of variation arise from the highly idiosyncratic and complex nature of housing (every home is unique). Both derive from the fact that real property has to be incorporated into going concerns, ordinarily households or firms, to produce the stream of benefits for which it serves as capital.

Households vary in the kinds of benefits they want to produce with a residence (for example, benefits for adults only, or for families with children), how long they expect to demand the particular benefits the property helps produce, how much they are oriented to capital gain, how much they enjoy maintaining a house, how much they have to spend (and consequently which built-in luxuries will determine the decision by balancing substantive utilities with costs), and how liquid they want their wealth and income to be and so how much of it they want to commit to residential investment. In short, homes are idiosyncratic goods that meet heterogeneous needs. Thus when appraisers want market information on what a given house is worth, they need to consider "closely comparable houses" (same neighborhood, same size, same luxury level, and so on). Households trying to construct lives that are easy to live in a given house, which constitute the micromarket for the house, would not consider other houses that were not "closely comparable." Thus the basic liquidity condition of many buyers meeting many sellers is not met at the bottom (the substantive assets that are the "security" for the mortgage) of the residential mortgage market.[8]

"Appraisal" by comparison with a few closely comparable residences, expertly turned into an estimate of market value, is expected to come within 5 percent of the actual selling price about half the time. Or to put it another way, "market consensus" on a house's value does not exist, so a marketable claim on that value has to be constructed in a special way before that claim is itself marketable to investors who value liquidity.

The magnitude of the income stream generated by a rental residential, commercial, or industrial property ordinarily enters in a simple fashion into the utility function of the owner—namely, as a return rate on the capital invested. But such investment properties are very much affected

8. Lewis (1989, 85) formulates this sharply. "Mortgages are not tradable pieces of paper; they were not bonds. . . . A single home mortgage was a messy investment for Wall Street, which was used to dealing in bigger numbers. No trader or investor wanted to poke around suburbs to find out whether the homeowner to whom he had just lent money was creditworthy. For the home mortgage to become a bond, it had to be depersonalized. At the very least, a mortgage had to be pooled with other mortgages of other homeowners. Traders and investors would trust statistics and buy into a pool of several thousand mortgage loans made by a savings and loan, of which, by the laws of probability, only a small fraction should default. . . . Thus standardized, the pieces of paper could be traded."

by fluctuations in local commodity and service markets, traffic flows, competition, shifting fashions, and the like. The risk is in the local market, rather than changing household utilities. Where such risks are hard to estimate (strictly speaking, where uncertainty rather than risk is involved), it is difficult for potential buyers to assess the true value of the property, and hence they become reluctant to unless there are high returns. But for a bank lending at a fixed rate, or a rate adjustable to a specific market criterion, the high returns may not be an option. The risk of losing the principal lent as well as the interest is therefore not compensated. The interest rates for such mortgages are therefore normally higher, and may not be available at all.

Further, the risks are differentially distributed to different kinds of claimants. Equity claims, for example, are usually more risky than mortgages. Leaseholds by occupying firms or residents ordinarily reduce risks to residual equity owners and mortgagors, but increase risks of renting firms if their own market positions change. The more predictable the income stream, the less local knowledge is required to assess its remaining uncertainty; and the more standard the leveraging, leaseholding, and other financial conditions, the closer a claim will be to owning a Treasury bill and so the more liquid it will be.

The more a residential property is held as a real estate speculation rather than as a household utility, the more its uncertainties are like those of income property, and the less dependent its future flow of benefits is on changing family conditions and the more dependent the flows are on market conditions. As the range of substantive utilities narrows down to financial ones, the remaining trade-offs in the utility functions of owners are likely to be those of financial theory: present versus future returns, quantities of net revenues, risks, and degrees of liquidity.

The statistical generalizations in appraisals then take on a "cellular statistical" form. The continuous form, for gross comparisons of markets (where the cells within which substitution is mostly confined can be ignored), is that the more heterogeneous the benefits valued in a market and the more heterogeneous the production processes for those benefits in terms of returns, the time paths of returns, and their risks, the less liquid the market as a whole is likely to be.

As one approaches small "cells" of the market where "comparable properties" produce substitutable benefits for productive households or firms, "appraisal" becomes possible. Nearby market cells containing "partially substitutable" properties also provide something like outer limits for estimating market value, as do new properties that could be built to the criteria of the market within the cells. The value of a house is, so to speak, "earmarked" as the value of a house like this one in an environment like this neighborhood for people with a life-style and financial resources like this client.

Such earmarking is rendered liquid by stratifying the claims on the benefits and income streams involved into senior and junior claims, with the junior ones taking more of the risk of getting the proper cell values wrong.[9] The appraisal, then, is concerned with sufficient knowledge of the cell of comparable houses so that the value and degree of risk of the benefit stream generated by this house can be assessed, stratified, and sold at more or less well-known degrees of risk, temporal organization, and rates of return: in short, can be liquidified. Generalized knowledge of value engenders liquidity.

Information in the appraisal can be added to information on the future income stream to be expected from the borrower. A "credit rating" of the going concern owning and managing the property (a family or a firm, usually) reinforces the value of that income and security information. The borrower assumes the risks of the value of the house being lower than its appraised value by paying a down payment, and this "equity insurance" for the secured value reduces risk. This risk bearing is also information about the borrower's seriousness. Both of these sources of information and security increase the probability that the equity holder will be able and willing to guard his equity by paying off the mortgage.

To this informational input from the borrowing process, a further stratification of risks helps make mortgages more liquid. In particular, mortgages can be sold or guaranteed in pools, and the risk stratification can be based on the (usually less variable) risks of the pool. But that further abstraction (by Fannie Mae) assumes that the basic properties can be accurately appraised on the average, and the households or firms owning them can be given a credit rating.

But in addition, the claim of the mortgagee (the bank) itself on the security (the house) must be legally actionable in case of the debtor's (the mortgagor's) default. In real estate this depends on the buyer's title of the house being clear, and the mortgage itself being a clear contingent claim on that title. Titles can be historically unclear (for example, if once sold by a nonowner) requiring title insurance, or can become unclear by nonpayment of taxes (requiring monitoring or escrow of tax payments), or a claim may become valueless by disappearance of the underlying property (requiring fire and other insurance).

9. This does not imply that all such stratifications of risk into junior and senior categories necessarily makes senior claims more liquid than junior ones. In the case of claims on a corporation, for example, shares (residual claims) can be as liquid as bonds (senior claims). What matters is that both are relatively homogeneous classes of assets. In housing the residual claims are more heterogeneous, so less liquid.

Uncertainties of Estimated Value, Formalization, and Liquidity

Let us define production of a liquid instrument as the production of a document or emblem recognizable by its formal features alone, regardless of its history or other symbolic features, that is accepted by a wide variety of people or organizations (and in particular by a capital market) as a valid social claim. Thus a dollar bill is a liquid social emblem—a liquid instrument—because by its formal features alone, regardless of whether it was once stolen, or should have been paid in taxes, or has references to God but is in the hands of an unbeliever, it is widely accepted as worth a dollar. The process of turning out such liquid instruments and endowing them with exchangeable value we might call, by an obvious analogy, "minting work" on a given claim.

Our argument in this section is that organizations that do minting work on a claim such as a mortgage do so by actively stripping it of its distinctiveness, by "formalization." But one of the distinctive organizational features of this particular kind of formalization is that much of it is required to be done by people other than the property buyer or mortgagor; a borrower would be likely to exaggerate the value of a house, borrow a large sum, and emigrate. The originating bank or mortgagee is often "paid a fee" proportional to the loan value, often in the form of a higher interest rate than it borrows the money for on the secondary market; that bank therefore also has a motive to exaggerate value, though it bears part of the risk.

For example, different pieces of real estate property have different degrees of uniqueness versus exchangeability. There is ordinarily in most cities an active market in houses, so an appraiser can find three quite comparable houses (neighborhood, size, upkeep, and so on) that have been sold recently. These can, with adjustments for such features as there being or not being a garage or for the estimated cost of deferred maintenance, provide an estimated market value for a given house "within the market cell of substitutability." This predicted value of exchangeability can then be combined with a down payment percentage (the equity of the buyer that bears the residual risk) that gives a predicted degree of security, and helps render a mortgage more liquid. One of the reasons very large mortgages on mansions often have a higher interest rate is that the estimate of what they can be sold for is much more uncertain.

A shopping mall in the same city may have to negotiate a set of leases with particular future tenants to provide a comparable degree of security. Then the credit rating and quality of business planning of those tenants form part of the assessment of those leases and hence of that security. The appraisal of the market value of that mall, then, is much more a matter of unique valuation and will have to be done by different means. We come back to this shortly in considering "equity insurers."

Residential mortgages require much easier minting work to produce a claim on the secure future stream of mortgage payments, or repossession and resale proceeds. It is therefore more easily liquidified, and therefore to become eventually a liquid mortgage security in the secondary market. A first requirement for minting work is a classification of different potential mortgages into categories defined by the market as a whole (compare the concept "negotiated information order" in Heimer 1985) by their degree of uniqueness. By "degree of uniqueness" we mean the inverse of the degree to which a large number of comparable risks are formalized by the same method and sold as comparable liquid instruments, perhaps in a pool of such instruments.

Because it is a member of a large class of comparable instruments, then, a residential mortgage is easier than a mortgage on a shopping mall to turn into a liquid instrument. And a first indication of why it is a member of a class of comparable instruments is that a competent appraiser can find comparable sales in comparable areas and adjust them by reasonable approximations of how much, for example, a garage costs, and so turn out a solid prediction of the future market price of the underlying gage (the house) pledged.

Minting Work Requires the Control of Moral Hazard

In addition to formalization or homogenization of a residential mortgage, the work involved in taking advantage of this multiplicity of comparisons in order to classify them together requires substantive judgments of three (or some other number) "comparable" sales. Since this is a corruptible process, it is best done either by a person independent of the client and of the originating lender or lender's broker, or by a rigidly incorruptible set of procedures. The problem with rigid incorruptibility is that the successful sales in, for example, a Houston neighborhood may have all been closed before the bottom dropped out of the oil market, and the price of Brent Light crude may not be built into the rigid Houston appraising procedure until too late. But it will be obvious to any real estate appraiser working in Houston at the time Brent Light went down that nobody is willing to pay the house prices they were paying the previous summer. Consequently the independent appraiser is probably more reliable in the long run, less corruptible by a mortgage broker with a rigid procedure that gives it an opportunity to finance a lot of weak contracts and collect the fees before Fannie Mae finds out that a Houston mortgage is not worth that much any more.

Connected to this appraisal by an independent professional is the upper amount of the loan. This serves as an estimate of the lowest value that can be got out of the house if it is taken over for nonpayment of the mortgage. This must necessarily include the amount it would cost to take over the house and sell it, a cost that is presumably an estimate of the future costs for the mortgaging bank and its agents. Loans on malls have to have either a quite separate appraisal system, or more participation of "equity insurers" in making that appraisal and backing it with reserves of their own.

Obviously the expected value of the future income stream from the house buyer depends on whether all these troubles, against which the gage is pledged, arise at all. If the mortgagor pays regularly and does not refinance, then the future income stream is more secure, more easily turned into a liquid instrument. Again the assessment of credit ratings would be corruptible if the broker (or first mortgagee acting with the intention to create a liquid instrument) were to do the credit check. For example, Stinchcombe discovered that neither his canceled check nor a receipt from the bank saying he had paid off a previous loan was enough to pass the credit check. Instead the bank had to notify the credit rating company that the debt was canceled before his loan could be approved. The check and the receipt were more corruptible than the bank's notice to an independent credit agency.

Finally the title insurance people have to certify that the trail of paper is perfect enough so that they will insure the mortgagee (and if pressed perhaps the owner of the house also) that the title is clear. Property ownership must be unambiguous.

A routine is set up so that it is not the mortgage broker, nor the mortgagee, nor the client that certifies or estimates any of the crucial questions about the value of real property, the legal documentation, or the owner's solvency. To do so would be to invoke the kind of information asymmetries that afflict markets for lemons (Akerlof 1970). So the issuing bank producing a liquid instrument for exchanges in the capital market, to be backed by a third party's (the mortgagor's) property, requires an arrangement of "fourth parties" to certify that various aspects of the expectable value of the instrument are indeed there.

Second mortgages presumably require more risk taking by the direct mortgagee before they can be passed on to become negotiable. Similarly special mortgages on shopping malls, balloon mortgages that involve a bet about refinancing in seven years, or mortgages on more precarious property rights (for example, mortgages where the security is a long-term lease), all require stratification of risks with some risk bearers charging more than others. In such cases the market makers need to know not only about the regular "insurers" like title and fire, but also what one

might call "equity insurers," who maintain reserves of equity to guarantee against "unique" risks. One indicator of this should be the margin between interest rate charged by the originating issuer of the mortgage
loan, compared with the secondary mortgage rate; the issuing bank
should be taking less risk when more of the risk is taken by equity participants with deep pockets, and so should take a lower margin on the interest rate.

The control of moral hazard in the mortgage origination process requires formalization because both the mortgagor house buyer and mortgagee bank may have an interest in misrepresenting the risks. As usual, it
depends on the interests of the entity making the abstraction how likely
the abstraction is to be accurate. Using fourth parties to certify aspects
of the mortgage origination process increases the "transparency" of the
market, in the language of chapter 2. The certification by an appraiser
rather than one of the interested parties of the estimated market value, by
a credit rating agency of the creditworthiness of the buyer, by a title insurance agent of the quality of the legal documentation of rights and
risks, by the buyer's bank for the certified check for closing costs and
down payment—all tend to eliminate moral hazard risks from the transaction. This formalization, by preventing misrepresentation, then allows
the acceptance of the mortgage document itself as a relatively liquid instrument, to be sold to the market maker (for example, to Fannie Mae)
for further liquidification.

Market Making in Mortgages

The market makers in the residential mortgage market are predomi-
nantly those created by the government itself to provide liquidity so that
more money would flow into mortgages (U.S. Department of the Treasury 1996, 17). The theory at the time was that owner-occupied houses
had a higher return in real utilities than houses costing the same but
owned by landlords.[10] There are many reasons to believe that resident-
owned residences can be designed and repaired to the unique tastes and
competencies of households better than can standardized rental housing
responding to an anonymous market. But that very policy preference
forced the government to confront the uniqueness problem in residential real property in a way that was evidently beyond the competence of
the real estate investment market at that time. The abstract theory of

10. Underwriting such liquidity has increased home ownership and thus also provided
political benefits, especially for those politicians and political parties most favorable to
property. The subsidy of mortgages by the tax break on the interest on mortgages both increases the market for single-family dwellings as compared with rented housing, and itself
makes politicians more popular except for those who raise local taxes.

capitalism says that capitalists would find out about the superior value of owned residences compared with rented residences for the same investment, would provide mortgages that paid a profit to people who wanted that added value, and would make money on it. The fact that capitalism did not in fact do so without government sponsorship suggests that formalization sufficient for the secondary mortgage market was not easy to create. Capitalism did not produce a functioning secondary mortgage market for housing; the government did.

Other government programs providing rental housing for the poor have been criticized on the grounds that they do not elicit tenant responsibility for maintenance the way ownership does and that they provide housing of a lower quality, especially in neighborhood amenities and security from crime, than people would choose for themselves. Therefore public rental housing is alleged to be worse than would be provided at equal total cost spent by the tenants themselves, especially if they owned their residences. The tax subsidy for homeowners involved in this program to increase home ownership is about ten times as large as the amount spent on public housing in the United States. The creation of a secondary mortgage market itself has, however, pretty much paid for itself.

But from the point of view of this chapter, the mortgage market is a uniquely valuable case exactly because it starts at the bottom with such uncertain flows of value, flows that unaided capitalism had difficulty dealing with on the scale that government intervention succeeded with. It is also uniquely valuable in that there is a public record of how the market makers operated, what spreads were necessary to make it work, who bore what kinds of risks, and how the stratification of streams of future income was specified on such a massive scale. This is macroscopic government operating on a massive scale of millions of homes, and doing it better than capitalists could do it for themselves, by making capitalists interested in liquidity willing to invest in private debts backed by housing with partial government guarantees.

By the beginning of Fannie Mae, the first deliberately organized government mortgage market maker, the Veteran's Administration after World War II and the Federal Housing Authority (FHA) had already acquired experience at guaranteeing mortgages. This meant that the "minting regulations" for the original mortgages to be saleable could be adapted from these precedents and made general for home mortgages. The procedures for "closing" on a house with a mortgage could be then standardized and routinized throughout the country for all potential participants in the secondary mortgage market, which included almost all the bankers and savings and loans organizations that wrote residential mortgages. Most other forms of commercial and industrial real estate were not routinely included in those regulations because they were not to be resold by Fannie Mae and are harder to standardize into pools.

Fannie Mae (and later Fannie Mac) had government guarantees that functioned much like creditworthiness of the market-creating bank in the regular market, so that it was a believable divider of various risks and guarantor of various financial features of the bonds. (Citibank's credit-worthiness served essentially identical functions in the private market for mortgages on malls and factories.) The implicit faith and credit of the U.S. government also enabled the federal market makers to promise an interest rate for a few months in advance so that the originators of mort-gages could set their interest rate, then go through the documentation part of minting work, and still be able to offer the mortgage at the end at the same rate. This required that they know what they could resell it to Fannie Mae or Fannie Mac for. It turned a discontinuous market caused by the delay of closing a large number of mortgages into a continuous one, created essentially by the market makers selling futures options to buy a loan from the federal market makers at a known rate of interest, thus satisfying points (4) and (5) of our definition of liquidity (page 000). Some government authorities are proposing to abolish the guarantee by the faith and credit of the government, and it is not clear whether the guarantees that government agencies now provide would be believable if they were privatized.

In a pool of mortgages there are still some common risks that people and institutions buying bonds do not want to run. An especially impor-tant one is that the rate at which people prepay their mortgages increases when the interest rate goes down, because then the mortgage they hold is more expensive than the market cost of a new mortgage, or because they can afford a more expensive house at some future lower interest rate. The market makers can then segregate the risks of prepayment from the other risks, selling the securities that bear most of that risk at a higher in-terest rate, and selling the securities protected from that risk at a lower rate. This enables different investors to buy the combination of risks and returns they prefer, and makes all of the resulting securities liquid in the secondary market (Fabozzi and Modigliani 1992; Lewis 1989, 136–37). But such segregation of risks in large pools of mortgages requires the minting work of turning sales of unique houses into highly standardized mortgages in large pools, and thence into sales of differentiated securi-ties of claims on those pools that bear identical risks in the different tranches of those pools.

Liquidity is not a natural feature of markets that arises automatically. In American home mortgages, government action was necessary to pro-

duce it. And the core of the achievement was to take extremely heterogeneous risks and to standardize them by minting work that involved assessment of the values of relatively unique objects, stratification of risks,
control of moral hazard, and government-sponsored futures in interest
rates. Only with all of these could homogeneous commodities to sell on
secondary mortgage markets be produced. In sum, this was a function that
government did not have to serve, as is shown by the fact that it was orig-
inated only after the agencies were created. In order to serve that function,
government had to produce a system that in its turn produced abstractions
that the secondary mortgage market would believe in. This in turn meant
that it had to create a sociology of knowledge of the claim on a mortgage
pool made up of comparably formalized mortgages, so that such claims
could have many buyers and many sellers at a known market price.

LEGAL LIQUIDITY IN THE ENGLISH STOCK MARKET AND ITS EXTENSION TO THE BRITISH NATIONAL DEBT

The Legal Basis of Liquidity of Financial Assets in London

Although there are many tangible assets and physical commodities that
can be used to think about the origins of liquidity, financial assets are particularly useful for illuminating its structure and determinants. Financial
assets are obligations that extend over time. They involve promises to
pay, so their value depends on the credibility of the debtor's promise. As
compared to a material object or tangible thing, it is difficult to find out
the value of base-level financial assets, for that value rests on the future
behavior of a particular individual or organization. Assessing their value
is not simply a matter of gauging the purity of gold, or the volume of
milk, or the number of board feet of lumber.

Some particular features of financial assets can reduce the demand for
them. For example, if a debtor issues a note promising to pay so much
money six months hence, then only creditors who are willing to do without their capital for six months will be willing to lend money—there must
be a temporal match between the debtor and creditor. As Berle and Means
(1991 [1932], 249) put it: "The owner of non-liquid property is, in a sense,
married to it." Furthermore, liquidity is defined by how easily a promise
made to one person or firm (to repay a debt) can be transferred to another.
In short, liquidity can be especially problematic for financial instruments,
and so how they can become liquid is particularly instructive.

In this section of the chapter, we trace in rough outline how liquidity
was "supplied" in the early days of the modern London stock market. To
begin with, to go back even earlier to around 1680, there were a number
of joint-stock companies (the only one of any considerable size being

the East India Company), but there was no stock market, nor was there sufficient trading activity to give company shares much liquidity. The market was thin and sparse, and there were no professional traders or brokers. Hence, company shares were a relatively illiquid asset. Other related financial instruments such as government bonds, bills of exchange, and promissory notes were also difficult to assign, and to transfer their ownership entailed high transaction costs. By 1710, however, a dramatic change had occurred: London's stock market was very active, highly centralized, and extremely liquid. Many financial assets were traded on it, and transaction costs were low. Furthermore, the market was populated by a group of full-time traders who acted as market makers (the so-called stock jobbers; "jobber" here has the traditional meaning of "wholesaler"). What happened during this thirty-year period? Where did the liquidity come from? Unlike in the case of the secondary mortgage market, there was in this instance no liquidity by design.

To be liquid, a commodity or asset must be easily transferable. Under modern commercial law, most commodities are freely alienable, and so can be bought and sold in an unconstrained manner. Under traditional English common law, however, private debts and company shares were "choses in action,"[11] a kind of intangible property that was difficult if not impossible to transfer from one person to another (Blackstone 1872 [1766], 396–97). In order to sell financial obligations, creditors would have to be able to transfer all the rights and claims they had over their debtors to a third party. For example, if a creditor had the right to sue a debtor in court if the latter defaulted on a loan, then for that claim to be liquid third parties would also have to be able to sue if the debt were sold to them. Or if the creditor had the right to claim certain of the debtor's assets as collateral, that right would also have to be transferable. In common law, however, such rights were considered personal, and so applied only to the specific debtor and creditor who originally contracted the debt. This meant that third parties could not have as secure a title to the debt as the original creditor, which obviously discouraged transfer of debts. There would be no liquidity-enhancing secondary market for choses in action.

The Legal Transferability of Financial Assets

Sovereign debts, which were transferable in theory, were in practice hard to buy and sell. The bureaucratic procedure dictated by the Exchequer

---

11. Literally "things in action." The meaning is roughly: "Things that exist only by the right they give to bring an action in court against someone." The ineligibility of a buyer to bring suit then made that "thing" nonnegotiable.

for transferring title was exceedingly cumbersome and inconvenient. Thus the market in government bonds also lacked liquidity.

Legal transferability distinguished many public from private debts, but the absence of a centralized financial market reduced the liquidity of both. Transaction costs were high, debts were hard to price, market makers were absent, and it was difficult to match buyers with sellers. Potential buyers and sellers were scattered about, and it was costly to bring them together.

A series of legal and institutional changes substantially enhanced the liquidity of public and private debts, and contributed to the emergence of an organized, active financial market based in Exchange Alley in central London. No one set out deliberately to "create" liquidity, but by emulating the institutions and features of the Amsterdam Bourse, that is what happened. The accession of William of Orange in 1689 to the English throne, along with his Dutch advisors, played an important role in diffusing Dutch finance across the North Sea. Even without this direct influence, however, English commentators had long envied the financial sophistication of Dutch merchants and investors, and tried to reproduce their success.

On the legal front, English laws were altered so as to be more supportive of financial contracts and property rights. Through specific legislative acts like the Promissory Notes Act of 1704 (3 & 4 Anne, c.9), and through more general changes like the absorption of the law merchant (*lex mercatoria*) into common law, debts and financial instruments became freely alienable commodities. Furthermore, the actual costs of transacting in them dropped as methods of transfer became routinized. For instance, standardized contracts for buying and selling shares or for purchasing options were published in London business newspapers during the 1690s. Buyers and sellers used model contracts to save themselves the expense of negotiating their own. Since these shares were intangible form of property, legal standardization effectively standardized shares as commodities. The costs of information also decreased as share prices and interest rates were published on a daily basis. Any member of the English reading public could easily find out how much various financial commodities and assets were worth.

Effective demand for assets was greatest among the wealthy. But not all rich Englishmen were eager to buy exotic financial assets. The landed gentry in particular were suspicious of them and during this period continued to invest in land, although compared to other investments land had a low rate of return and little liquidity. The economic deficiencies of land were more than compensated, in the eyes of the gentry, by land's considerable social and political benefits, and by its comforting tangibility.

Merchants and traders, in contrast, were more familiar with financial assets and were eager to buy them. Thus, the number of potential buyers increased along with the expansion of trade and commerce at the end of the seventeenth century. The numbers and wealth of wholesale and manufacturing merchants grew substantially, and most of the biggest ones lived in the London region. In addition, as the stock market grew, it concentrated in the coffee houses of Exchange Alley (Jonathan's and Garroway's coffee houses, in particular). This geographic consolidation facilitated liquidity by bringing together in one place all those wishing to transact in the market, a crowd of buyers and sellers. It helped to produce a more nearly continuous auction. According to contemporary accounts, Exchange Alley was a small and easily identifiable location (it can still be found in central London, off Lombard Street).

The Extension of Stock Market Liquidity to the Public Debt

Of course, not all financial commodities were equally liquid. Company shares were probably the most liquid—they could easily be bought and sold in Exchange Alley (although the London stock market did lack one liquidity-enhancing feature characteristic of modern stock exchanges: official market makers). The procedures for transferring title were simple and involved a quick visit to the office of the relevant company and registration of the transaction in the stock transfer ledger.

Annuities-for-lives and lottery tickets (both issued by the British government), in contrast, were less liquid. Although legally alienable, the bureaucratic procedure for transferring title to both of these instruments was cumbersome. Furthermore annuities-for-lives were idiosyncratic assets whose true worth varied considerably, because these annuities obliged the Exchequer to pay out a sum so long as a particular person (nominated by the purchaser) was still alive. The annuity holder paid a sum to the Exchequer in exchange for annual payments contingent on a nominee's (who need not be the holder) life. Life-expectancy varied from person to person, and knowledge of another person's health could be hard for potential purchasers to obtain. Other nonfinancial assets were even less liquid. Land, for example, was very hard to buy and sell.

For sophisticated buyers with other assets and income streams already evaluated by the stock market, such as the British East India Company and the Bank of England, national debt was an investment with good returns. With the development of a practice of parliamentary approval of debt issues, together with laws assigning tax revenues to repayment, these debt instruments came to seem secure. Further, by adding to company assets by issuing new stocks and investing the additional money in the national debt, the debt became implicitly liquidified; one bought a salable interest in the national debt by buying salable shares of East India Company or Bank of England stock.

The consequences of liquidity were dramatic.[12] The long-term national debt grew substantially not only because government bonds paid an attractive rate of return, but also because they were liquid assets. Liquidity reconciled differing interests over loan maturity; it meant that the government could borrow long-term even though its creditors did not want to lend long-term. Should public creditors wish to recover their capital, they did not have to get it back from the government because they could simply turn to secondary markets and sell their company shares or bonds to someone else. And liquidity meant that there was no shortage of potential buyers. It also benefited private parties since they could now diversify their investment portfolios without fear of being financially "locked in" to a particular asset; in some sense it made shares themselves into portfolios of investments.

Although English students of the Amsterdam Bourse wished to emulate Dutch finance, they were not interested in liquidity per se. They believed that English economic, military, and political strength would benefit from the existence of an active capital market, but they did not set out consciously to create liquidity. Instead, they constructed a set of institutions that subsequently produced liquidity.

EXTENDING THE CONCEPT OF LIQUIDITY TO ORGANIZATIONAL BUDGETS AND FLEXIBLE ADAPTABILITY

Earmarking by Budgeting for Liquidity of Operations

The core document that reflects the decision of a firm or other organization to shift resources from one use to another is the budget. Budgetary changes, monitored over time, therefore reflect the different degrees of liquidity or flexibility of resources, with "overhead" (see Clark 1929 [1923]) and debt service being less liquid, operating expenses more liquid, and cash balances most liquid. As an authorization for future expenditures of departments, the budget gives them limited liquidity in pursuing assigned purposes and so is an instrument of limited operating flexibility. The capital budget's main purpose is to authorize turning liquid resources into illiquid buildings, machines, or research and development.

A robust organizational strategy is one that will produce positive returns (or for nonprofits nonnegative balances) under widely varying conditions. Robustness, then, means having internal liquidity when re-

---

12. For an interesting general discussion of the consequences of liquidity, see Berle and Means 1991 [1932], 249–50.

sources are being committed to highly volatile products and services, and authorized illiquidity—for example, in single purpose capital investments or tenure commitments in the wage budget—only where conditions are stable. Robustness of strategy depends on matching the degree of internal liquidity of resources to the volatility of conditions. Robustness in strategy is making long-term commitments only when the expected payback is quite secure, and "preserving options" in volatile areas. The process of budget making is a central part of the management of liquidity of resources within a firm, a government, or a nonprofit organization.

Short-term adaptability of budgets, as in the construction industry or the ladies garment industry, reflects wide fluctuations of the total budget of firms over periods of weeks or months. These drastic changes in money flows are, then, measures of the flexibility of activities within the organizations, required by rapid changes in what is sustainable or profitable.

A budget reflecting a distinctive relation to liquidity is a "project budget." Obviously the very idea of a project budget is that an organization will devote some expenditures to a given purpose for a period of time, which then will be sunk costs. During the project, resources have to be moved quickly among different expenses of the project. Except for the commitment of resources to the project, the regular budget of an organization need not be unstable in order to have the flexibility of having a project. Money for the project often comes bank loans or reserves, rather than the operating budget. Project budgets themselves are highly volatile and adaptable, but the capital assets often produced by projects are very inflexible and illiquid. Flexible construction projects, for example, produce rigid real estate rents for long periods of time. After the project is over, no new resources (except perhaps "maintenance") are to be devoted to it. A project, then, typically represents turning liquid resources into illiquid capital resources. Quite often it uses highly liquid labor and specialized construction capital resources, hired by contracts.

Organizations typically segregate such project budgets from the regular budgeting process, and create a special structure to approve those budgets. For example, the formalization of a short-term construction contract creates liquidity in the contractor to get the project done, in order to then freeze the completed construction as an asset of the firm or government. The formalization of specifications, tenders, bid acceptance, and the like (as discussed in chapter 3) is a special case of a client formalizing and segregating an operational budget for a temporary purpose, so that the rest of both the client (in its regular operations) and contractors can use resources in a liquid fashion. The general effect of project budgets and capital budgets, then, is to make resources of departments or projects liquid for short periods of time and for prespecified general purposes, to be reviewed for the following period by superior authority.

Earmarking to Create Liquidity above Departments

The earmarking of funds in the operating budget makes resources liquid at the department level (or in, for example, a construction contract) at the expense of rigidity at higher levels. The higher level cannot spend what it has turned over to the lower level (or promised to a contractor). Flexibility below is created by rigidity above, and vice versa. Lower units cannot spend the contingency reserves of the higher levels until these are turned into authorized budgets. Compensatory flexibility at higher levels has four main components: (1) annual budget reviews and changes; (2) strategic managerial reserves ("slush funds"); (3) board-level portfolio or endowment reserves; and (4) risk management (insurance and options) contracts. There are also (5) supraorganizational bankruptcy or estate liquidation institutions for freezing internal organizational liquidity in order to provide creditor, or heir, liquidity.

From the point of view of the sociology of liquidity, these reserve funds at higher levels are comparable to the risk-bearing market makers in securities markets. Market makers provide risk-bearing and risk-division functions by the use of funds "earmarked" in property law (the equity of market makers). Comparable funds in organizations are earmarked by formal budgeting, especially budgeting of reserves under a given executive's or committee's control. In the market, the market maker's equity reserve is supplemented by high-speed management of the market maker's portfolio, his "short" or "long" position, in the light of prices in a more or less continuous auction. Committees or other authorities in organizations that have internally earmarked reserves have a comparable higher level liquidity creation function in organizations.

We might distinguish the funds "authorized" to a lower level department as "operating liquidity," like the liquidity provided by short-term loans to market makers or by discount houses to exporters, allocated perhaps in yearly reviews. In contrast, the liquidity of higher level reserves or slush funds is "strategic liquidity," like the overall liquidity of the mortgage market that Fannie Mae provides. This latter strategic liquidity is in general, more closely related to liquidity in the capital market, in the sense that its spending is more an investment function. Earmarking funds in budgets to operating departments or executive reserves, then, divides flows of money between operating and strategic reserves whenever a budget is authorized. Strategic reserves within the firm, in turn, reflect the faith by the capital markets in the firm's strategic vision, letting it invest in future unspecified adaptation rather than declaring it all as dividends.

Liquidity is then created by a system of earmarking, or rigidification, that gives authority to make some resources liquid *in a particular way* by specifying that they are not liquid for numerous other purposes. Similarly, only if the market maker's equity is not to be spent on personal purposes can it be committed to the risks of matching a sale at this instant with a buy a few minutes later or earlier. Likewise only if premiums are committed to a fire insurance contract by a risk management committee can a finance committee borrow money in the mortgage market to build a factory that might burn down. Only if the residual, after that committee's payment of the mortgage, is committed to stockholders will the board of directors, a committee elected by stockholders, take the risk of borrowing to build a factory.

Budget authorizations serve the same function as property rights in the market. Property rights are wealth in the hands of the owner who can dispose of them, make decisions about them, and so make his or her situation liquid. This liquidity may be confined by contract to a given purpose, such as buying a house. Similarly a budget authorization for a department or division routinely has a purpose attached—it may be approved for buying a new machine but not for covering overtime work, for example. But the whole series of decisions by the buying department, engineering, purchasing, and the like represent power delegated by the budget authorization to make the relevant subordinate decisions. It is important to look not only at the fact that the purpose is part of the exercise of higher authority; one must look at how the pursuit of that purpose is delegated to the routines and authorities of the subordinate departments.

Liquidity in organizations, then, depends on the structure of believable earmarking of funds and streams of income. Far from being the opposite of liquidity, earmarking is generally a device for producing liquidity by dividing risks, and then by providing reserves and authority to run those risks while other money is put at the disposal of other authorities, and so liquidified. Earmarked money provides against risks and expenses of a given kind, so that *other* money can be moved about. In organizations such earmarking with corresponding authority is ordinarily hierarchically arranged, with the most general and long-term risks managed by a general board or committee of trustees, partners, or directors. A brief discussion of the main types of risk-bearing "liquidity managers" illustrates this point.

BUDGET COMMITTEES

As Padgett (1980, 1981) has explained about the federal Office of Management and Budget (OMB), a budget committee usually gets general directives of how the budget has to add up from higher authorities ("macroeconomic goals" in Padgett's words), which it then breaks down into departmental or agency total budget goals. In addition some parts of each department's budget are fixed by higher organizational mandates or contracts with the outside, so that the totals given by macroeconomic criteria ("strategic level management") give implicit goals for those parts that are not precommitted. Earmarking or precommitting parts of departmental budgets then focuses liquid management by that department on the manipulable parts. Precommitted parts of the budget can only be changed when a crisis causes higher authorities' involvement. But setting goals for the budget committee can produce substantial reallocations over the medium term, for example in universities, by slowly starving arts and sciences while the business school is expanding and flush.

STRATEGIC MANAGERIAL RESERVES

Often departmental budgets have one or more lines for contingency reserves or (lower down) petty cash. A salary budget may have a line for "substitutes," "temporary" staff, or "overtime." Building maintenance budgets often have a reserve for contracting for major repairs. Frequently reserves are tied to estimates of expected sales, or (negatively) to excessive inventories of unsold goods (Chandler 1962, 114–62, on General Motors; 1977, 224–33, 235–39, on department stores). That is, budgets are often deliberately structured with reserves to increase liquidity within departments or divisions, with a corresponding creation of authority to respond to contingencies.

PORTFOLIOS OR ENDOWMENTS

Boards of trustees or directors quite often create endowment or portfolio management committees to buy and sell financial claims outside the going concern. These claims are often chosen to be highly liquid (for example, stocks and bonds, or certificates of deposit), so as to be available for medium- and long-term contingencies. The liquidity component is frequently indicated by calling the process something like "the management of the cash flow." Often the policy of such a committee is closely coordinated with (or included in) the management of organizational debt and equity financing. This committee is often part of the board or reports to it directly.

RISK MANAGEMENT

When a contingency is highly specifiable (for example, a fire, a change in cotton prices), the risk is large, and causes of losses (or gains) are sufficiently out of the control of the organization, it is often wise to have contingency reserves held outside the organization. Insurance contracts, by convention, only cover losses, whereas options contracts can provide contingent gains (for example, to hedge losses due to the same contingency). But both insurance and options buy outside coverage of risks, backed by reserves held outside the organization. This frees up the reserves inside the organization to cover other contingencies, rendering the whole more liquid.

LIQUIDATION

Bankruptcy of firms or families, and estate liquidation (probate, estate management) for families involve transferring illiquid organizational resources to an authority to "realize" the assets in more liquid form. Some of the going concern value of the firm or household may sometimes be realized as well, by financial reorganization. The general purpose is to destroy the previous organization of claims on the assets (including the set of claims represented in the budget) and on the going concern value, so that creditors' claims may be rendered liquid.

The central thing one has to realize in importing ideas of liquidity into organizational studies is that the purpose of liquidity is, in general, to be able to create or buy illiquid assets to be used for a purpose. What liquidity does is to allow one to pursue now one purpose, now another. Liquidification of the residential mortgage market had the explicit purpose of allowing people to buy or build quite illiquid houses. Rendering secondary mortgage bonds then allowed capital to flow into illiquid consumer investments, as well as into illiquid factories and irrigation canals. Insurance reserves are maintained in relatively liquid forms so that they can be devoted to the purpose of replacing a burned house, when that contingency comes up. The matching of liquid resources to illiquid expenditure, but doing it in such a way that the response to future contingencies can be flexible, is the core of financial markets. It is the core of budget making in organizations as well. More concretely, the place to look for organizational flexibility is not only among its skilled workforce, but in its administrative contingency reserves, insurance and options contracts, and the like.

Toward a Sociology of Organizational Flexibility

In *The Great Transformation* (1985 [1944]) Karl Polanyi argued that people or political systems would not tolerate the flexibility required for economic development unless there were believable social insurance claims. Similarly, we have argued that organizational flexibility at a given time depends on believable commitments, or earmarking, to other resource holders and claimants. Organizational flexibility, then, depends on the structure of rigidities, just as running depends on a stable relation between flexible muscles and rigid bones.

The need to gain flexibility by earmarking is partly due to people being very bad at calculating even a single probability, let alone the great vector of risks that constitute the organization-as-portfolio. If risks at a given organizational level can be properly segregated, by known and authorized rigidities, so that the risk each department or division must run is of the sort they routinely calculate,[13] then more of the risks can be well managed. Having to simultaneously manage, for example, the financing of major repairs on a contingency basis in the capital budget, buying insurance for the contingency that one will have to rebuild after a fire, as well as selecting the stock portfolio of the strategic reserve would greatly strain the powers of a risk-management committee.

People's common sense usually regards all aspects of the environment as stable except the part they themselves currently act on. If organizational budget rigidities recognize this limited cognitive capacity to manage risks, they encourage flexibility in dealing with them by making some resources liquid for the department for risk management, but rigidly segregating that from the budget of other departments managing other risks. Internal organizational liquidity rests on the earmarking of resources and income streams because earmarking segments the cognitive problem of a vector of risks, assigning each segment to those who are good at managing it (Stinchcombe 1990).

In the fruitless debate between organizational ecology's assumption that organizations are rigid and the old institutionalists who assumed they were adaptive, the correct resolution is not "some of this, some of that." Instead the solution is the one that vertebrates came up with—that flexibility of the limbs and head depends on the rigidity of the backbone. The vertebrae of an organization's budget are earmarked resources, so that the muscles and eyes and ears of the organization can manage orga-

---

13. Jean Lave (1988, 56) documents how people whose calculation is embedded in routines of activities are much better at such embedded calculations than they are at solving abstract "word problems" that are mathematically equivalent.

nizational adaptation to the environment. Jellyfish move where the environment takes them; monkeys are agile structures of rigidities that actively adapt to the environment.

CONCLUSION

Liquidity in the market is the ease with which an asset can be bought and sold (Stiglitz 1993, 260). That ease is greater when the costs of selling are low and where sellers can quickly find buyers. Bank savings accounts, for example, are highly liquid because the bank will always buy back the customer's claim, based on the deposit, by allowing easy withdrawals. Houses, in contrast, tend to be illiquid. In general, information asymmetries between buyers and sellers will reduce liquidity. Value that is difficult to discern, or to communicate credibly to a large number of potential buyers, makes an asset illiquid. We have outlined a variety of institutional mechanisms that can reduce transaction costs and make assets knowable; such mechanisms consequently enhance liquidity. Liquidity gives the asset holder a desirable measure of flexibility. But it does so by creating claims on illiquid flows of profits or use values that can themselves be traded. By making it possible to use a lender's money to build a house, who may want that money in five years, while the house will last thirty to fifty years, the liquidity of the secondary mortgage market facilitates both flexibility in the lender's money management and rigidity in investments in real estate. Liquidity also means that buyers do not need as much specific or detailed knowledge of the assets they purchase. Transacting in standardized, homogeneous commodities with predictable features and risks is easier, so they tend to be more liquid.

Liquidity is created in different ways in different markets. Sometimes the liquidity is the direct result of government policy consciously aimed at its creation. Fannie Mae and Freddie Mac deliberately enhance the liquidity of secondary mortgage markets, facilitating the flow of investment funds into home mortgages and consequently increasing home ownership. The institutional underpinnings of the early-eighteenth-century London stock market are equally evident, although no Fannie Mae equivalent orchestrated the creation of liquidity. Organizational liquidity emerges out of a combination of illiquid commitments or sunk costs, authorizations to adapt by spending liquid resources, and holding reserves to facilitate future adaptation. But spending those resources in turn creates illiquid resources that can be productive, or can be kept in inventory until sold.

Liquidity in the market facilitates flexibility and adaptability, which are useful attributes in uncertain environments; we have tried to extend the concept to states (and how they can use the market to gain liquidity) and formal organizations, and how they can allocate resources to real activities ("invest in illiquid revenue producing resources") without losing that flexibility.

We have then conceived liquidity more generally as the degree to which an asset is a fungible, generalized resource. As uncertainty increases, the demand for liquidity increases. In hard times, for example, firms try to increase their holdings of cash. During a credit crunch, banks enhance their own liquidity by piling up cash and other liquid assets. Real environments are mostly a selective combination of stability and instability, and so rational organizations will match liquid assets to the unstable parts of the environment, and illiquid assets to the stable parts. Or they might follow a quasi-Thompson (Thompson 1967) strategy and use their liquid assets to buffer their illiquid (core) assets. Organizational slack (March and Simon 1993 [1958]) can also be seen as a kind of liquidity.

Liquidity has some disadvantages, and so few organizations try to be completely liquid. Generalized resources are usually not as useful or productive as specialized ones. Fixed costs invested in useful productive machines may pay off better than the same resources paid to flexible human labor. Flexibility often comes at the price of being less efficacious. In a highly stable environment, it is rational to cut back on liquidity and invest in illiquid assets that are adapted to relatively unchanging environments. Where special efforts or particular institutions are necessary to create liquidity, the price of liquidity will include the cost of such efforts. For example, securitized home mortgages are a liquid asset, but the government mortgage programs, the premium over the market interest rate for secure assets that is charged by a mortgage issuing bank, and the "closing costs" of real estate deals are part of the price of that liquidity.

Demand for the asset helps to create liquidity. Having many potential buyers gives the asset owner the liquidity he or she demands. In general this means that the more a given asset is a substitute for (or nearly identical with) something demanded on a large scale, the more liquid it is. Thus a debt of the sovereign in England, when owned by the British East India Company, became a component of a highly liquid EIC share, very similar to the share already being sold. But liquidity, created by institutions, itself frequently enhances demand, and so has a self-reinforcing quality. That is, demand can be decomposed into direct demand and indirect (or "reflected") demand. I may want an asset on its own inherent merits, but I might also want it because there are many others who want it (thus my demand reflects their demand). If many others want it, it becomes a liquid "store of value." Should circumstances change, and direct merits become less attractive, then it will be easy for me to sell it off. Or it could be that I would retain the asset simply because of my "liquidity preference." People often die with wealth in housing, an illiquid investment from which they had been getting use value; but they often die also with liquid financial instruments in their estate, evidently held as useful for contingencies up to the end (Palumbo 1999).

Money is an example of one extreme: the demand for modern money is entirely indirect or reflected (Simmel 1978 [1907], 131–203). Excepting Midas, people only want money because others want it, and will accept it in exchange for goods and services. Money issued by a solvent government without exchange restrictions is, of course, the most liquid of assets.

The "supply" of liquidity can be met in a number of ways. Anything that makes an asset easily transferable, or that reduces transaction costs, or that raises demand for the asset enhances liquidity. Legal transferability, the alienability of a commodity or asset, is basic. Depending on the structure of property rights, some things are inalienable or are difficult to alienate. Alienability is therefore a necessary but not sufficient condition for liquidity. Low transaction costs, the second factor, are determined by the costs of information, among other things. It is easier for the buyer to know what he or she is buying when the commodity is highly standardized along a small number of easily measurable dimensions. Transaction costs are higher when dealing with an idiosyncratic or difficult-to-measure asset. Intangible commodities are easier to standardize than tangible ones because one does not have to deal with the inherent variability of the material world (for example, it is easier to standardize futures contracts than it is to standardize wheat; wheat futures only exist after standardized wheat, but are easy to develop after that). Standardization can also help resolve the problem of information asymmetries between buyer and seller. Those who wish to enhance liquidity can try to standardize or homogenize the relevant assets. Transaction costs can also be affected by the legal framework for market transactions generally; predictable law of exchange can make whole classes of assets more liquid.

Sometimes liquidity is created deliberately, as in the organized New York and Chicago financial markets. There, in addition to low transaction costs and standardized financial assets, market makers, whose job it is always to be willing to buy or sell at a price, generate liquidity. Even when no one else wants to buy (as during a market crash), it is still their job to do so, with an occasional brief closing of the market to get a grip on changes in a crisis. Sometimes liquidity happens more unintentionally, as in the liquidity of the London stock market at the end of the seventeenth century, when "stock jobbers" did the work of market making without being specifically assigned that as a function. Sometimes liquidity represented in the already liquid money streams of an organization can be preserved while investing most of it by a combination of ear-marking money streams for things that have to be done, holding reserves for contingencies, and maintaining access to financial markets at the top so that the overall cash balances can remain sufficiently liquid.

A state facing the radically increased expenditures of a seventeenth- or eighteenth-century war had a great need to increase the demand for the national debt. Thus if it could exploit the liquidity preference reflected in the willingness of Londoners to buy share in corporations traded in Exchange Alley, by having parliament approve and guarantee the debt with future taxes and then borrowing from a traded company, it could get more money faster and at a lower rate. Similarly if the U.S. government believed that the whole population would be better off if more capital were invested in single-family owner-occupied housing, then by making a market by various guarantees to bondholders and forward contracts with mortgage originators, it could increase the demand for mortgage debts in the financial community.

An organization's careful matching of authority and reserves with various kinds of contingencies structurally looks a lot like market making. By using nested authorizations and contingency reserves, it can achieve an overall level of flexibility comparable to the agility of an institutional investor in the stock and bond markets. It is, so to speak, exploiting the opportunity for flexibility created for it by the liquidity of its income stream in money. It does so by entering the market for raw materials and parts, labor, or investment goods, and devoting these to productive activity, and also by maintaining enough liquid reserves, strategically placed, to change its activities quickly. Thus institutions of market making spread flexibility throughout the polity, to nonprofit organizations and firms with budgets, and to households that might like to buy a house for a while and sell it (when they have to move) to someone else who also does not have enough money at the time.

What we hope to have shown in this chapter is that some kinds of flexibility require formalization of uncertain elements, combined with formalized risk-taking to split up risks into unique and standard categories. The formalization involved in a modern real estate transaction is partly the ancient formalization of a contract transferring possession of a piece of real estate for a payment. But it is partly minting work so that formalized and identical financial claims can be produced for the mortgage market. This stratifies the risks by requiring of the buyer an equity contribution, the down payment; by insuring for fire and unclear title; by arranging for the issuing bank to take some creditworthiness risk after a check with credit rating agencies; a risk of interest rate changes by Fannie Mae giving a forward interest rate to issuing banks, pooling and guaranteeing mortgage pools so that the securities have different but homogeneous risks; and so on. None of this could be reasonably done with heterogeneous informal risks at the bottom, and without formal specification of the nature of the resulting multiple claims on the house buyer's repayment stream.

Similarly, without the formal limitations and authorizations of a budget for various spending authorities it governs, all the risks of all parts of an organization would have to be estimated by everyone before anyone could spend. Liquidity inside organizations likewise then depends on the core formalization of the accounting system and its connection to the authority system. In these situations, one can create flexibility by strategically rigidifying things by governing them with abstractions. But one then had better adjust the rigidifying abstractions to the world, or one will go broke.

Flexibility, Abstraction, and Formalization

We have argued in this chapter that liquidity in markets and flexibility in organizations depend on abstraction and formalization. Only if mortgage-backed securities are abstracted from houses, made equal by pooling and stratification of risks, and made formally legally identical can they become liquid. Only if one department's expenditure is formally limited by abstractions can another department confidently spend its budgetary allocation. But how does formal rigidity produce flexibility?

A common stock in General Motors can be traded in the securities market because it abstracts from everything but a share of ownership in the aggregate fund and the government of the company. That fund, and that government, change over time. But the risk of fluctuating returns, or of succession of managers, are the only risks it bears. Because of this abstraction, it has a consensual price; because of that consensus a continuous auction can track its current consensual price; because of that continuous auction, it is liquid at that consensual price.

The accountants of General Motors and of its auditor do the abstraction of valuing the current fund of resources and the net revenue. We did not study that abstraction process in this chapter. The central feature required is that the abstraction process satisfy the auditors and the tax authorities.

In the mortgage market, however, the certification of the continuing value of the gage pledged by the client as security for the loan (the house) is a much more public process. That process is formalized into several dimensions that must be certified separately. The market value is abstracted by the appraiser. The quality of the legal title is abstracted and certified by the title insurance company. The credit rating of the mortgagor is certified by a credit rating company, and current employment by the buyer's employer. The cashability of the check for the closing has to be certified by a bank that holds the money. The fire insurance coverage has to be certified by the fire insurance company. The issuing bank has to evaluate the combined information as a satisfactory security for the loan, and to bear at least for a while a part of the risk. The multiple certifications of various abstractions of the deal being made are required for the market maker (as well as the issuing bank) to provide access to the secondary mortgage security market, from which much of the money ultimately comes.

None of these abstractions, individually or jointly, represents in full the eight or so years that an average mortgagor holds the house, nor its beauty, its roof problems, its electric meter on the back lawn, the slight slant of the basement floor and walls toward the southwest because of a historical pattern of drainage that made the soil soft there, its neighbors who hang a disemboweled deer, head down, to drain in the back yard, or the divorce that stimulated the sale of the house after eight years of the thirty that were anticipated. It abstracts from everything irrelevant to the mortgage market.

But there is still a great deal of information in the pile of documents at the closing, all of which may bear on the present value of the expected stream of income from mortgage payments. The solidity of each of those pieces of abstraction is secured by complicated social arrangements. The core function of many of those arrangements is to secure transparency in the mortgage market, *and so* in the secondary mortgage securities market. Part of this foundation of transparent closings of real estate transactions derives from historical practice in the capitalist mortgage market. But they have been regularized and formalized by the government market makers, which fundamentally reshaped the flow of funds from the capital market into single-family housing.

The key abstractions here are procedures, which abstract, then provide against, the ways in which key elements of the mortgage transactions can be corrupted. They are features of the government of social activity by such abstractions. Insurers and Fannie Mae and Fannie Mac certify that they are willing, after proper evaluations, to take the risks involved. The other validations in the closing documents are specified so that they come on a fee-for-service basis, but the fee payer generally does not get to choose the certifiers; instead the issuing bank specifies who they will be. The extensive validations by fourth parties have the function of creating a minigovernment for each transaction.

The liquidification of the British national debt created pools of bonds held by the Bank of England and the British East India Company. The stocks in the companies then served much the economic function of the securities on pools of mortgages, except that the stocks also reflected other assets and streams of income of the companies so they were claims on more diverse portfolios. Both sets of institutions are in this respect similar to the mutual funds and pension funds that invest on behalf of claimants in a common portfolio of financial assets, a "fund." Claims on a portfolio or fund, administered in a formally governed way so that the claims are strictly equal and more or less transparent in administration, are quite often the instruments that are traded in financial markets. These funds abstract from all the variety of businesses, governments, and real estate in which they hold shares or debt claims simply by taking the sums of income streams and ignoring their differences. The pool—the fund of assets of a corporation or the fund of the insurance company or the fund of the mortgage pool—then has its own financial and risk characteristics. Claims are identical, or differ in known ways, so that large numbers of claims exist and can be traded. The formation of such pools, such "funds," is then a central aspect of the economy of abstraction that we took to be central in chapter 2.

CHAPTER SIX

FORMALIZING RIGHTLESSNESS IN IMMIGRATION LAW AND ADMINISTRATION

So far I have treated cases in which formalization's main functions are improved, the better the information in the abstractions. When the abstraction was radically inadequate to make a good decision, I have been predicting failure of the abstraction system, formality as only ritual. In this chapter I take up a case in which the purposes of the abstraction system are best achieved by specifying that parts of the environment will be systematically ignored. In particular, the right to have one's case intelligently treated by the formalities is formally very much restricted in the law and administration of immigration regulations.

The "due process" rights that are denied to aliens are deep in the constitutional tradition of the United States and other English-speaking countries. However, even American citizens discover those rights are restricted when they cross national borders to enter the United States: for example, the protections against "search and seizure" are very limited for citizens at the border. But if one is not a citizen (or a near-citizen, as I discuss below) and is at the border, one not only has certain rights in suspension, but moreover there is no right to a hearing about whether that suspension was justified. This rightlessness of aliens (and partial suspension of rights for citizens) at the border is very highly formalized, and it is defended in the law as a central component of sovereignty.

Institutionalized ignorance about an alien's wanting to come into the country is positively sought and defended by the legal and organizational traditions that we have been analyzing for their intelligence. Immigration law and administration is therefore a deep challenge to the whole scheme of analysis here. That a legal system devoted to due process of law—with appeals courts perhaps using the criterion of due process more than any other principle of law to revise, retry, or overturn lower court cases—devotes itself to carefully denying due process to aliens suggests the whole thing is perhaps cant and ritual. Perhaps Karl Llewellyn's great judges are as comfortable creating formalities to go against the great principles of our law as to conform to them.

I argue in this chapter that the key abstractions in this system of law are *a priori* probabilities, in this case probabilities that due process will defend the rights of people "We" (in the sense of "We the people of the United States of America") want to ensure are protected. I show judges and administrators trying to make their system work by improving the estimates of *a priori* probabilities that some claimant to due process has a right that "We" want to defend. I then try to extend the same reasoning to the informal rightlessness for review of one's status as on the lower tracks, leading to working-class jobs, in American high schools. It is, then, a matter of choosing to use a set of concepts about probabilities, rather than concepts of due process of law, as the basis of formalization.

THE BURDEN OF PROOF AND *A PRIORI* PROBABILITIES

In immigration law and administration in the United States, there are two categorizations of cases by *a priori* probabilities that affect their legal fate; they may be broadly denominated "administrative" and "legal" category systems. The administrative categories generally determine how much search effort the government should put into sorting out a few aliens who would make "good" immigrants from among the very large numbers who would like to come or to stay in the United States. The burden of proof that one is a good immigrant rests on the immigrant and his or her sponsors. The legal categories sort out those who have "rights" that might be damaged by being denied entry, being deported, or being given a visa that does not give the right to stay, *once they have the right of appeal.* Once in court, the burden of proof is on the government that believes it worthwhile to "invade" that right for cause, or to show the right to due process does not exist.

By and large the categorization of aliens by the *a priori* probability that they will be good immigrants, or will leave if they are not, is an administrative matter. The courts generally grant wide discretion to the Executive to decide on these questions according to procedures and substantive criteria the Immigration and Naturalization Service (INS), or Congress, have arranged. This administrative categorization is most powerful where the *a priori* probability that the person can establish a legal right is minimal. For example, questions of right rarely arise when an person without documents appears at the border (Gilboy 1991; 1992), or when people without documents speaking only Spanish are found working with many others with the same characteristics in a factory or field near the Mexican border, or when a person with a tourist visa has overstayed its term.

In particular, when an administrative process exists in the U.S. consular service in the country of origin to select immigrants for the United States, then the likelihood that someone who has not gone through that process has a right to enter or be in the United States is presumed to be negligible. That is, when a successful claim of right to enter or remain in the United States is *a priori* improbable, the administrative classification in terms of *a priori* low probability of desirability as an immigrant tends to rule.

The probability of a claim of right in the legal category system has an upper extreme when exile is forced on a native-born citizen of the United States. Exile is conceived of as analogous to a serious criminal penalty, destroying liberties and freedoms in much the way that prison does. The *a priori* probability then takes the form of "innocent until proven guilty," with all the burden of proof on the government. For aliens within five years after the date of entry, conviction of certain crimes (crimes involving moral turpitude) may carry with them the "additional punishment" of deportation, without further factual basis (Aleinikoff and Martin, 1991 [1985], 503–24). Conviction of such crimes of course requires due process of law as understood in the criminal law, so the standards and burden of proof are the same as for citizens but the punishment is greater.

The opposite end of the claim of right is that of a person who has entered the country illegally, as compared with one who is at the border but has not yet entered. Ordinarily the person who is illegally in the country has a right to an administrative hearing with some elementary due process before being deported, but (for example) they often need not be informed that they need not agree to "voluntary repatriation." The alien at, but still legally "outside," the border does not have even these elementary rights to a hearing, nor any warnings whatever, nor any right to be listened to at all.

The general point here is that the *a priori* probabilities are matched to the location of the burden of proof. When the alien and his sponsors have the burden of proving that they deserve admission, as in the application for an immigrant visa or for entry without a visa, the *a priori* probability that any particular person applying or trying to enter is deserving is ordinarily presumed to be low. Showing that a higher probability pertains to a particular individual then is the burden of that individual and the sponsors. But if a person is in the United States with no *prima facie* case that he or she does not belong there by right, the presumption is that the *a priori* probability that they have the right is high. The government has to show good cause to deprive him or her of that apparent right, either by a serious, and contestable, showing that he or she *does not have* the right, or by a showing that the factual basis of a *legal cause exists to deprive* him or her of that right. In the usual language, the potential immigrant has the probabilities, and so the burden of proof, attached to the government's giving the individual a "privilege" to which he or she has no right. The hearing to deport has the probabilities that require the government to have sufficient evidence to deprive the individual of a right, and the burden of proof is on the government.

At entry, "formality" for an alien without a visa has the meaning that the American government has no obligation to listen to a rightless alien. Further, having specified American consuls in the country of origin as the agents for listening to aliens (who are making a case that they should have an immigrant visa or some other kind), the INS agent has no responsibility to listen at the port of entry. The government is almost always formally immune from charges of failure to have a good cause for exclusion at entry (the main exceptions have to do with refugees). This saves time for the immigration inspectors at the border, and avoids circumvention of the specialized listening apparatus (the consulate); one can use the procedural ground that listening is supposed to be done at the consulate, but this procedural requirement is the burden of the immigrant, because there is no inherent ground to believe this is a good immigrant.

For an alien with permanent residence or a naturalized citizen, formality of the immigration law is a set of requirements on the government to listen to him or her, with procedural protections of how such a hearing should be conducted and what opportunities of the alien or citizen to present supporting evidence. The object is to make the government live up to the requirement that they bear the burden of proof, that the *a priori* probability that the national interest requires deporting such a person is very low, and that errors of letting an undeserving resident stay are less damaging than errors of deporting a deserving resident. It should be very cheap to reject aliens whose probability of justifying entry is low, and be very expensive to deport aliens or citizens whose rights are assumed to have an important value to the government.

A SEARCH COSTS RATIONALIZATION OF
A PRIORI FORMALITY

Another way to understand this formalization is to use the way economists model "search costs" of unemployed workers for jobs, or "vacancy costs" of employers looking for workers. If a worker's search costs are to be rational, the benefits of search (for example, the wages of the job) have to be multiplied by the probability of getting the job before saying that the search was worth its costs. The full cost of eventually getting a job should be paid by getting one—though good luck may lead a particular worker to get a job cheaply, bad luck to paying more to get a job than it was worth. The general solution to a search cost problem is that the worker should spend the costs (say monthly costs) up to the point where the increase in probability of finding a job (or of finding a job with higher wages) due to the last dollar's worth of search in a month, multiplied by the value of the job's net wages, is equal to that last dollar.

We can think of the search by an immigration officer through the undocumented workers caught in a sweep of a sweat shop near the border as a "search for good immigrants." If the probability of finding good (for example, "eligible") workers is small, and the reward for finding this eligible worker illegally in the country over finding another an equally eligible one waiting in a queue for a visa at the consulate in his or her home country is very small, then very small search costs are justified. It is then not "rational" to spend very much time warning them that their statements may be used to deport them, allowing them time in the United States to build their case, giving them the right to representation, setting up a hearing with a special hearing judge, and so on. What is crucial here is that the damage to aliens due to their not being able to come to the United States is not usually considered a cost to be taken into account. The INS is not considered a welfare organization for aliens, except perhaps for refugees.

On the other hand people well settled in the United States have a very high utility for staying where they are, with their family, their job, their house, their children well adapted to the school. Most crucially, *that* welfare value for them *is also* a value in U.S. policy. If in addition deporting them would destroy many values for their citizen relatives, their employers, and their neighborhoods, the presumption is that they have a right to stay in the United States.

In order to protect such people (both the deported person and their relatives and employers) from "arbitrary" government power, the U.S. government provides extensive rights to answer government reasons for deporting them. Because that person is thought to have rights, unlike the person without a visa at the border, due process of law is guaranteed by the courts or by formal hearings much like courts in the Immigration and Naturalization Service. The destruction of individual rights of such people has an external negative effect on the social order and on people's investments in their relatives, neighbors, and employees. The courts, and (sometimes reluctantly) the INS, therefore insist on a high level of protection by requiring due process of law in cases of deportation—higher for citizens and long-term resident aliens than for tourists, lower for felons convicted by due process of law than for the unconvicted, and so on.

Another way to look at this is by twisting the formulation about search costs for good immigrants on its head. We substitute the benefit derived by a citizen or permanent resident from a more thorough search process for evidence that might defend his rights, and in particular one in which he has a right to be heard, for the cost to the government. Requiring the government to pay the costs of a fair hearing, then, is reconceived as an incentive effect on the government to bring only those deportation cases that they think are very sound. But this further means that the costs for the immigrant (or in rare cases, the citizen) of defending their rights is much reduced, and in particular they are not subject to the refusal of administrative officers to hear their case because it would be too expensive.

THE LEGAL RECOGNITION OF *A PRIORI* PROBABILISTIC REASONING

In a dissent in *Jean v. Nelson*, 472 U.S. 846 (1985), Justice Marshall wrote:

> To the extent that this court has relied on *Mezei* [a case permitting summary justice for entry decisions] at all, it has done so only in the narrow area of entry decisions [case citations omitted]. It is in this area that the Government's interest in protecting our sovereignty is at its strongest and that individual claims to constitutional entitlement are the least compelling. (*Quoted in* Aleinikoff and Martin 1991 [1985], 434.)

Justice Marshall here used both kinds of categorization to describe why entry decisions are ones in which the Court should allow greatest administrative discretion, and should not worry much about protecting the rights of the person not allowed into the country. My argument above amounts to translating Justice Marshall's dictum into a language of two series of *a priori* probabilities. One is the variation in "individual claims to constitutional entitlement," the *a priori* probabilities that a person has a substantive claim of right and therefore a claim to have the government assume the burden of proof that the right should be abrogated. The other is the variation in "interest in protecting our sovereignty," where a low *a priori* probability that the grant to an alien of a right to be a visitor, a student, or a resident (perhaps eventually a citizen) will be in the interest of the United States puts the burden of proof on the alien. The minimal (or nonexistent) duty of the government to listen carefully, the "summary justice" rights and immunities of the immigration inspector at entry, saves the costs of investigating people who are unlikely to be able to justify entry.[1]

The basic idea then is a slope of the trade-off between immigrant interests and the sovereign interests of the United States, as represented in immigration policy. The low probable value of an immigrant and the low justification of rights of a noncitizen both describe an alien at entry at the physical border.[2]

Much the same reasoning appears in an opinion by Justice O'Connor in *Landon v. Plasencia*, 459 U.S. 21 (1982):

> An alien seeking admission to the United States requests a privilege and has no constitutional rights regarding his application, for the power to admit or exclude aliens is a sovereign prerogative. [H]owever, once an alien gains admission to our country and begins to develop the ties that go with permanent residence his constitutional status changes accordingly.[3]

The administrative simplicity and rightlessness that derives from being at the bottom of the slope was crisply formulated by Justice Minton in *United States ex rel. Knauff v. Shaughnessy*, 338 U.S. 537, 544 (1950): "Whatever the procedure authorized by Congress is, it is due process as

---

1. A similar set of trade-offs is suggested in an Australian report on the review by administrative panels of migration decisions (Administrative Review Council 1986, 31–32): "[R]efusal of entry to . . . Australia may affect significant interests of members of the Australian community with whom the person directly affected by the decisions has close ties of a family personal, business, or employment nature . . . . At the same time the Council considers that . . . it is important to achieve sensible balance between the desirability of providing individual justice and . . . the costs of review; the volume of decisions of a particular class; the need to avoid excessive delay . . . ; whether those affected . . . are located within Australia or overseas; and whether those affected . . . have engaged in unlawful conduct. These considerations are taken into account in [our] discussion of whether particular classes of decisions should be subject to [review on appeal] . . . ."

2. Or at interior airports receiving planes from abroad, where barriers create a small physical space temporarily considered legally outside the border, with booths marking the place of "crossing the border."

3. During much of the history of immigration law, particular kinds of ties (for example, ties created by a labor contract with an American employer at the time of immigration which might create peonage, or might be in competition with American workers who would otherwise be employed) actually told against immigrants. During the period when the United States was very worried about subversion from aliens who might be communists, the ties with communists within the United States actually become more troublesome. No doubt a careful formulation of Justice O'Connor's point would include a classification of ties that are "citizenlike," and that would not include peonage ties as specified in the Contract Labor Law (Aleinikoff and Martin, 1991 [1985], 385), ties of comembership in the Communist Party (ibid., 315–31), or ties between a madam and a prostitute (ibid., marriages of single women meeting a fiancé on Ellis island to prevent white slavery). A justice writing on the intuitive idea behind the formalization of rights has, of course, no reason for such specificity.

far as an alien denied entry is concerned" (*quoted in* Aleinikoff and Martin 1991 [1985], 353).

Spending low search costs to find good immigrants in unlikely categories is thus justified by the low probabilities of finding an eligible immigrant, and low probabilities of their being able to justify a claim of right. They are therefore formally denied any expensive Immigration Agent search for evidence justifying exclusion. Note that here the abstraction in the formality is not even thought to be an accurate description of an alien seeking entry. It is supposed to be a protection *against having to describe aliens well*, if they fall into classes with low probabilities of justifying the search costs.

Resident aliens and naturalized citizens have a high *a priori* probability of being desirable "immigrants." Furthermore, fruitful participation in American society requires the use of rights, and justifies public investment in reducing "arbitrary" authority. Resident aliens have "relied on" the implicit contract of permission to settle, from which reliance they have the same rights freely to pursue their own and their kinsmen's welfare, to work and start businesses, to give birth to children who have the right to live here, as do other residents. Thus they have a good claim to due process by the liberal moral system that undergirds our notions of justice. Further, a society that freely disregards such individual rights and takes back the fruits of investments made on such reliance would be an unpleasant place to live.

SOCIAL AND LEGAL BOUNDARIES AS SLOPES OF PROBABILITIES

Social boundaries are in general slopes, so that if one were to graph the proportion of the population Spanish-speaking or the proportion English-speaking from five hundred miles south to five hundred miles north of the U.S.–Mexican border, it would show a steeper slope near the physical border. This would reflect the proportion of all communication ties that use Spanish or English (or both within one conversation, see Gumperz 1982). A graph against distance from the legal border of competence in either language, or a graph of the proportion of all conversations that were monolingual in either, might well find the steepest part of the slope at the physical boundary itself. Perhaps the maximum of bilingual residents would be very near the physical boundary as well.

That is, where there is a linguistic difference between countries, one would expect the density of "ties" that go with permanent U.S. residence in Justice O'Connor's opinion to be measured by the proportion speaking English. For example, a program for legalization of illegal immigrants involved training both in English and in civics (Baker 1990, 170–77), suggesting that linguistic and constitutional status are expected to be interdependent.

While we think of the boundary between countries as a line that divides points in geographical space, the U.S. Supreme Court justices are saying that the deep structure behind that abstraction is a slope of density of "American" ties. That slope is affected not only by geography, but also by the amount of time spent in one or another country (for example, it turns out not to be "entry" into the United States if a resident alien returns after being out of the country a short time), investment, communication competence, civics instruction, applications for changes of status, place of birth, citizenship of parents at one's birth, and the like. If the formalization is serious, then the abstraction system that is socially legitimated as formally having jurisdiction should, according to the argument of this chapter, reflect the reality of the slope accurately. Further, it should tend to develop in the direction of more accurate representation. It is comforting, then, to find the description of the system at the highest legal level does not just draw lines in the sand, at least for "We the people" rather than for the aliens.

But accuracy of abstraction is costly. Especially when the law grants rights to make trouble for the administrative and judicial system, it is allocating the right for citizens and resident aliens to be expensive. Thus we can use as an indicator of the seriousness of abstraction the degree of legal expense a person (or a legally defined situation) can put the government to, to make sure they are classified correctly by the immigration authorities.

The simplification of the slope into a theoretically one-dimensional boundary is clearest when "entry" means "crossing the boundary," as is most common at land boundaries. This is because the rights to use legalized coercion are strongly bounded at boundaries, so the first possible application of American coercion to an entrant is "at the boundary." Fences or walls or machine gun emplacements are often located "at the boundary," which actually means just sufficiently on this side so that it will not be challenged by the government on the other side. That is, the boundary is concretized in a great variety of ways, of which the authority of the Immigration and Naturalization Service over "entry" is only one. One then has to create simulations of boundaries with machine gun emplacements to serve the same function when the entrants are disembarking from a boat or an airplane with a foreign origin.

A *PRIORI* PROBABILITIES FORMALIZED

Bayesian statistics is built on the basis that people judge (or should judge) evidence about risks by using the evidence to modify their *a priori* probabilities about that risk, that is, the probabilities they believed before getting the evidence. In making individual decisions, people "use their own judgment" by taking account of such *a priori* knowledge as they have, or think they have. Organizations, in order to be as rational as individuals, have to have a way to take account of what they think they already know. They often do that by formally assigning categorizations that can be thought of as estimates of *a priori* probabilities. I have asserted above that the categories of the administrative and legal system of immigration are, on the one hand, *a priori* probabilities of an alien in another country, or at the entry point, being a desirable immigrant, and, on the other hand, of an alien or citizen "in" the United States being able to assert a right to have more information collected about his or her case. Now we want to go deeper into the nature of *a priori* probabilities and therefore into what formalization of them might mean.

In particular, people or organizations may use *a priori* probabilities to judge whether it is worthwhile to collect evidence at all. Most people most of the time are not interested in buying an encyclopedia, for example. Only if there is some indication that a family may use encyclopedias and might want one in the home is it worthwhile for a salesperson to investigate the evidence further. Special offers of a first volume for a dollar, for example, are a strategy to sort people out by their probabilities of buying a set. Only after a client has made a first buy is it worthwhile to collect information on whether an actual sale of the whole set is at all likely.

The point is that buying one volume for a dollar is itself information on the probable value of further evidence about the client. Advertising of a special offer of the first volume is a cheap way of getting a bit of further evidence, and the evidence of that higher probability for a particular customer only costs the difference between a dollar and the cost of producing and shipping a volume. Only if the cheap evidence is favorable is it profitable to collect better evidence.[4]

Formalization by encyclopedia producers of such categories of *a priori* probabilities unjustly denies encyclopedia sales efforts to those who

4. For example, people are required to "look for a job" in order to collect unemployment insurance. In a case in Australia, a person running for a political office held that this was "looking for a job," and so he should remain eligible for the payments. The relevant official apparently used *a priori* probabilities to say that such an application for a job had to be accompanied by evidence that there was some possibility of winning, before it could be accepted.

would like to buy but do not see what value a single volume would be, given the way they use encyclopedias. After all, one does not need those encyclopedia articles whose quality one is competent to judge. It is an exceptional customer whose competence to judge an encyclopedia is well tapped by the "A" volume. From an actuarial point of view, such people not buying a volume for a dollar because they could only use the set are rare enough that it is not worth the while to go looking for them. The *a priori* probability that someone who did not respond to the offer to buy one volume wants a set is even lower than the one describing the population as a whole, which justified such a cheap sales strategy in the first place.

Justice Marshall's two dimensions ought to create four quadrants of the space defined by "claims of right" and "desirable residents." He describes a point in that space as "entry decisions [about aliens]." Citizens also have less rights at entry. For citizens as well as aliens, for example, the constitutional standing of "search and seizure" is much different at entry (see, e.g., Aleinikoff and Martin 1991 [1985], 583). Customs officers go through your bags without "probable cause" required in the law of search and seizure. Customs boundaries and immigration boundaries, with free movement and free trade within countries but not across borders, create a motivation for smuggling both goods and people at entry. If one can get far enough beyond the boundary for a long enough period of time, both goods and people have a high *a priori* probability of "belonging" there, so search and seizure is *a priori* more justified at the boundary than inland.

This centrality of entry in the sociology of smuggling means that citizens, as well as aliens, have a high *a priori* probability of being a customs or immigration problem at the border. If a customs inspector had to apply for a warrant with probable cause to search a suitcase for an extra bottle of Kalua, the interest in sovereignty that Justice Marshall talks about would be undermined. Sovereignty has to be enforced on citizens as well as foreigners when at the point of entry, so the Sixth Amendment provisions on search and seizure must be put to one side. The very existence of the boundary makes crimes of boundary violation have a high *a priori* probability at the point of entry. The boundary creates a motivational potential for increasing the value of goods at the boundary, and for securing *de facto* rights of residence of illegal aliens at the boundary.

This geographical variation in the invasion of citizenship rights, abrogation of the presumption of innocence of the contents of one's bags, extends for some ways into the geographical interior. The motivational potential for smuggling that is greatest at the boundary is still great for some distance. Sometimes this is legally explicit, as when one has still not "entered" the Unites States when one is inside the terminal building at O'Hare airport in Chicago, but still has not passed immigration and customs inspection. These geographical limits may be extended inward for special purposes, as when goods to be shipped out later are kept "in bond" in warehouses near the port, or when aliens are allowed into the United States, without approved entry, "on parole." But one occasionally finds police stops a little ways inland where luggage is reinspected, or where it is suggested that the *a priori* probability that one is a smuggler could be reduced by a small payment under the counter.

To put it another way, "entry" is itself a gradient with a high-point near the formal boundary, sloping off on both sides. The gradient may be steeper on one side of a boundary than another, as when Spanish-speaking, dark, poor-looking people are stopped for questioning farther inside the United States than English-speaking, lighter-white, rich-looking people are in Mexico. The probability of being a problem for sovereignty then depends on distance from the boundary, and an administrative history of a particular shipment of goods or person having "entered." One can enter quite a ways geographically without having formally entered, and one can formally enter but be subject to further inquiry for quite a ways inland.

SEMIFORMAL ROUTINES WITH *A PRIORI* PROBABILITIES IN SPARSE FIELDS

The core mechanism that ties selling encyclopedias to administering immigration law is that both operate in sparse fields. Only a very small part of the population want encyclopedias in a given year. Only a very few of the aliens who might prefer to live in the United States have any chance of getting in. In such sparse fields, it is administratively very important to minimize "search costs." Hunting animals that hunt must have keen senses of sight and smell so as to quickly distinguish have to see far and smell very dilute aromas, and to distinguish possible prey rapidly from everything else. The same is true of bureaucrats hunting for a good immigrant, or a salesman for an encyclopedia sale "prospect." If the aroma of a good immigrant is too faint, the immigration officer does not hunt it.

This problem of minimizing search costs is thrown into bold relief in immigration matters because American citizens have extensive protections, "due process of law," against losing their citizenship. This means that an alien at the border without documents must be very cheap to reject, while forcing citizens into exile must be a very expensive administrative and legal enterprise, searching the evidence until their extreme undesirability is established beyond all reasonable doubt.

I now want to discuss the police administration of the criminal law (compare Stinchcombe 1963) as a structure with mechanisms very similar to the Immigration and Naturalization Service, except that it is conviction rather than a good immigrant that is the end of the search process. Further, the quick categorization by a police officer at investigation or arrest occurs in stark contrast to the due process in a regular criminal trial (Black 1971; Emerson 1969; Gilboy 1988). I then discuss streaming in American high schools (Rosenbaum 1976; the consequences are studied in Stinchcombe 1964, esp. chaps. 3 and 4) as a case of great legal informality, where *a priori* probabilities that an adolescent can learn well in a more advanced or faster-moving class are used to categorize people. Reclassification based on performance is always possible, but low search effort by the school is put into moving people among streams.

The minimization of search costs for good immigrants is thrown into high relief by the guarantees of due process of law for citizens. The U.S. courts tend to talk the language of absolute kings with arbitrary power (whatever Congress provides, that is due process) only when addressing foreigners. Similarly the categorization by *a priori* probabilities of possible criminals in police practice shows up in the probabilistic language of the law of arrest or of search and seizure, of the law of what kind of case has to exist for an indictment, and the law of criminal procedure in adversary criminal courts. That is, the *a priori* police arrest system is illuminated by the same contrast with due process as immigration law has.

The *a priori* probability that a given kind of citizen in a given situation (for example, a young male on the street in the early hours) will have been involved in a crime is judged very informally by police, but a suspicion gives rise at first only to stopping for inquiry. Suspicious behavior (say, carrying a glass cutter) warrants further investigation. A pocketful of jewelry may justify an arrest. But for a prosecutor to seek an indictment, evidence of a form acceptable in court or to a grand jury has to be quite convincing, at least enough to build a *prima facie* case. In the United States, if the evidence is overwhelming it usually leads to plea bargaining rather than an adversary trial, while if it convinces a prosecutor, but might not convince a jury, it is more likely to lead to trial.

In police administration, the cost to the citizen is graded from (1) being stopped to answer questions, checked for a prior record of illegitimate use of a glass cutter, and perhaps given a warning, to (2) being arrested and (usually) let out on bail, to (3) being indicted and so to stand trial, and finally to (4) being convicted or convinced to plead guilty. With each of these increases of cost to the defendant, the citizen gains new due process rights before the decision is made. This in turn requires the state to pay increasingly expensive "search costs" to gain evidence to increase (or perhaps decrease) the probability that someone has committed a crime and that we have the right someone. Obviously sorting through all suspicious pedestrians in the early hours at the cost of a full adversary trial would be impossible.

The *a priori* probability that someone stopped for questioning or contacted after a complaint can be shown in court to have committed a crime is, for most crimes, very low indeed (Stinchcombe 1963). That means that the cost to the citizens and to the state of the deeper search involved in an arrest and a hearing are, *a priori*, not worth paying unless there is some other social good than a conviction (such as preventing more family violence) to be obtained by an arrest. Consequently, only if police questioning on the street or in the doorway turns up some evidence that increases that probability of conviction substantially is an arrest worthwhile. But that probability is still, normally, not high enough that either the citizen or the state is ready to pay for a full adversarial hearing on the issue of the arrest. The prospect of such a hearing may rationally induce the suspect to contact a lawyer after an arrest and to offer evidence (for example, an alibi) on his or her own behalf. Defendant investment generally increases as the probability of a conviction increases in each step of criminal procedure.

To put it another way, the graduated sequence of stopping, arresting, indicting, and convicting a citizen is arranged so that it is not worth the while of the state to go forward unless the probability of conviction is high enough. The least expensive procedures (for both the citizen and for the state) have the loosest criteria for the probability. The higher the *a priori* probability of a conviction at each stage, the greater the cost to the citizen of defending himself or herself. But the rights to put costs on the state, costs of ensuring due process of law, also increase with the increases of *a priori* conviction probability.

Turning now to the policy of streaming in secondary schools in the United States, school counselors have quite good evidence from a student's previous performance and their age, and perhaps from standardized tests, about the probability of fruitful performance in advanced classes. Thus the age-grading and the streaming-within-age-grade decisions are relatively defensible, and the probabilities of success are fairly well estimated in advance.

But such decisions, fateful as they are, are very little subject to formal review with an impartial judge, calling teacher witnesses for cross-examination, and the like. Teachers are supposed to be fair, but the chances to impugn their objectivity are few and far between. It is true that secondary schools often follow an informal policy that "the squeaky wheel gets the grease." An insistent parent is quite likely to manage to prevent a student who is apparently having trouble from being moved from Honors English to regular College Preparatory English, but somewhat less likely to overcome a transfer from Algebra to Algebra Preparation (cf. Hallinan and Sørensen 1983; for some of the ethnography on informal resistance to moving students among high school curricula, see Rosenbaum 1976).

This may of course prevent a student who blossomed in College Preparatory English from moving up into the honors space not, therefore, vacated. And yet, another squeaky parent may manage to get an average college preparatory student into Honors English, and then that student is unlikely to be moved back out if they perform badly: more likely the teacher will be urged to give more help for his or her special problems, and then the student will be placed in Honors English again the following year. But aside from these informal responses around the edges of categories, most students and parents, most of the time, have little appeal against streaming decisions.

Parents and students have even less appeal against the *a priori* judgments of what one is ready to learn at a given age. Studies show that students of a given age know nearly a year's worth more if they have been just barely qualified by birth date for entry into school (for example, born on November 30 rather than December 1). So in fact what students are actually ready to learn is apparently routinely misjudged by nearly a year, as predicted by age, because those a year younger just on the boundary learn almost all their older classmates learn.[5] This strict age-grading is, however, probably most tragic at the low end of learning capacity, where students struggle and fail to learn "what everybody should learn" at their age. An advanced student who could have managed the material a year earlier only loses an extra year in the labor market at the end of school, so being just under the age boundary costs only a year's wages (say in year 2000 about $7 X 2,000 hours, or $14,000); one who is always placed a year ahead of what he or she is ready for faces about twelve years of suffering and humiliation. An obvious solution would be for people who learn more slowly to attend school for correspondingly more years.

5. In the United States I believe there is another year or so lost in middle school (grades six through eight), while most of the class marks time so others can catch up. The proportion of all mathematics in a middle school textbook that was also in the previous year's textbook is astounding. Most of the reading assigned in middle school is routinely at the fifth grade level, preparatory to a sudden jump in grade nine. Middle school history and civics routinely avoid giving explanations, and particularly avoid giving evidence for or against any explanations (though this often lasts on into secondary school). An American middle school, then, is a social institution devoted to carefully not teaching anything that one's age-peers are not ready to learn. This has a democratizing effect, and an effect of producing problems of school discipline. But that trade-off is a different subject.

The difficulties with this, especially in screwing up the societywide age-grading system, are obvious. But those difficulties are the ultimate origin of routinely demanding that such people should fail to reach the standards *a priori* appropriate for their age group, year after year.

In the streaming system the categorization is so set up that there is little search for the possible flash of brilliance in the lower streams. Children who are placed in a lower stream because they are trouble in the classroom, rather than because of slower learning (Milofsky 1976), learn considerably less than they might have.

FORMALIZED PROBABILITIES AND INJUSTICE, SEEN FROM THE BOTTOM

A common result in sociology is that lower-status people find the system less fair, less trustworthy, and more corrupt than those farther up (for example, for secondary schools, see Stinchcombe 1964). Part of this is due to the administrative costs of searching, against the probabilities, for a prize winner in an improbable category. Those in improbable categories have less effective right to have evidence of their merit taken into account. They then see the formality as a barrier to being heard at all, to having a fair go, a barrier to being looked in the eye by the rich, the wise, and the well born who run the schools. They see it that way because that is the way it is in fact.

For the police stopping suspicious young men, all the evidence shows that, for example, even "delinquent gangs" on the average go months without committing "gang-related events" worthy of police recording. The difference between gang members and others in the probability of having recently committed a crime is thus very small, enough so the police should take it into account, but not enough to send many of them to detention. The great majority of times they are stopped by the police, then, they are as innocent as the men in cars driving by at the same hour who are not stopped. Slight differences in *a priori* probabilities, then, result in disproportionate "hassling." And those who do get hassled in this way know a lot of people not stopped who have committed similar crimes to those they are wrongly suspected of, and that grates even if at some other time they have committed those crimes and not been stopped.

Thus the formal barrier between categories justified by probabilities is also a barrier to being treated justly, to being heard, to having due process rights respected. Just treatment of people who are not going to win in schools is expensive, and the only way to catch any of the criminals is to go where most of the crime is, as best one can bet. Administrative rationality creates the experience of injustice in people who have little going for them, but a lot going against them.

CONCLUSION

Chapter 3 is about formally arranging gaps in blueprints so that someone else can formalize them better. The whole system of construction planning uses "switches" of the sort "Details will be supplied by . . . ." In immigration matters formal switches say instead, "We will not be bothered with further details whenever . . . ." The purpose of the first kind of formality is to achieve better abstractions in the gaps. The purpose in immigration law is to achieve better abstraction by due process where it matters, with citizens and near-citizens, and carefully *not* to fill the gap for aliens. I think it would be wise foreign policy, more than worth its cost, to give more due process and concern for fairness to aliens than we presently do. Besides, treating people fairly and giving them their say is inherently valuable. But as long as people of poor nations want to go to rich nations that do not want many of them, the burden of giving due process in hopeless cases will "need to be" reduced.

Similarly, students in secondary schools learn more if the material in a class is slightly, but not far, over their heads. This means "tracking," either within classrooms or between them. In all classrooms, half are above the room average, half below it; the distances between students can be reduced, so that the teacher aiming for the seventieth percentile puts the material slightly, but not far, over the heads of those at the bottom; the ones at the top usually learn something. Students and parents see the higher classes as desirable privileges, as evaluations of the prospects of the student. They are indeed error-full estimates of the prospects of the students.

But the administrative trouble of moving one student down out of an honors class, in order to move another up who has worked very hard, makes correcting teaching mistakes very expensive in teacher and administrator effort. The same dynamics that produce formal rightlessness of aliens thus tends to produce informal rightlessness of the hardworking but slower student. The pressures toward formalizing rightlessness for the aliens are produced by the high value of correct abstraction about the rights of citizens and near-citizens. In the normal routine of tracked classrooms, the question of reassignment never comes up. When immigration agents roust a group of Spanish-speaking workers without papers from a workplace near the border, likewise, the question of a hearing is not likely to come up. But if an appeal for a hearing does come up, the formal culture allocating rightlessness carefully is called on to classify the claimant as deserving, or not deserving, a chance to have his or her claim to a right heard. That formality is not formally available to classify the student who worked hard in the lower track.

People and organizations rationally abstract a rough probability of success or failure from situations. They use these to determine whether to explore further or to listen to contrary evidence. The question in this chapter has been to ask when such normal intuitive abstractions are likely to be formalized. In particular, a very low probability that a person will be able to establish that he or she has a right might be formalized as rightlessness. The chilling words, "Whatever the procedure authorized by Congress is, it is due process as far as an alien is concerned," is just what we feared that formalization was all about.

But we find a similar informal rightlessness in the lower tracks in secondary schools. And we find it even where people have formal rights to a hearing, as in the rousting of Spanish-speaking workers, but there it is formally defended in the sense that the INS agent does not need to warn them of their rights.

CHAPTER SEVEN

FORMALIZING EPISTEMOLOGICAL STRATIFICATION OF KNOWLEDGE

THE SOCIAL PRODUCTION OF EPISTEMOLOGICAL STRATIFICATION

By the epistemological stratification of a body of knowledge, I mean a commonly understood classification of pieces of knowledge into more or less fundamental. We will be interested in such stratification when it has an impact on how the government of social activity is organized, when, that is, more fundamental parts of knowledge are more central to the government of the activity oriented to the body of knowledge. The most obvious case is science, where the activity to be governed is the production new fundamental knowledge. Thus when much-cited papers in a science are more likely than other papers by the same authors to cite previous much-cited papers (Cole and Cole 1973, 26–27, 176–79, 221–28), the obvious hypothesis is that more fundamental new knowledge will have more to do with more fundamental old knowledge than with experimental details.

My argument in this chapter relies on science as an obvious case in which more fundamental knowledge at present will be more used by the highest status people in future cohorts (high status because they themselves as scientists contribute more fundamental new knowledge), because it is more relevant to finding new knowledge. Those high-status people, then, will govern social activity by virtue of their generating more fundamental knowledge. For the purposes of this chapter, I am not very interested in the resulting stratification of people, though I will prefer famous scientists to illustrate the argument when possible.[1] Specifi-

---

1. It is very important for readers of this chapter to keep in mind that scientists and other scholars use citations even when the ideas or facts of the paper cited have no scien-

cally, I treat Imre Lakatos's analysis of this phenomenon in science, and contrast it with the different stratification of the same sort of knowledge by usefulness and reliability in engineering and other technical fields.

But we find clear statements of such a stratification by fundamentalness in the law as well, as in the following dissenting opinion by Justice Jackson:

> Procedural due process is more elemental and less flexible than substantive due process. It yields less to the time, varies less with conditions, and defers much less to legislative judgment. Insofar as it is technical law, it must be a specialized responsibility within the competence of the judiciary on which they do not bend before political branches of the Government, as they should on matters of policy. (*Shaughnessy v. United States ex rel. Mezei*, 345 U.S. 206 [1953], *quoted in* Aleinikoff and Martin 1991 [1985], 363)

There are two sorts of fundamentalness asserted here. One is an assertion that procedural matters are "more elemental" and more invariable. ("It yields less to the time, varies less with conditions, and defers much less to legislative judgment.") The second is that procedure is "technical law" over which courts in general preside, rather than the Legislative or the Executive. So there is a segregation of the parts of law that are matters of "policy" over which the legislature presides, and appeals courts' role is only to say concretely in particular cases what Congress says policy is, and parts of the law that are "technical" over which courts in general preside. Then within that stratification, procedure is more elemental and more invariable, and so more central.

An incidental part of the earlier argument in chapter 3 is that dimensions or measurements on blueprints that treat of the interdependence of weight-bearing members are "more central," because none of the rest of the provisions in the contract will work unless the weight-bearing parts are done right. This is an epistemology of purpose, that unless the building can bear its own weight and the weight of its contents, none of the other features of the building can serve their purpose either.

These examples show three different ways abstractions can be "more fundamental" than others. In science, more fundamental findings, theories, or constants are more often used to find new knowledge, are them-

---

tific use to them. In the extreme, some scholars are reputed to require students, and other scholars whose papers they referee, to cite them. People often cite their spouses more than they rightly deserve, though most spouses in the same discipline are actually more useful to their spouses than to other people, so it is hard to sort out. In short, like all formalities, citations can be corrupted. My purpose is to identify what is being corrupted, for the corruption would be of no value unless citations carried authority.

selves rarely tested or questioned, and are usually replaced only by new fundamentals. In law, by Justice Jackson's account, procedure is more fundamental because more unchangeable, and more central to "technical law" as compared to decisions of other branches of government. In construction, the dimensions of structure are central to holding the building up, so everything else depends on them. They are therefore more planned in advance, less at the discretion of a craftsperson. They are more central to the government of the project by the wishes of the client, as formalized in the blueprints.

The analogy among these cases of stratification of knowledge by fundamentalness, then, is that there is a congruence of the epistemological status of an abstraction and its role in the government of further science. Fundamental notions in science play a central role because they generate solutions to a wide variety of problems, and therefore govern the course of scientific research. A particular application of such fundamentals, to improve the accuracy of a measuring instrument in another subfield of science, is more peripheral, and more changeable as new instruments are developed.

The "fundamental fairness" central to judgment of legal procedure is central to the government of legal activity because it helps courts give substantive justice in a wide variety of circumstances. The fundamental fairness of housing policy (say, the large aggregate subsidy in the United States to home mortgages, the small one to public rental housing for the poor) is much more variable through time, much more a matter of policy rather than technical law, and does not help courts think in any but a very few cases. We would not then expect appeals courts concerned with technical law to decide on the fairness and justice of much larger subsidies to homeowners than to the poor living in housing projects. That would instead be in legislation determining policy. Only if the poor in housing projects had large mortgages, and large income tax obligations to take deductions from, would larger subsidies for the rich be "fundamentally unfair."

The dimensions of structural members of a building are central because heavy structures cannot stand up unless structurally sound, and structural members with the right size, materials, and angle to the force of gravity are principal determinants of structural soundness. The size, materials, and angle of electrical conduit, on the other hand, make very little difference to anything else.

EPISTEMOLOGICAL STRATIFICATION IN SCIENCE

Science gets its authority in a different way than law or blueprints do. To see this, it is useful to look at the way fundamental scientific numbers (for example, Planck's constant, the speed of light, the valence of hydrogen, the rate of expansion of the universe, and so on) get their authority.

The first feature of such numbers is that there are many ways to estimate them. A constant gets to be fundamental because different ways of estimating it give "the same" answer. This is, of course, an achievement that takes place over time. It happens quite often that the early days of estimating such a constant are filled with questions of whether it is indeed a constant, of whether there are some systematic biases in the first ways of estimating it, or in how to resolve disagreements among the estimates. Hubble's first estimates of the rate of expansion of the universe suggested that the universe could be no older than about a 1.5 billion years, while several estimates of the age of rocks suggested that the earth was approximately 4 billion years old. Clearly a constituent of the universe could not be older than the whole. But the postulate that, whatever its value was, it was a constant was partly confirmed by the fact that Hubble's method of estimating it gave about the same answer with observations of different nearby galaxies. Present (year 2000) estimates suggest that Hubble's first calculation of the age of the universe might be off by a factor around ten. Recent estimates of the constant using very distant supernovas instead of relatively nearby Cepheid variable stars suggest that it may in fact not be constant after all, but may decrease with distance (or with time). It may be, however, that estimates based on relatively nearby variable stars give underestimates. The empirical result, then, can cast doubt on the basic theory, or instead only on a theory of the measurement process quite far out on the universe's periphery.

A constant cannot have a great many estimates that converge unless the theory in which it is embedded has a great many consequences or causes in many different empirical situations. Thus the gravitational constant as estimated by Galileo with inclined planes (and tested by him for constancy by dropping balls of different weights to see if they landed at the same time) has implications for how much people and objects should weigh on the moon, and so how far a given mass should stretch a spring there.[2] Thus having several ways of estimating a constant itself shows the theoretical scope of the concept it represents; those several ways provide

---

2. Because gravitational force is smaller on the moon, a given mass will be lighter. But it will still balance the same mass on the other pan of a scale. At the same temperature steel will require the same force to distort it, so a spring scale on the moon will show a smaller weight, while a balance scale will show the same weight. Thus the equality of the gravitational constant demonstrated by Galileo does not hold when we move from the earth to the moon; Galileo did not try that. In modern science the gravitational constant of Galileo is a variable. It was treated as a variable by Newton, a function of the masses and distance. A balance scale equalizes masses, a spring scale weights.

the motivation for correcting or recalibrating each; and the convergence of the corrected estimates allows a high degree of accuracy of the abstraction, and allows that degree of accuracy itself to be estimated.

This in turn allows the estimates themselves to serve as tests of the theory of the measuring instrument, which often comes from quite a different branch of science than the one in which the instrument is used. Thus fundamental constants having many independent estimates gives evidence of several ways in which they are fundamental—by having large scope, high correctability, high and estimable accuracy, and great usefulness in tests of other scientific theories. That is, the features that make them "fundamental" are those that make them useful as abstractions, as described in chapter 2. But that means also that by the time they come to be fundamental, they are unlikely to be challenged. There are multiple indications that one has the theoretical concept correctly defined and understands very well how it works in a wide variety of situations. Thus when there are fundamental scientific constants, they tend to be important in scientific research, to lead to new knowledge, and rarely to be challenged. They thus form part of the "core" of a scientific research program.

The existence of fundamental constants (or other more complex mathematical forms), then, is a measure of a discipline's stratification of bits of knowledge by epistemological status. Jonathan Kelley, an Australian sociologist, used to define "Duncan's constant"[3] as "for anything of social importance, measurements on the father are correlated with measurements on the son at 0.4." Sociologists immediately recognize this as a joke, moderately near to the truth for a wide variety of characteristics in a wide variety of societies, but far from what real scientists would recognize as a fundamental constant. The fact that this is the best sociologists can do indicates that sociology is not as strongly epistemologically stratified as physics or chemistry.

LAKATOS AND STRATIFICATION OF SCIENTIFIC KNOWLEDGE

Imre Lakatos (1978 [1970]) undertook to develop a stratification of substructures of knowledge inside "scientific research programs." This was incidental to his purpose of analyzing how rational scientists would select among research programs, which then in turn would give them a framework for dealing with empirical anomalies and theoretical inconsistencies. His fundamental point was that one would stratify knowledge

3. Named after Otis Dudley Duncan, then the leading scholar in the study of social mobility.

differently for the task of betting where new knowledge was to be found (the basic purpose of a "research program") than one would to estimate the degree of epistemological certainty of knowledge. Then, in turn, if the advance of science did not depend much on epistemological certainty, the philosophical difficulties of the task of assessing epistemological certainty would not be very important to science's progress. In order to use these notions for present purposes, I have to tweak bits of them. For now the main point is that fundamentalness is a very different thing than certainty. Hubble's constant was very fundamental to cosmology from the first, even though its first estimate was obviously impossible, and seems to have been about ten times too small.

Lakatos differentiates the pieces of a research program into a "generative" core and a "protective belt" of mathematical derivations, problems, measurement procedures, experimental protocols, and the like. He argues that people working in the program routinely take some large share of the generative core as unchallengeable. That does not mean they are certain it is true; only that if it is false in some other way than "mere" failure of the protective belt, that will be fundamental. The protective belt and the core together generate what Thomas Kuhn (1970 [1966]) calls "puzzles" for scientists to work on. The puzzles actually consist of complex entities, which are partly derivations from the core and partly the theories embedded in observational protocols.

For example, Hubble's constant[4] describing the rate of expansion of the universe has a protective belt that at least includes how to measure redshift by observing emission lines in the spectrum, one relating red-shift of those lines to speed of recession (the Doppler effect), one observing brightness of certain objects thought to be of roughly known inherent brightness, so as to estimate distances by observed brightness of such objects, and various theories about how errors in these observations could be estimated. I already mentioned the anomaly in the apparent brightness of supernovas in very distant galaxies that challenges either the traditional method of estimation or the constancy of the expansion. But the estimation protocols for calibrating the red-shift are in the periphery of cosmology, while the notion of the expansion of the universe is still central to generating new knowledge in cosmology and is "assumed."

4. The postulate that Hubble's constant is a constant over the history of the universe is not as solid a part of the core of cosmology as the notion that the expansion it estimates is really going on and has gone on in the past. To a distant observer of these sciences it seems that Planck's constant being a constant is more solid than that Hubble's constant being a constant is. But as we will come to see, that does not mean that Hubble's constant is not continually used in the generation of new knowledge, and that many current uses of Planck's constant are only of technical, not scientific, interest.

These theories and practices in the observation and measurement part of the protective belt may themselves have different scientific status. For example, the hypothesis that Cepheid variable stars have a roughly constant relation between their period and their brightness did not, when it was first used, have a good theory of why it should be so. Similarly in estimating the red-shift, the smearing of spectrum lines by gravitation, by mixtures of radiation from gas jets traveling rapidly in opposite directions from a star, and so on, involves theories of how one tells what such processes do.

In particular the theories built into the instruments or adjustments of the data are often part of other research programs, so that there was a research program estimating emission and absorption lines in laboratories, while the inherent brightness of Cepheids cannot be studied in laboratories. The emission lines have been thoroughly theorized in quantum mechanics for several generations (though this was quite new when Hubble first worked on the expansion constant), so are now deeply embedded in the hard core of physics as a whole, taught to undergraduates. A smearing of a hydrogen line is therefore unlikely to result in astronomers' postulating misbehavior of very distant hydrogen. It will instead result in their postulating gravitational anomalies such as black holes near the light's origin, or jets moving at different speeds, or massive galaxies along its path.

Thus the periphery of a theory—connecting hypotheses derived from the core to observations, connecting them to "puzzles"—is itself stratified into periphery and core (often in other research programs). Not all the periphery is easily adjusted by *ad hoc* hypotheses, as Lakatos sometimes suggests. Hubble could not casually throw out all of quantum mechanics that had to do with emission lines, for it was at the foundation of that subject.

Great chunks of the derivation of phenomena from a core theory, that creates the first step of the observational "test," are done by logic and mathematics. Usually the mathematics is quite stable and well founded.[5] Usually therefore the derivations in physics and chemistry are reasonably solid. This means that the transmission of probative (or falsificative) value from the observations back to the theory is not problematic. This in turn means that observed falsifications imply that either the formula-

---

5. Newton, however, used a great deal of calculus that depended on "infinitely small" mathematical entities behaving in some respects like ordinary numbers, so one could add them up in an integral, for instance. Newton knew a great many paradoxes connected to such entities, but that did not slow him down much. We can be glad he did not wait to apply it to gravitation until modern analysis, addressed to the limits involved in the calculus, was invented (Lakatos 1976b [1961]).

tion of the "axiomatic" core, or the auxiliary theory embedded in instrumentation and calibration, is likely at fault; the mathematics is likely solid.

The phrases Lakatos uses for these theories that create observations are "background knowledge" and "initial conditions." Background knowledge in a given program does not occupy center stage, although it may be at the center of informal teaching in "laboratory life" (Latour and Woolgar 1979).[6] Outside the research program, it may be in the core of other research programs, or in well-established parts of research programs no longer generating much new knowledge but still taught in elementary textbooks. Like a contract of adhesion (an example of background formality in the law), one does not look into the fine print except in extraordinary situations. When one has to look, one may well change it to fit the circumstances. Inattention is not an epistemological commitment any more than it is a strong commitment to live by the boilerplate in a contract. It just reflects the fact that even great scientists and great negotiators cannot pay attention to everything at once.

Some background knowledge is developed only for instrumental purposes. Factor analysis in the social sciences is specifically designed to explore hypotheses having the general form: "This set of measures all measure the same underlying variable, whatever it is." The last clause is essential, for it shows that the technique is useful in a wide variety of research programs. It also says that the technique is not much good for studying what the substance of the factor is. Factor analysis is especially useful for finding ways to measure subjective states or predispositions that cannot be measured directly, such as intelligence or attitudes. The central mathematics has to do with the hypothesis that a matrix of associations among measures has rank one (after suitable discounting of the association of a measure with itself). This theoretical technique is rarely useful for testing any substantive hypothesis, but only for testing hypotheses about whether one is measuring anything at all that is common to several observables. If that hypothesis fails, it means the measures do not point to *any* underlying variable common to them, which includes not pointing to the one the scientist hoped he or she was measuring. A substantive theory almost never fails merely because one thought a given set of measures should have a great deal in common, and they do not. One just tries again with a different—purified—set of measures. A serious scientist is hardly ever theoretically interested in the results of a fac-

---

6. Bruno Latour's habit of insisting on chasing the assumptions that scientists borrow from the background science created by other research programs reminds me of Karl Llewellyn's phrase (1960, 185): "One must not in these matters chase fireflies into the marshes of absurdity."

tor analysis. This is then a very good case of a quite well-developed theory that is virtually always on the periphery of any research program where it is found.

But obviously *if* a given observation contradicts a theory *and* that observation depends on a set of measures that supposedly measures a concept, *then* one can investigate whether the set of observables measures anything, and if it does, whether it measures only one thing. If the auxiliary observation theory fails this test, then one need not adjust the core theory at all. One need only to try to develop measures by refining the empirical content of the concept that failed to be manifested in the empirical measures first chosen.

The existence of such general purpose tools for checking on observational theories shows that rejection of observational theories itself is divided into core and periphery. A core postulate of psychometric theory is that measures of the same thing, applied so as to yield a large enough sample of simultaneous measures, must have greater than chance relations with each other. Various devices for sorting out chance from a common thing that is measured then should give approximately equivalent answers to this question. *What* the measures have in common is then a question for substantive theory and investigation, and from the point of view of psychometric theory is peripheral and *ad hoc*. "Naming the factors" is something psychometricians rarely deal with.

The general point of this inherently tedious example is that the stratification of the whole body of knowledge in a scientific research program is not along a single dimension. In fact, some of the periphery is indeed *ad hoc* empirical generalization, as in Hubble's empirical hypothesis that Cepheid variable stars were of approximately known inherent brightness, supported by those whose distance could be estimated by parallax methods. Some of it is the core of a different research program, as the constancy of the frequency of emission lines was at the core of quantum mechanics at the time Hubble started working, generating new results in that subdiscipline. Others may be the subject of a research program in methods, itself having a core and a periphery but very little new substance, as factor analysis has been in behavioral science, or refinements of measurement of spectra of astronomical objects has been in astronomy.

OPERATIONALIZING FORMAL STRATIFICATION OF KNOWLEDGE IN RESEARCH PROGRAMS

Lakatos proposes two main features of the stratification of knowledge into core and periphery. The most fundamental is *generativity*, that the core of a research program generates new results. The more such results are "true enough," and the more they are not easily generated by competing programs, the more the elements of the core are worth working with. In essence this generative feature is the rate of change of what he sometimes calls the "empirical content" of the program.[7] Lakatos, having written a good deal on the calculus, must have been aware that a positive rate of change of empirical content implies a larger mass of empirical content over time.[8] He sometimes requires that a new research program also explain the empirical content of the research program it replaces, but does not take that requirement very seriously.

His main point is that the anomalies for a theory at a given time are opportunities to increase empirical content, rather than disproofs of the core theories of the program. He also requires that, in incorporating anomalies, one not add as much information to the axioms as one adds to its empirical content. If, for example, one simply adds to the Newtonian theory of gravitation a postulate that Mercury's perihelion is an exception, and then says what rate of change it has instead, the program's empirical content is not thereby increased. This means that what Lakatos calls "monster barring" cannot be counted as a positive rate of change of empirical content.[9]

The second, less important, feature of the stratification of knowledge is that the generative core is used without rethinking its fundamental structure during the generative process (I prefer "can be used," since sometimes it *is* transformed; I'd say for example that the Copernican heliocentric theory was fundamentally transformed by Kepler in his empirical fit of orbits,

7. One can also increase the mathematical content of either the core theory or parts of the protective belt (Lakatos 1978 [1970], 51 n.2). New approximations of solutions that were too complicated to derive or calculate explicitly, or that behave better near the limits, were frequent in the early development of quantum theory of atomic and molecular structures. A concrete example is the mathematical analysis, by Francis Crick and independently by W. Cochran, of the pattern of x-ray diffraction produced by a helix with its regularly repeated parts on the outside. The analyses of Crick and Cochran were stimulated by the attempt of V. Vand to solve the same problem, and is described by James Watson (1980 [1968], 40–41, 43. In the central papers reporting the discovery of DNA, reprinted as appendices to this edition, the mathematical finding is cited or discussed on pp. 247, 252, 253, 257, 278, 292). They all worked on the problem because it was useful for the DNA work and related crystallographic work in biology.

8. For example, Lakatos says (1978 [1970], 51 n.4) that "verification" is a corroboration of excess content in the expanding program.

9. Einstein explained Mercury's orbital behavior without "monster barring," but as a natural part of his relativity theory. One of Lakatos's original "monster barring" examples is the development of a theorem of Euler about the relation between the number of vertices, faces, and edges of a polyhedron; a cylinder has no vertices, three faces, and two edges, and violates the theorem, and the best we could at that time say was that, as a polyhedron, a cylinder is a monster (see Koetsier 1991; Lakatos 1976a [1961]). Lakatos thought that was in general a bad strategy, but he could not find a way out of it at the time.

because after all an elliptical orbit has no center—or has two "centers"—
to put the sun in.) Otherwise put, if we think of each potential test or theoretical elaboration as a combination of a derivation from the core and a
supplemental observational, experimental, and measurement theory, then
the effort can be spent on the derivation and observation part, rather than
modifying the core. But it can modify the core as well.

Lakatos sometimes writes as if this entailed a high degree of belief in
the core, and it probably usually does. But sufficient confidence that one
is working on the same research program as someone else need not mean
identical views on what is most important in the core in generating new
results. In fact, the "consensus" of people who believe in "the same" theory, program, or operationalization strategy is often each scientist's pro-
jection onto others of his or her own interpretation of the core (see
Gilbert and Mulkay 1984, 112–40). Thus it is more nearly true that scientists can contribute to a research program by using whatever parts of
the core they find convenient, true, or beautiful, and rejecting the parts
they do not. As long as they are not too dogmatic about the parts they
reject (at least pay attention to them), they can be perfectly reputable
among fellow researchers working on the same core.

The same is even more true of the hard core of theories used to build
observational machines or protocols. Most social scientists get by perfectly well without factor analysis tests of the number of dimensions (for
example, to reject the hypothesis that that number is zero) in their sets of
measures of their concepts. They can always use the alternative test that
if different measures have different causes or different effects, then they
cannot measure the same concept. For example, many survey questions
measuring approval of public policies do not predict well whether people
are willing to vote to pay for those policies, or to use coercion to enforce
them, so votes on practical legislative proposals do not evidently measure
the same thing as positive attitude answers. It is a matter of taste and talent whether such scientists use an abstract general tool like factor analysis, or a specialized substantive tool like predicting votes in favor of paying for policies one approves of, and finding a lot fewer in favor.

An abstraction system to govern a research program, then, must be
pluralistic because scientists need to use different parts of the structure
for different purposes, depending on what their particular puzzle is. If
their proposed solution to the puzzle does not work, the problem may be
with something fundamental in the core, something scientifically trivial
in the protective belt, or some deep problem in the theory of the measuring instrument in a different discipline entirely.

INDIVIDUALIZED COLLEGIALITY AND STRATIFICATION BEHAVIOR IN SCIENCE

Refereeing (including editorial and granting agency judgments, and in some disciplines book reviews) and citation are the central processes that "authoritatively" stratify bits of knowledge in modern scholarly disciplines. Both involve combined judgments of relevance (or "usefulness" to the discipline) and solidity (or "credibility"). If it is true, as I have argued above, that the various parts of a research program may have separate stratification criteria for knowledge, then we should expect to find separate clusters that could be defined as stratification by coreness and stratification by epistemological certainty. We should expect these clusters to overlap or be correlated with each other. Most of our information on scientists' judgments of pieces of work derives from citations, because referees' reports are not published. And, as Lakatos's analysis of research programs would suggest, they do indeed cluster into citations to theories and methods citations. Generativity and solidity are then somewhat separable criteria for stratification of scientific knowledge.

The refereeing process and the citation process are often tied together by referees and editors who require authors to cite the core papers. Often one is specifically required to deal in the text of one's own paper with core method, evidence, or theory contrary to one's own conclusion. Citations to pieces that once were part of the core, but that have been superseded, only show one is out of date.

When citing a particular paper, there is an internal stratification by how near the core the subparts of the paper are. Thus among Euclid's axioms, the one on parallel lines was traditionally the most vulnerable. For example, the meridians of longitude occupy a place in navigation, perpendicular at different points to the equator, closely analogous to the place of parallel lines in Cartesian analytic geometry, but they meet at the poles. In the days when Euclidean geometry was still generative, that was something to worry about. But when spherical trigonometry became central to navigation, one discarded the parallel postulate with no trouble. When non-Euclidean geometry was generalized, Euclidean geometry was for mathematicians a mostly uninteresting special case, though still of interest to people (some of them at least) in the tenth grade. But the core point here is that the parallel postulate was not part of the main core of Euclidean geometry; it eventually became the core of a research program on non-Euclidean geometries exactly because it was so easy to dispense with.

Very often there are special abbreviations to cite only the core part of a fundamental paper. The extreme of core citation only is the naming of constants after the person who conceived or first estimated them, such as Planck's constant or Hubble's constant. The fact that Hubble's constant is now thought to be very different from Hubble's own estimate (Planck's was very near) shows that it is the coreness of the concept, not Hubble's observational achievement, that is being cited. That achievement is now not even on the periphery. The relevant paper itself is probably cited only in the history of science. To call the constant instead "the rate of increase of the red-shift of stellar objects with apparent distance" (except in a text-book or a history of science) would be to announce the possibility that the expansion of the universe might not be the thing measured. The other parts of Hubble's papers on the subject are of the nature of *obiter dicta* in the law, easily dispensable parts of the periphery of the research program. Very often the core part of a classic paper is in fact the most general part.[10]

Although acts such as printing a citation or submitting an authoritative referee's report constitute the main formal acts of the stratification system, the connections between these formal acts are not formally specified. Lakatos's generalization is that such stratification, and thus presumably such differentiation of the indicators of formal refereeing and formal citation, reflect continuing usefulness in leading to new knowledge. That is, the informal valuation of generalizations or observational procedures is by their usefulness in finding new knowledge, which is then formalized in referees' reports and other scientists' citations.

APPLIED SCIENCE AND EMPIRICAL REGULARITY

Applied science usually has a different stratification of knowledge than academic science. For example, one of the things that specifically cannot be patented is a law of nature, so a core formalization of applied knowledge is unavailable for formalizing a law of nature. The more fundamental it is, the less it can be patented. The applied science occupations are taught science rearranged into a form so that it can be reliably incorporated into machines, or into protocols of medical treatment, or into providing synthetic substitutes for leather soles of shoes.

Often in application, the applied science from one discipline will have to be combined with applied science from others. Sciences may be quite

---

10. In sociology, it is likely to be a phrase rather than a constant that is the object of coreness. For example, it is not legitimate to use the phrase "world system" without citing Immanuel Wallerstein's classic three-volume work on the subject (1974–), even if his *obiter dicta* in that work, for the problem at hand, are false or inapplicable. I know because I once forgot to. That was equivalent to renaming Hubble's constant for oneself because one had corrected Hubble's estimate.

differentiated by what they find useful for generating new knowledge, yet intimately intertwined in making a dam strong enough to hold a valleyful of water.

Civil or structural engineering therefore needs the physical chemistry of concrete, including physical qualities of sand and gravel as well as of crystallized ("cured") cement. But structural engineering also needs the metallurgy of steel, joint strength at various angles of welded, glued, and nailed joints, and of reinforced steel embedded in concrete joints, the economics of procurement of construction materials, average weights per square foot of floor for various uses of space, resistance to failure for expectable temperatures in fires, and so on. In short, applied science would often be a disaster if it were pure—devoted only to, say, the physical chemistry of the setting of cement.

These are much like the combinations of disciplines in the observational machines in the protective belts of pure sciences. The concrete under a telescope must not break, nor the tracking mechanism be too responsive to the vibrations of trucks going by. The observational machines of pure sciences are themselves examples of applied science; they require solid results from other disciplines. They also usually require a high degree of original theory of the things to be observed. Astronomers need the physical chemistry of cement only to keep their telescopes still, not to interpret the spectra of very distant galaxies; they need complex and sometimes original theories in order to know what to measure about those spectra.

Applied science has to be generative in a different way than the core of a research program is. It usually has to form a reliable part in many different applications. The theoretical similarity of rough reinforcing steel so the concrete binds well to it in concrete pillars to the roughening of a rubber tube before gluing a patch on it is of no applied value (nor I suppose of much generative value in materials science). As long as reinforcing steel as it comes from the steel wholesaler, and cement as it comes from burning limestone in a furnace and grinding it up, reliably produce good bonds, one after another building reliably stands up. And it is quite a separate technological fact that patches stick to rubber tubes that have been roughened.

In particular, the radical increase in the empirical content of "materials science" in recent years, so that the theory of those good bonds is sounder, need not change a single entry in the tables of strengths of reinforced concrete beams or foundations. Even the variations in epistemological certainty between theories in undergraduate textbooks and theories at the frontier of science need have no effect, as long as the technically useful effects of the uncertain theories reliably appear under known conditions. Animal breeding with a "bloodlines" theory of genetics produced fast race horses long before chromosomes and genes were known, and improvements in horse speeds between generations are not much greater now that we know more about chromonsomal genetics. Similarly, as long as tunneling of electrons reliably goes on with imperfect theories, semiconductor devices can make use of it.

FORMALIZATION BY USEFULNESS DECENTRALIZED

Decentralized formalization of a stratification of knowledge by its usefulness for changing knowledge does not sound like authoritative formalization of bureaucracies and laws that sociologists usually study. The particle theory of radiation of Planck and Einstein formed one of the bases of the development of a theory of the variation of specific heats with temperature (Kuhn 1978, 210–20), the theory of atomic structure, and the theory of atomic emission and absorption of radiation. How could that usefulness arise in the face of particle theory's incompatibility with interference phenomena? In some sense the Planck theory was "known" to be epistemologically unsound, because some obvious phenomena in radiation could not be derived from it, and seemed on the face of things to contradict it. This shows that scientists were clearly distinguishing "coreness," in Lakatos's sense of generativity, from epistemological soundness, and were preferring generativity.

The deep tendency of sociologists of science to imagine that scientists are taking a position on epistemological questions when they are preferring generativity is confusing enough to the sociology of science. It was fatal to most of the philosophy of science of the mid–twentieth century, which did not distinguish between an uncertainty that was an interesting anomaly to work out and the uncertainty of not knowing whether something was true or not. But if the authoritativeness of being useful for finding new knowledge is different from the authoritativeness of being epistemologically sound, it is even more different from the authoritativeness of the batallion commander. Any scientist can challenge it at any time, or not pay any attention to it at all if he or she chooses.

The central difference is, of course, that scientists in their work are betting on where new knowledge is to be found. But if they *knew* where it was to be found, it would be merely engineering, not science. This does not mean that they do not care what is true. Planck paid a great deal of attention to experiments on "black body radiation." He figured out that adopting binomial statistics that were based on discontinuous phenomena would produce a fit to the experiments, while Maxwell's equations would not (Kuhn 1978). He may have been comforted by the fact that, in the limit as the number of units goes to infinity, the binomial approaches a well-known continuous distribution. But when Einstein showed that this fact was not enough to make Maxwell's received continuous theory acceptable, Planck went with what fit the black body data (Kuhn 1978, 170–87); the wave theory that generated an understanding of interference did not generate an understanding of black body radiation, nor later of specific heats or emission and absorption lines in solar and stellar spectra.

Going ahead with what works does not, of course, mean not worrying about the contradictions. But the presumption of physical science is that the world cannot have contradictions in it; only the imperfections of our theory make it look as if it did. So the Lakatos solution is to put up with known epistemological unsoundness in favor of what works. What works must work for some reason, which in the long run we will understand. There is a sort of temporary, and useful, soundness to things known to be ultimately unsound. That is what betting where new knowledge is to be found is all about.

The air of wry surprise at scientists' epistemological "assumptions" in Latour and Woolgar 1979 comes first of all from not understanding that the theories on which the measuring instruments and laboratory practice are built mostly come from sciences that the experimenter is not expert in and does not care about advancing. But a good part of it is Latour and Woolgar's notion that the usefulness of a fact or idea in the search for new knowledge is a function of its soundness alone. For new knowledge, an idea is best if there is an anomaly implied by it, which the scientist has a good bet about how to go about resolving. If, as in Planck's case, the resulting solution turns out to work merely to make the anomaly deeper, more troublesome, that is still new knowledge. If the anomaly gets deep enough, as in the long run the contradiction between the theory that explained interference and the one that explained black body radiation did become, then the elaboration of the contradiction itself becomes a fundamental innovation in the science.

In the meanwhile, technological uses of science do not need to worry about the contradictions. It is perfectly all right for a civil engineer not to know why the crushing strength of concrete is nearer to the crushing strength of steel than the tensile strength of concrete is to steel's tensile strength; even less does he or she have to know whether these two are the same phenomenon as the lesser tensile strength of cast iron versus rolled steel, or of "fatigued" steel versus newly rolled steel. If one's theory of the formation of crystals in cement and its relation to concrete's tensile strength contradicts one's theory of the effect of rolling on steel crystals, so in turn on its much higher tensile strength, no worries. Reliability of empirical consequences of a disintegrated knowledge of the world is fine, and only research engineers need to try figure out whether they could have something like a rolling mill for concrete.

Likewise the standards for foundations that are an abstract component of construction blueprints need not bear any relation to the abstractions that are strategic to the advance of materials science. The "realistic" answer to Latour and Woolgar, that after all airplanes fly and buildings stand up (so science must be sound in the real world), is no answer to the real question a scientist asks: "What is a good bet for finding new knowledge, and what a good bet for establishing that it is good enough knowledge to be valuable in finding still more?" And that is the question Lakatos understands and answers.

The fit between citations as the formalizing device for stratification of bits of scientific knowledge and the theory of what is being stratified in this chapter is exact. For a paper to be a source of a citation, it itself has to be refereed and published as a contribution to knowledge. For a citation to be worth the while, it has to bear either on the newness of the knowledge (for example, what is the best we knew before) or on whether or not it is knowledge. In either case, the work cited is being useful to the paper from which the citation comes.[11]

Further the citation refers, in general at least, to a paper that was refereed before as being new knowledge, conceived as new, as a contribution to science. The citation says that indeed it was a contribution to science, at the very least as something worth refuting. One would not cite a foundations foreman who said that if the slump of the concrete is too quick (indicating too much water), the concrete will be too weak, as the basis of an experiment on the form and packing of crystals in cement with varying water content. The foreman's statement was never intended to be a contribution to knowledge, and in any event would be known to anyone in the foundations business. Further it was not organized so as to be valuable for the advance of concrete technology. It is, of course, very likely that no one who reads this paragraph will know why too much water makes concrete weaker; nor would anyone think that the foreman's statement was a worthwhile criterion of epistemological soundness of whatever theory he or she did have.

Thus the stratification of pieces of knowledge by scientists in their work has very little to do with their epistemological soundness, nor does the applied use of science bear on the sort of soundness that scientists use

---

11. To remind the reader, this is a statement about what the formalization of scientific knowledge for research purposes demands. Citing a senior professor who will vote on one's tenure case need not contribute to the advance of knowledge to be explained.

to generate new knowledge. Instead citations formalize a different sort of usefulness of findings and ideas, namely, usefulness for betting where new knowledge is to be found. A paper is valuable if someone using it in making their bet has been successful in finding new knowledge, and that is what is formalized in a citation.

CONCLUSION

A referee's report on a draft paper, or a citation to the published version, both come out of the informal life of a science, just as a blueprint comes out of the informal life of a construction contract. It is an abstraction of that informal life, useful for telling what was the generative core that was used to produce the paper and which particular parts of the protective belt it uses. In using it, of course, one needs to take account of whether the citations are by a junior faculty member to a senior professor with a vote on his or her tenure. But that is not what is wrong with viewing a citation as an assertion of epistemological soundness in the philosophical sense. The generative core that generates new knowledge and so citations may not be very certain at all. And even more, many of the things in the protective belt of the theory may be false, or untested, or apparently anomalous, and not challenge the core of the research program at all, because their imperfections do not suggest (at least not very strongly) where new knowledge is to be found.

Improving the cement contractor's performance by developing a theory of what too much water does to the strength of concrete might improve the technology. For example, extra water might produce voids where the crystalline structure that gives strength to concrete is discontinuous, and that might explain why firing of bricks, or stressed concrete beams, or concrete with additives that make it pourable without as much water all increase the strength of concrete. (I have no idea whether this is true or not—I am trying to show that this "scientific mechanism problem" is a different problem than a concrete contractor and the architect have.) Such a theory, however, might not suggest any new (cheap) ways not to produce voids nor to divert from the voids those forces that propagate cracks in concrete, and might then only reproduce what the relevant crafts already knew about, say, mortar being softer and more easily degraded than brick.

The construction specification on slump is a different kind of abstraction than a scientific theory, or even than a series of speculations in applied science such as I have given. The specification has a different purpose: that the foundation be sound enough to hold up the building. *That* purpose is improved by noticing it is strong enough, but in the wrong place to hold up the roof, which has nothing to do with water in concrete at all. None of these applied purposes has a main purpose of making good bets on where new knowledge is to be found. It has epistemological certainty about a scientific dead end, at least until theoretical speculation opens it up; its "protective belt" of auxiliary aids to effective applied thought is putting the concrete under the supports for the roof, not locating where the core theory leads to anomalies that a scientist might be smart enough to resolve.

The key function of citations or referees' reports is the collective government of attention by pluralistic consensus. The consensus of a liquid market, as discussed in chapter 5, has to result in exactly one price of exactly one standardized commodity. The consensus of a science ideally has to lead *each* scientist to a *distinct* puzzle that he or she can solve. Lakatos's core of a scientific research program is then a focus of attention, not a focus of belief or certainty. The common focus of attention causes each participant in a research program to read the papers of the others. But that focus has to be blurry, or they would all see the same thing. If each scientist had only one citation, the way the financial pages have only one closing price (and that a citation to the one market maker), there would be only one possible option for further research. If an elementary science text has single, or no, citations in an argument, it shows it is not a part of a research program in Lakatos's sense. Multiple citations in a single paper, including some core citations and some protective belt citations, are exactly the kind of government by abstractions a research program needs.

This does not mean, of course, that government of attention is all that is needed. The body of a scientific paper is not, except for review articles,[12] the citations. Instead it is an argument combining measurement or experimental techniques and tentative generalizations from the periphery with fundamental but uncertain theory and evidence from the core, in order to extend knowledge. There is also government by the abstractions embedded within the published papers that are cited, and in published collections of mathematical formulas, in tables of constants, or even from textbooks. One does not ordinarily cite textbooks, except from other sciences or mathematics, for purposes on the periphery.

The core of a research program need not be theoretically deep and abstruse. In the late-nineteenth-century geology of the high plateaus of Utah, Nevada, and Arizona, a central piece of the core had to do with the ages of rivers versus mountains. In the lowlands, we expect rivers to *follow* slopes—rivers run through valleys. In the high plateau, as John Wes-

---

12. Review articles usually do not count on a scientist's vita except as "teaching," or as "service" to the profession.

ley Powell observed, one sees rivers ignoring valleys and instead cutting through mountains. Since water does not run uphill, and probably did not in ancient times, this means that the river must have been there *before* the mountains and continued cutting as the mountains rose. The protective belt of the technology for finding rivers by slopes is rejected by this simple idea. We ordinarily assume that rivers follow the stable geology, rather than being stable in the face of changing geology. The idea of the river's stability in the face of geological change went to the core and transformed geological investigation (Stegner 1954 [1953], 152–58).

The observation that water cannot run uphill to cut its way through mountains involves no mystery about wave equations or the uncertainty principle. But it did direct attention to the lifting forces, sometimes associated with volcanic penetration of layers of sedimentary rock, which in particular pushed bits of the ancient surface upward into the path of a river. Which rivers were there before which mountains, and which after, became an important topic, governing the attention of geologists after the crucial Powell observations. That in turn implied some mountains were formed by cutting away their sides and some by uplifting, explaining different elevations of the same layers on the lifted ones. There were, in short, lots of puzzles for a lot of geologists, all citing each other, and all driven by what was, from the point of view of physics, a triviality; a very certain triviality compared to Schrödinger's equations on particles being also waves, but just as much a core of attention government.

Attention government in humans originally dealt with something moving in the periphery of vision, which might be a lion. Careful split-second study after that government of attention, by turning its head and focusing its eyes, told the humanoid whether to run or continue eating. If one governed one's attention only by the *certainty* that it was a lion, one would pay attention only as one's neck was broken. A government of action in the face of uncertainty cannot start from the certainties. The abstractions that govern attention cannot therefore respond only to certainties. The hypothesis that the river was there before the mountain was based on a certainty about gravity and water, but also on the uncertain hypothesis that rivers could stay their course while the rocks moved. That reckless hypothesis opened up a lot of new territory to explain, and explained a lot of anomalies other than having trouble finding the headwaters of the Dirty Devil River. It is *a priori* epistemologically uncertain that it would be the water, not the rocks, that was the basic stable force of the geology, shaping the rocks instead of being shaped by them.

Thus the contrast between the citation practices of the concrete foundations contractor versus geologists acknowledging Powell for seeing a consequence of water not being able to run uphill, or quantum physicists citing Schrödinger's ungrounded equation (Treiman 1999, 85–90), along with data on emission and absorption lines, is expectable. Scientists, unlike early hominids, must govern their attention in order to find the lion, not to avoid it. But pluralistic attention government with careful consensual confirmation works in both avoiding and in finding the lion; or finding why rivers cut through mountains with lava intrusions, in strata that are higher on the mountain than on the plateau, and why mountains without lava intrusions have strata at the same level as the plateau;[13] or why electrons as particles behave as waves. Referee and citation formalization of epistemological stratification therefore solves the distinctive problems of attention government when scientists have to bet on where new knowledge is to be found, not when they have to make an idea solid enough to build an airplane with.

13. The famous characterization of the Grand Canyon as "a mountain range in a ditch" depends on all those mountains in the ditch having been cut around by erosion, rather than uplifted into the river. The level of strata of these mountains in a ditch are well predicted by the level of those same strata on the sides of the canyon. The igneous rock is largely on the bottom, not intrusive in the sedimentary strata, as it tends to be in the mountains higher than the plateau, cut through by a river.

CHAPTER EIGHT

CONCLUSION: THE VARIETIES OF FORMALITY

THE THEORY AND THE BOOK

Chapter 2 might be described as a theory of what formality—government by abstractions—must be like to be good for anything. In short, the abstractions that govern in formality have to be embedded in a social process that produces accuracy, communicability, and a trajectory of improvement in order to be good for anything. Government by those abstractions, to produce social formality, has to be characterized by formal validations, assumption of risk, organization of attention, and standards, or routines, or protocols. To be more exact, the more the abstractions of a system and government by them have the features described, the more such a formal system can be expected to be able to fulfill some purpose or function. I have usually defined the variable of "good for anything" by its high end, because that is what is missing in sociology and related fields. Most sociology of formality applies especially to formality that is not good for anything.

There is, then, a whole subdiscipline in organizational studies showing my variable has a low end, that a lot of formality is good for nothing, except maybe to celebrate and ritualize rationality that is not there. We know so much about formality that is cant and ritual that we have forgotten that the rationality that we ritualize or corrupt would not be celebrated unless it was *sometimes* good for something. To some degree I have had to be a Pollyanna, a Dr. Pangloss, in order to describe what the high end of the variable of rational formality is like. That is an uncomfortable role for a sociologist, and should have been assigned to an economist.

The other five chapters specify that general argument by locating the crucial features that make it possible for *specific* functions to be performed. Just as functionalism of saying the liver-pancreas system regulates sugar levels is supported by showing that it is exquisitely adapted to that function, showing that the tiny details of blueprints (not tiny compared to the islets of Langerhans, of course) are exquisitely adapted to relating structural integrity to shapes and sizes of rooms and walls. Chapter 3 argues that special characteristics of blueprints might make them a good formality to connect a client and its architect to craft contractors, and, with that connection, to build a building that would stand up and would look and function like the building the client thought it was buying. The central feature of that formality is its being embedded in a system that fills in the blanks in the blueprint with formalities or informal competencies worked out elsewhere, especially in the institutions of the separate crafts.

Chapter 4 argues that the civil law needs gaps filled. The civil law courts fill gaps by distinguishing a case from closely related cases, then applying some of the legal principles relevant to the nearby cases to the distinct features of the case in the gap. Those reasons that still apply to the new case in the gap then apply in the gap *as well as* to the others covered by the old precedent. The argument is that this system of improving abstractions does better at producing a nearly everywhere gapless system of legal abstractions, and therefore better remedies governing the disputes, than does the formally rational system described by Max Weber.

Chapter 5 argues that highly liquid markets with a continuous price for a given kind of commodity, security, or option contract can only operate if the legal information on the real goods at the base of the market is abstracted reliably. Multiple third-party or fourth-party guarantees of the validity of the values that ultimately back up the financial instruments serve as a transparent abstraction system, making income streams generated in the markets into abstract commodities of known values and risks. This allows the prices of abstract securities in the secondary market to be flexible, because the formality governing risks at the bottom is rigid enough so that the abstractions in the finance markets accurately reflect the aggregated and formalized, and identical, risks of given securities.

Chapter 6 argues that a formality designed for protecting the rights of citizens and near-citizens may be too expensive for treating aliens at the borders. But that implies that there have to be constant corrections and special decisions for cases close to the boundary between alien and citizen or potential citizen. Limiting the scope of formalities that protect noncitizens then makes national boundaries less expensive. And there are limits on the protection of citizens at national boundaries as well—for example, limits on the search and seizure provisions of the constitution.

The economy of effort produced by the rightlessness of foreigners is then limited by the formalization of indicators of the *a priori* probability that a given alien would be eligible to immigrate.

Chapter 7 argues that the key function of formalities of refereeing and citation in science is to govern attention of scientists, not to allocate truth value. The core of a research program as described by Imre Lakatos is a set of things to pay attention to, not a set of things one is required to believe. The core often involves assertions of great epistemological uncertainty. But core ideas and evidence are supposed to provide ways to bet wisely where new knowledge is to be found, that will in their turn be useful in finding still more new knowledge. Citation and refereeing are types of formalization that can govern attention without necessarily governing belief.

The overall point, then, is that socially instituted abstraction systems, when properly designed, are a very useful way of governing some kinds of social action. To be good at governing action, they have to be so arranged that they tend to be accurate, communicable, and on a trajectory of improvement so they will stay accurate and communicable. But what they have to be accurate, communicable, and improvable *about* will depend on the concrete purposes and functions of the social action they are supposed to govern. Treating foreigners worse than citizens, and citizens crossing national boundaries worse than citizens living at home, is a different purpose or function than building buildings, liquidifying mortgage debts, or betting where new scientific knowledge is to be found. It therefore requires abstractions to be accurate about different things, to govern different things, to be improved in different ways.

Broad features of the process of abstraction make abstractions and their government of social life functional. Lack of those broad features is therefore a fairly reliable indicator of ritual or corrupt formality. Distinct features of formality in different niches make the sorts of formality that are functional for pouring concrete different from those for advancing geology, and different yet from those for adapting the law of contract to large flows of contracts about homogeneous legal instruments, traded by telegrams or Internet connections.

Another way to put all this is that formality has to be substantively as well as formally rational to be better than informality, if the informality is itself substantively rational; if people are trying to be substantively rational, they will only prefer formality if it has *fidelity* to that informal rationality. I have argued against the notion that formality is always less substantively rational by showing that the different kinds of formality analyzed in chapters 3–7 differ in ways that achieve different substantive ends or functions effectively. The distinction between formal and substantive rationality is perhaps Max Weber's central mistake. The purpose of this book, especially the purpose of its case studies of different sorts of formality, is to persuade the reader that this distinction is not a valid one, *if* the formality is any good. That cause may be forwarded by analyzing where it was Weber went wrong; some of this has been built into chapter 4 on civil law, but is used for a different purpose here.

MAX WEBER ON FORMAL VERSUS SUBSTANTIVE RATIONALITY

Max Weber (especially 1954 [1924]; more generally 1968 [1924]) was interested in explaining three aspects of formalized social action: (1) formalized action can be improved ("rationalized") by systematic thought and then taught as a system; (2) formalized action can be predicted, because formality reduces arbitrariness and encourages social routines that give the same outcomes in the future as now (for example, formal law is more certain law); and (3) formalized action (especially in bureaucracies and lower courts) can be controlled by law or by a prince or a board of directors (can produce "discipline"), and so allows large-scale social action to be controlled by policy.

But when Weber came to formalization in the law, he was tempted into contrasting formalization with "*Khadi* justice," "arbitrary" judgment in the light of substantive justice in particular cases (Weber 1968, vol. 2, 809–15; more generally for law, 641–900; Rheinstein's introduction in Weber 1954 [1924] is especially valuable on this point). I believe this distinction between formality and substance gave him trouble, *especially* in his sociology of law, in explaining the three things he wanted to explain; it was a scientific mistake.

It was this temptation that was continued in the contrast between "formal organization" and "informal groups" in American industrial sociology (for example, Roethlisberger and Dickson 1950; Whyte 1961, 38–51); between law as part of the "great tradition" as opposed to the "little [or local] tradition" in anthropology (Redfield 1971, 40–59); between law, or the written contract, and "custom," or "business practice," in the history of law (Llewellyn 1960; chapter 4 above); and between science and "laboratory life" in the sociology of science (Latour and Woolgar 1979; chapter 7 above).

What these all do conceptually is to focus on a situationally specific *meeting* between some system of formalized action and some action or detail that is either less formalized or is formalized in a different way. Weber's contrast between law and "*Khadi* justice," for example, is an attempt to describe law in contrast to what happens in a such a meeting (of abstract law and welfare or justice) within a great religious tradition, Islam. That tradition was only partly designed to give reliable guidance to a court organization in producing a decision to fit the local details. But *Khadi*s were a part of a Muslim empire with a great deal of continuity through time, as well as being judges of the empire's religion. They occupied a regular and formalized position and did their jobs in such a way as to maintain the empire and its religion. Their role cannot have been much less formal than that of modern police (I have explained in chapter 6 in what sense police are the least formal part of the modern criminal justice system). But they were located in a system that formalized law in a different way for different purposes, so that the role of the *Khadi* looked informal to Weber.

Whenever such a meeting between formal and informal life takes place, something about local life has to be abstracted in order to be treated by the formal system. But I argue that this fact, and consequently the whole set of traditions that points with wonder to the fact that some informal system has a dynamic that is not completely captured by its formal description, cannot explain the central things that Max Weber wanted to explain by rationalization and formalization. These traditions fail because all formalization contains such meetings; a successful formalizing system builds parts (abstracted parts) of informal social life into the formality. The meeting itself, then, is part of a larger structure that eventually, to some degree or other, produces a formalization; all formal abstraction comes from informal details. Even the *Khadi* could produce a final judgment on a case to set in motion an enforcement apparatus enforcing a narrowly conceived, formalized, resolution of the case. And the Ottoman Empire, after all, managed to administer law to a wide variety of peoples over many centuries, not obviously sinking back into an informal group of friends and enemies.

Similarly the calling together of the witnesses of the "seisin" (roughly "ritual of entering into legitimate possession") as a jury in early Anglo-Norman law, to testify collectively on a transfer of land tenure and its conditions, stabilized land tenure. It was more informal than the writing of a contract, but it served the same function. And in order to serve that function, it had to be so arranged that the original contract could be produced (by the jury, not the writing) in a formal legal dispute. In short, it was an abstraction formalized for the purpose, and worked much like a writing.

In some ways seisin and juries led eventually to the pile of papers that must be certified by various kinds of experts and financial people at a modern American real estate closing, as discussed in chapter 5. The point of the hearing of neighbors as a "collective witness" was to produce an abstraction of the local facts for future formal decisions on the *legal* facts of the transfer of land tenure, establishing a property right that would not have to be investigated by the court again. The jury in modern English courts looks to Weber as a very first step to replace a "charismatic" legacy in law with reasoned consideration of this worldly evidence. It was only a first step, so its persistence seemed irrational, or traditional, to Weber; juries still abstract the legal essence of facts rather than having expert judges do it (Weber 1968 [1924], 767–68).

But much of the law of evidence in British and American law is a formalization of what the jury must, and must not, be told, and must be charged to do as their duty, so that the abstraction of the legally relevant facts may be entrusted to them. One cannot read even a bit of *Wigmore on Evidence* (1940) and believe that Anglo-American law is unrationalized, and that juries would be free to say: "It is written . . . , but I say unto you . . . ," as Weber says charismatic authorities do.

The first of Weber's purposes, explaining rationalization—that is, explaining why a formalized system can be cumulatively improved by thought—can be best approached by remembering Alfred North Whitehead's observation, "We think in abstractions, but live in details." We have to start with the relations between details and the abstractions that we can use to think about those details, rather than imagining that some ("informal") systems manage details, while some ("formal") systems work exclusively with abstractions. Some of the substance gets into English law through the law controlling juries. That control over the abstraction process of juries has been done differently in different historical periods. Weber evidently thought that the intelligence of a legally controlled jury was less rationalized than the intelligence of a legally trained judge, typically used for trying facts in Continental systems.

But the "informal" part of abstraction of the legally relevant factual conclusion is in the common sense of the judge in a bench trial rather than in the common sense of the jurors. The common sense of both is informal, in the first instance. As the judge's common sense is trained in the course of learning a more complex system of distinctions (of abstractions, that is), it surely becomes more formal, more "legal." But jurors also think more formally in their special role, for which they are socialized and instructed by the judge, and they produce a single abstraction of a decision rather than a jumbled picture of the reality they have heard about during the trial.

The location of Continental judgments of facts in the judge's common sense does not make that common sense either more or less essential to formality than the common sense of the jury. Weber was led astray in interpreting the difference between Continental and English law, because he had drawn the wool over his own eyes by contrasting what is formal and informal in the wrong way. Formality is the informal abstracted; formal devices for abstracting can, and usually must, use common sense to pick out the relevant parts of reality and abstract them for the use of the formal system. Juries and judges can act in much the same way in doing that. They do not act in exactly the same way, but the final decision of the court is in both cases still abstracted from all the facts and made simple, and communicable to the police and other enforcement agencies, and made improvable by the appeals court. That is, it can be made into a system that grasps the relevant parts of reality as well as, or better than, informality, and it can start there and get better. Chapter 4 is about how it could get better, and what the conditions in the abstracting process of appeals courts should be to make it regularly get better. Chapter 5 is about how creative use of the law of contract and the certification of the abstracting process by "fourth parties" to a transaction can render states' debts and secondary mortgage markets more flexible, can move money around faster to more distinct houses and more new house owners.

ROUTINIZATION

The second of Weber's purposes, explaining routinization—that is, explaining the predictability of life governed by formal laws, formal regulations in organizations, formal procedures, formal capital accounting— is best achieved by asking what are the conditions under which abstractions do in fact govern social life, and when they fail to govern. I have argued that they fail to govern, among other reasons, because they sometimes do not abstract the details that are critical for action.

The purpose of going through the details of different abstraction systems (blueprints, civil law, market making producing liquidity, immigration administration and its law, and science producing focused disciplined creativity) is to show that routinization has to be done differently for different substantive purposes, because different things are relevant in the different situations in which those purposes are pursued.

Weber himself was fascinated by the great variety of ways things can be formalized. His beastly dull outline of the "forms of appropriation" (1968 [1924], vol. 1, 144–50) could only have been interesting to him if he thought different purposes required different forms. I have not tried to make a complete list of the forms, as Weber seemed to be aspiring to do. I have instead chosen to study in detail how blueprints can leave some kinds of rationality to formal systems of the crafts while leaving others authoritatively in the drawings, and how the civil law and the three other examples do something completely different. So far that is obvious. But that is like saying that all different sorts of organs can get oxygen to cells in different animals and plants, so nothing is explained by the function of respiration. To show why this is bad biology, we have to show in detail how lungs, gills, leaves,[1] and cell membranes of single-celled organisms in seawater all in fact work to supply oxygen, and how all the organisms will die if one interferes (in different ways for different organisms) with their oxygen transport system. The argument here has a similar structure: the variety of abstraction systems described in this book all make it possible to govern social life by abstractions, that in their turn can be improved. If one takes away the possibility of improvement, or of government, the formality withers and dies, and informality takes over again.

But during a time in which an abstraction system is not being improved, its shaping of the social life under its government is what we know as "routinization." It involves routines to ensure that the world is being accurately abstracted, that those abstractions are effectively communicated, and that they are checked not only for nonconformity, but also for inaccuracy and ineffective communication. We see the end product as people's behaving as they have in the past, or with slight variations so as to adapt routinely to variations in the environment. Our argument is that such routines tend not to stay routinized unless the abstraction system accurately specifies effective action, accurately communicates it to the actors, improves it over time, and arranges for it to govern action effectively.

Weber's list of forms of appropriation cannot therefore show us very well why they are routinized in a given situation.

THE AUTHORITY OF WHOLE SYSTEMS OF ABSTRACTIONS

Weber's third purpose, explaining authority—that is, explaining how reliable social routines can be built that embed abstractions in social life—requires us to conceive *the whole system* that manages a particular abstraction, rather than a particular meeting of an abstraction with a group of details. This last, the inattention to the origin and improvement of abstractions is the most crucial part of my disagreement with the tradition of law versus custom, formal organization versus primary groups, the great tradition versus the little tradition. Abstraction into formality is a central part of law, but it is a central part of most things. Formality has its greatest effects when it is not formalizing one abstraction, but a system of abstractions, along with a social system for improving that system of abstractions.

1. Leaves are more famous for producing food than for supplying oxygen, but they do both.

For example, if an architect has forgotten to draw a vent on a sewage drain stack, the system includes the fact that the client, the architect's boss and peers, and the plumber will all consider that a "mistake," to be formally corrected if necessary. The plumbing contractor who notices this mistake will often supply the missing detail and include it in his or her bid. If the correction will entail costs elsewhere (for example, other omitted details, such as adequate space or greater continuity in a partition), the plumbing bidder will call up the architect or client. If the plumbing contractor overlooks the missing vent as well, the plumbing craftsperson will either just do it right or will call the contractor. This is part of "good workmanship" as specified in the contract; good workmanship is to know plumbing better than an architect does.

All of this informality is, however, supported by the fact that the vent is specified in the building code, in the reference book on plumbing standards that one can check out of the local public library, and in the curriculum of a plumbing apprenticeship. And it is even included in a blueprint reading class, a cut-down version of what the architect had to go through.

Finally, if none of this informal correction happens, and the issue of the missing vent is taken to arbitration or a court, the court decision will be such that it is formally decided that somebody pays for putting the vent in and the damages caused by the mistake to which everybody, by now, has contributed. Thus the "informality" *and* the "formality" that corrects the contract are built into a system so that sewer gases, in the great majority of cases, are vented into the atmosphere rather than exploding in the sewer, and so that someone is to blame if they do explode. Such abstraction is central to the good politics of keeping sewer gases from exploding, as well as the bad politics of preserving the market position of plumbers and plumbing contractors.

In the long run the formality of the final result (the vented sewer), achieved by both formal and informal means, is quite highly correctable by knowledge of sewer chemistry. The final result is highly predictable because it is formally written in several ways in several places and enforced by a large number of social arrangements, including both informal ones of "good workmanship" and calling up the architect on the telephone to change the formal drawings. It is built as well into formal routines such as inspection in the light of building codes. It is made authoritative by arbitrators' willingness to make business practice formally binding, and can be authoritatively enforced (though perhaps less reliably) through contractual law. For example, the contract may contain a boilerplate provision that construction will be carried out in compliance with the building code. Code compliance therefore becomes part of the contractor's required performance, and may be achieved through apprenticeship provisions in the union contract and plumbing licensing law.

This success of the whole system does not mean that in some particular meeting between the competent plumber and the incompetent architect, the formal blueprint may be resorted to, and overruled. But my argument is that this is the result of the criterion that the meeting of the formal blueprint with the knowledgeable plumber is embedded in a system that is trying hard to govern so as to ensure that a sewer vent goes into the proper building partition. That system will, quite likely, secure the abstract characteristics that get explosive gases out of sewers and diluted in the atmosphere. The blueprint on which the contract formally rests will be overruled when it is not a good abstraction of the details it was supposed to abstract. To study this success,[2] I believe we have to build a different conception of how formality governs, one in which any given abstraction can be re-abstracted. And we have to keep our eye on what it takes in such a system to make the whole more rationalizable with the advance of knowledge, more routinizable so that it can be reliably predicted, and more authoritative because it can really abstract what needs to be abstracted in order for authority to work. These in turn involve the capacity of authority to correct itself when it has "made a mistake."

I have tried to refute the idea that the essence of formality is rigidity, that abstraction necessarily loses contact with reality and details, that routines are frozen and never improved, and that the central source of legitimacy is dogmatism rather than reason. I have attacked the distinction between formal and substantive rationality that, I believe, led Weber and the rest of us astray. The idea that formality is rigidity is part of a sort of Platonist view of abstractions, that they are the permanent reality behind the "accidents" that produce phenomena. On the contrary, abstractions change very fast, and all the faster when they are part of better abstracting systems. There is no reality behind abstractions except the same world that is embedded in informal social life, and informal social life is often more rigid than bureaucracy or law. When a system of formality has good abstractions in it, and governs those parts of social practice that it is essential to govern, then formality is nimble, and informality traditionalistic and sluggish.

---

2. And, of course, its failures. For example, the formality of Stalinist apartment buildings did not routinely work well when built—and I heard that the worst insult one could give the architect of Stockholm University buildings was that they are in the modern Bulgarian architectural tradition. People who knew better how to construct Stalinist buildings than the planners could rarely correct those planners.

EMBEDDING OF FORMALITY IN CONCRETE SYSTEMS OF ACTION

The functionalism of this book works when formalism makes it possible to do something that would be difficult to do with spontaneity. This means that it necessarily creates power to do those things, and then to exchange those achievements for resources to support the formality. Inputs into these systems of power all come from concrete interpersonal interactions at the base level, among the details. A few of these are so dominated by the governing abstractions that their output to the system is only a manifestation of the system itself, as I suppose the cockpit of a passenger airplane landing at a busy airport might be. At the other extreme might be a causal conversation over hot chocolate at home just before going to sleep, or a pickup game of kickball on a playground in the park. Only the legal right to use the space, the chocolate powder, and the ball are really abstract and formal government.

Between those extremes are the little worlds of people in interaction, with abstract government of activity to different degrees. All of these are encounters between the informal and formal. The power of abstractions, then, is generated in social interaction embedded simultaneously in details and abstractions, in informality and formality. Government by abstractions fails if, in thousands of concrete interactions, it does not dominate those parts of the action it claims to govern. It may fail by reason of the informalities in the setting, or by reason of the other formalities there.

I once studied social interaction in a steel rolling mill in South America (Stinchcombe 1974). I noticed that in the last few minutes of a shift, the foremen disappeared into their offices. I found out they were filling out the hours and materials used and the amounts of various products rolled for the cost accounting system. In the meantime, the workers stopped working to be ready to leave at the end of their shift, when most got on busses to get a ride home. Many of the foremen also rode those busses. The new work force was recruited from dispersed nearby towns, and public transportation was not up to moving them efficiently, so the plant provided the busses.

The formal system demanded the numbers from the foremen, his simultaneous supervision to the end of the shift, and for all to be ready to leave and catch the bus at the end of the shift. Thus the formal system came up against itself, as well as against the informal adaptations of the workers and foremen to its pressures. It was not the purpose of the cost accounting department to increase costs by taking away supervision just when workers had the most motivation to stop. It abstracted from the costs of the activities it demanded from the foreman.

This is a common failing of abstractions by management of all kinds; it is a common failure of university administrators not to count the costs of students' standing in long lines at registration, or writing distinctive essays for each of several different college admissions offices, or sitting outside a faculty member's door in a queue the day before a paper is due. The time of people not paid wages is a much-wasted resource. There is no abstraction that measures this loss so that a university administrator can reduce it. It can be justified by the common maxim of intelligent administration, "Do not sweat the small things"; it applies especially if they are the small things of low-status and powerless people. Such small things can in fact be the big ones in the lives of aliens, and the Imigration and Naturalization Service and the the law it administers are carefully set up not to collect information on aliens' costs.

But in the rolling mill the workers' time after the shift was not paid for by the plant, and it was hard to get them to agree to get home a quarter of an hour later by cleaning up and walking to the company bus on their own time. It was difficult for the plan to switch the costs of closing down a bit early to the workers, when management themselves had got the supervisor off the floor, and were not willing to pay for the quarter hour after the shift. In short, the failure of the formal system was due to the other parts of the formal system.

BUT WE WOULD HAVE ABSTRACTED DIFFERENTLY

I heard of an English teacher who had previously been a restaurant manager, whose black friend had been denied promotion and finally was fired, over his protest. He then collected extensive evidence of bigoted speech, policy, and practice by carrying a tape recorder with him. When he quit the restaurant, after playing a copy of the recording for his boss, he took it to the Equal Employment Opportunity Commission (EEOC) as evidence that they should investigate his (now former) employer for discrimination. The EEOC officer asked him if he had had permission to make the recordings from his employer. (The officer might alternatively have asked whether he had asked for court approval, on the basis of his preliminary evidence, to record). When he said no, they refused to accept it. He decided teaching English would be better. This is the sort of social conflict that puts the fire back into the distinction between formal and informal governance of social life, between substantive and formal rationality.

The argument above implies that I believe that the disagreement between the EEOC officer and the English-teacher-to-be was not due to the formalities, but to a conflict over substance. The employer's right to trust the privacy of conversations is in substantive conflict with an employee planning to collect evidence of criminal wrongdoing by intentionally being secret about the recording. The EEOC is responsible to the norms that protect privacy. The employee's probable cause to believe that a crime was being committed, and that the employer's managers were the criminals, is also a substantive point.

The employee's informal evidence might have persuaded a judge to issue a warrant for secret evidence collection. Thus there is a formality that abstracts the aims and purposes of the informal actor and governs activity in the light of that abstraction. My argument implies that this formal government of secret data collection is just as substantive as the employee's aims and purposes of punishing discrimination, and would use those aims and purposes as part of the justification for formal action. The carefulness about invasions of privacy for purposes of crime control, and the reliance of employers who discriminate on both the informal career interests of their employees to go along with organizational crimes, and on the search and seizure provisions of the law that protect that privacy, is no less substantive because imposed by an EEOC officer faced with clear "informal" evidence of criminal discrimination.

Because substantive rationality has trade-offs among values, so formal rationality that abstracts that substance will have conflicts among the abstractions representing those values. Sometimes those trade-offs are themselves abstracted and systematized, as in the provisions for warrants for secret data collection. Sometimes when formal provisions conflict, the wise thing to do is to "go informal" to discuss what the substance is about and what is the best way to decide on the trade-off for this case. This tends to result in "casuistry" rather than "legal craftsmanship." But sometimes if one is not ready to decide the case as a precedent, as modifying the abstractions, casuistry is wiser. The inequality of power to start an investigation between the EEOC officer and the employee, of course, determines how the casuistry will come out for the particular case.

In chapter 6 we studied a situation in which foreigners wanting to enter the United States ordinarily get no chance to provide the system with evidence that its abstractions are bad. The immigration laws and regulations are designed to discriminate against foreigners, while protecting citizens and near-citizens. It is, for example, specifically provided that secret information may be collected and used against a foreigner seeking admission, without allowing the foreigner to confront his or her accuser. Immigration officials, then, would be allowed to listen to the future English teacher's secret recordings, though given that their job is to discriminate they might not have receptive ears. Similarly the norms that might permit a parent or a student in regular high school English to collect and give evidence that the student could write better than a specific other student in honors English, and so deserved the honors student's place, are very weak indeed, though not quite as weak as the norms governing immigration officials' dealing with aliens.

The general point is that the representation of one set of values in the informal part of a formal–informal encounter, and a different set in the formal part, is not inherent in abstraction and government of social life by abstractions. One can usually think of abstractions somewhere in social life that represent the values left out of a given abstraction system.

CONCEPTUAL CLARITY AND EMPIRICIST CONFUSION

I have defined formality as a process of abstraction for particular purposes and then government of social life by those abstractions. Thus in chapter 3, when I found a foundations contractor correcting an architect, I looked to see whether there was an abstraction governing that correction. If there were, the architect would recognize the abstraction and correct the government of the activity in the light of it. The abstraction in the mistaken blueprint gave way to the foundation contractor's correct reading from the blueprint of where the foundation ought to be. That is, it turned out not to be really informal. Similarly Karl Llewellyn found that what appellate judges did to distinguish cases was not really informal. Instead the judges were governed by their responsibility of filling the gap so revealed so that business could go on, and the actual agreements of the contracting parties could be adequately represented by the abstract distinctions being created in the common law. Further, they generally filled the gap with legal principles from nearby cases, often, in fact, from the precedent they were overturning.

That is, the foundations contractor and the appellate judges might be looked at as "informal" elements in the system of abstractions, but that is to misconstrue what the abstract system is. The abstraction system is a way of thinking about details in such a way that, when they don't fit, the system can recognize it and correct itself. The future English teacher with the useless tapes showing criminal discrimination, the foremen in their offices in the last quarter hour of a shift, and the architect drawing the foundations so that they would not support the roof were all part of interaction systems that the formalities had abstracted, and had abstracted badly. The problems with those troubles are not with informality, but with other parts of the formal system. They manifest themselves in concrete systems in which people simultaneously deal with the details, and with the abstractions governing some of those details. The abstractions never grasp all the details one has to live with in the situation.

Sometimes that means that the abstractions have to be corrected; sometimes it means that people live their lives in details that escape the system; sometimes it means that the details are, from the point of view of what is mainly going on in the situation, merely noise and error; and sometimes it means only the metaphysical proposition that we can never know everything about anything, never get to the *Ding an sich*.

The great mistake here is to fall into reification, so that the group of workers leaving the steel plant when the shift ends are understood to have been acting informally, because their boss would have liked them to clean up and get to the bus on their own time. Or that the EEOC officer is understood to have been acting legalistically in respecting the privacy of people who had been using the privacy to discriminate. No doubt many EEOC officers do not care whether the rules protecting privacy have any deep constitutional justification, and are glad to get rid of a troublesome ideologue on whatever ground is convenient, and the Constitution happens to be convenient. But the groups of interacting people are neither formal nor informal in any given situation, but rather are a mix of formalities, informalities, and irrelevancies. Early juries are not informal versions of rationalized use of evidence, but are groups of people tending the abstractions of legal possession by reporting on rituals of seisin—that represent the contract of land tenure—while taking account of how to live with their powerful neighbors.

It is not situations, nor groups of people, nor social systems that are formal or informal. It is processes that make abstractions and govern by them that make things more or less formal. Those processes go on in the same times and places as people live in details. All thinking goes on in situations with details in them, by people who attend to some of those details. The type-situation of formality as a process is a foundations contractor looking at a blueprint and seeing that the foundation drawn will not support the roof. And in the case described, it is the mistake of the architect and the drawing that is informal, not the competence of the craftsperson, because that's the way the abstraction system is socially embedded.

REFERENCES

Administrative Review Council. 1986. *Report to the Attorney-General: Review of Migration Decisions (Report No. 25).* Canberra: Australian Government Publishing Service.

Akerlof, George A. 1970. "The Market for Lemons: Quality Uncertainty and the Market Mechanism." *Journal of Economics* 84: 488–500.

Aleinikoff, Thomas Alexander, and David A. Martin. 1991 [1985]. *Immigration, Process and Policy.* 2d ed. St. Paul: West Publishing.

Aubert, Vilhelm. 1963. "The Structure of Legal Thinking." Pp. 41–63 in *Festskrift til Frede Castberg*, ed. Johannes Andenaes. Oslo: Unversitetsforlaget.

Baker, Susan Gonzales. 1990. *The Cautious Welcome: The Legalization Programs of the Immigration and Control Act.* Santa Monica: Rand Corporation; Washington, D.C.: Urban Institute.

Barzel, Yoram. 1982. "Measurement Cost and the Organization of Markets." *Journal of Law and Economics* 25: 27–48.

Berle, Adolf, and Gardiner Means. 1991 [1932]. *The Modern Corporation and Private Property.* New Brunswick, N.J.: Transaction Books.

Bernstein, Lisa. 1996. "Symposium: Law, Economics, and Norms: Merchant Law in a Merchant Court: Rethinking the Code's Search for Immanent Business Norms." *University of Pennsylvania Law Review* 144: 1765–1821.

Black, Donald. 1971. "The Social Organization of Arrest." *Stanford Law Review* 23: 1087–1111.

Blackstone, Sir William. 1872 [1766]. *Commentaries on the Laws of England.* Edited by Thomas M. Cooley. Chicago: Callaghan.

Boswell, Terry, and John Brueggemann. 2000. "Labor Market Segmentation and the Cultural Division of Labor in the Copper Mining Industry, 1880–1920." *Research in Social Movements, Conflicts and Change* 22: 193–217.

Burawoy, Michael. 1979. *Manufacturing Consent: Changes in the Labor Process under Monopoly Capitalism.* Chicago: University of Chicago Press.

Carruthers, Bruce G. 1996. *City of Capital: Politics and Markets in the English Financial Revolution.* Princeton: Princeton University Press.

Carruthers, Bruce G., and Arthur L. Stinchcombe. 1999. "The Social Structure of Liquidity: Flexibility, Markets, and States." *Theory and Society* 28: 353–82.

Carruthers, Bruce G., and Wendy Nelson Espeland. 1991. "Accounting for Rationality: Double-Entry Bookkeeping and the Rhetoric of Economic Rationality." *American Journal of Sociology* 97(1): 31–69.

Chandler, Alfred D., Jr. 1962. *Strategy and Structure: Chapters in the History of the Industrial Enterprise.* Cambridge: MIT Press.

———. 1977. *The Visible Hand: The Managerial Revolution in American Business.* Cambridge: Harvard University Press.

Clark, John Maurice. 1929 [1923]. *Studies in the Economics of Overhead Cost.* Chicago: University of Chicago Press.

Cole, Jonathan R., and Stephen Cole. 1973. *Social Stratification in Science.* Chicago: University of Chicago Press.

Collins, Randall. 1979. *The Credential Society: An Historical Sociology of Education and Stratification.* New York: Academic Press.

Commons, John R. 1974 [1924]. *Legal Foundations of Capitalism.* Reprint, Clifton N.J.: Augustus M. Kelley.

Congressional Budget Office. 1996. *Assessing the Public Costs and Benefits of Fannie Mae and Freddie Mac.* Washington, D.C.: Government Printing Office.

Cronon, William. 1991. *Nature's Metropolis: Chicago and the Great West.* New York: Norton.

Douglas, Mary. 1981 [1980]. *Edward Evans-Pritchard.* Harmondsworth: Penguin Books.

———. 1986. "Institutions Remember and Forget." Pp. 69–80 in *How Institutions Think.* Syracuse: Syracuse University Press.

Eccles, Robert C. 1985. *The Transfer Pricing Problem: A Theory for Practice.* Lexington, Mass.: Lexington Books.

Eccles, Robert C., and Harrison C. White. 1988. "Price and Authority in Inter-Profit Center Transactions." In *Organizations and Institutions: Sociological and Economic Approaches to the Analysis of Social Structure*, ed. Christopher Winship and Sherwin Rosen. *American Journal of Sociology Supplement* 94: S17–S51.

Emerson, Robert M. 1969. *Judging Delinquents: Context and Process in Juvenile Court.* Chicago: Aldine.

Espeland, Wendy. 1998. *The Struggle for Water: Politics, Rationality, and Identity in the American Southwest.* Chicago: University of Chicago Press.

Fabozzi, Frank J., and Franco Modigliani. 1992. *Mortgages and Mortgage Backed Securities Markets.* Boston: Harvard Business School Press.

Fletcher, G. A. 1976. *The Discount Houses in London: Principles, Operations, and Change.* Toronto: Macmillan.

Friedman, Edith J. 1968. *Encyclopedia of Real Estate Appraising.* Englewood Cliffs, N.J.: Prentice-Hall.

Friedman, Lawrence. 1966. "On Legalistic Reasoning—A Footnote to Weber." *Wisconsin Law Review* 1966: 148–71.

Gage, Daniel D. 1937. *Land Title Assuring Agencies*. San Francisco: Recorder Printing and Publishing.

Gilbert, G. Nigel, and Michael Mulkay. 1984. *Opening Pandora's Box: A Sociological Analysis of Scientists' Discourse*. Cambridge: Cambridge University Press.

Gilboy, Janet. 1983. "Holistic Effects in Social Control Decision-Making." *Law and Society Review* 17: 425–55.

———. 1988. "Administrative Review in a System of Conflicting Values." *Law and Social Inquiry* 13: 515–79.

———. 1991. "Deciding Who Gets In: Decisionmaking by Immigration Inspectors." *Law and Society Review* 25(3): 571–99.

———. 1992. "Penetrability of Administrative Systems: Political 'Casework' and Immigration Inspections." *Law and Society Review* 26(2): 273–314.

Gouldner, Alvin Ward. 1954a. *Patterns of Industrial Bureaucracy*. New York: Free Press.

———. 1954b. *Wildcat Strike*. Yellow Springs, Ohio: Antioch Press.

Green, Thomas F. 1940. *Practical Summary of Negotiable Instruments*. New York: Longmans, Green.

Gumperz, John. 1982. *Discourse Strategies*. Cambridge: Cambridge University Press.

Hallinan, Maureen T., and Aage B. Sørensen. 1983. "The Formation and Stability of Instructional Groups." *American Sociological Review* 48 (December): 838–51.

Heimer, Carol A. 1985. "Allocating Information Costs in a Negotiated Information Order." *Administrative Science Quarterly* 30: 395–417.

Heimer, Carol A., and Arthur L. Stinchcombe. 1999. "Remodeling the Garbage Can: Implications of the Origins of Items in Decision Streams." Pp. 25–57 in *Organizing Political Institutions: Essays for Johan P. Olsen*, ed. Morten Egeberg and Per Lægreid. Oslo: Scandinavian University Press.

Inhelder, Barbel, and Jean Piaget. 1958. *The Growth of Logical Thinking from Childhood to Adolescence: An Essay on the Construction of Formal Operational Structures*. Translated by A. Parsons and S. Milgram. London: Routledge & Kegan Paul.

Joel, Adrian. 1984. *A Practical Guide to Obtaining Permanent Residence in Australia*. 3d ed. Woolloomooloo (Sydney) NSW: Legal Books.

Koetsier, Teun. 1991. *Lakatos' Philosophy of Mathematics: A Historical Approach*. Amsterdam: North-Holland.

Krygier, Martin. 1998. "Common Law." *Routledge Encyclopedia of Philosophy*. Vol. 2, pp. 440–46.

Kuhn, Thomas. 1970 [1966]. *The Structure of Scientific Revolutions*. Chicago: University of Chicago Press.

———. 1978. *Black Body Theory and the Quantum Discontinuity. 1894–1912*. New York: Oxford University Press.

Lakatos, Imre. 1976a [1961]. *Proofs and Refutations: The Logic of Mathematical Discovery*. Edited by John Worrall and Elie Zahar. Cambridge: Cambridge University Press.

————. 1976b [1961]. "Another Case-Study in the Method of Proofs and Refutations." Pp. 127–41 in *Proofs and Refutations: The Logic of Mathematical Discovery*. Edited by John Worrall and Elie Zahar. Cambridge: Cambridge University Press.

————. 1978 [1970]. "The Methodology of Scientific Research Programmes." Pp. 8–101 in *The Methodology of Scientific Research Programmes: Philosophical Papers, Volume 1*. Edited by John Worrall and Gregory Currie. Cambridge: Cambridge University Press.

Landis, Michele. 1998. "'Let me Next Time Be Tried by Fire': Disaster Relief and the Origins of the American Welfare State 1789–1874." *Northwestern University Law Review* 92(3): 969–1036.

————. 1999. "Fate, Responsibility, and 'Natural' Disaster Relief: Narrating the American Welfare State." *Law and Society Review* 33(2): 257–318.

Latour, Bruno, and Steve Woolgar. 1979. *Laboratory Life: The Social Construction of Scientific Facts*. Beverly Hills: Sage Publications.

Lave, Jean. 1988. *Cognition in Practice: Mind, Mathematics, and Culture in Everyday Life*. Cambridge: Cambridge University Press.

Lempert, Richard. 1997. "After the DNA Wars: Skirmishing with NRC II." *Jurimetrics* 37: 439–68.

Levi, Edward. 1949. *An Introduction to Legal Reasoning*. Chicago: University of Chicago Press.

Lewis, Michael. 1989. *Liar's Poker: Rising through the Wreckage on Wall Street*. New York: Norton.

Llewellyn, Karl N. 1960. *The Common Law Tradition: Deciding Appeals*. Boston: Little, Brown.

Lopez, Mary D., and Carol A. Heimer. 1996. "Exercising Control in the Face of Uncertainty: A Comparison of MS and Other Chronic Illnesses." Paper read at annual meeting of the American Sociological Association, August 1996, New York.

Lurie, Jonathan. 1979. *The Chicago Board of Trade 1859–1905: The Dynamics of Self-Regulation*. Urbana: University of Illinois Press.

Macaulay, Stewart. 1996. "Organic Transactions: Contract, Frank Lloyd Wright, and the Johnson Building." *Wisconsin Law Review* 27(1): 75–121.

MacEachern, Alan M. 1994. *Some Truth with Maps: A Primer on Symbolization and Design*. Washington, D.C.: Association of American Geographers.

March, James G., and Herbert A. Simon. 1993 [1958]. *Organizations*. Cambridge, Mass.: Blackwell.

McCarter, Robert. 1999 [1997]. *Frank Lloyd Wright, Architect*. London: Phaidon Press.

Meyer, John W., and Brian Rowan. 1977. "Institutionalized Organizations: Formal Structure as Myth and Ceremony." *American Journal of Sociology* 83(2): 340–63.

Milofsky, Carl. 1976. *Special Education: A Sociological Study of California Programs*. New York: Praeger.

Neal, Larry. 1990. *The Rise of Financial Capitalism*. Cambridge: Cambridge University Press.

Padgett, John. 1980. "Bounded Rationality in Budgetary Research." *American Political Science Review* 74: 354–72.

———. 1981. "Hierarchy and Ecological Control in Federal Budgetary Decision Making." *American Journal of Sociology* 87: 75–129.

Paige, Jeffery M., and Herbert A. Simon. 1966. "Cognitive Processes in Solving Algebra Word Problems." Pp. 51–119 in *Problem Solving: Research Method and Theory*, ed. Benjamin Kleinmetz. New York: Wiley.

Palumbo, Michael G. 1999. "Uncertain Medical Expenses and Precautionary Saving Near the End of the Life Cycle." *Review of Economic Studies* 66(2) (April): 395–421.

Polanyi, Karl. 1985 [1944]. *The Great Transformation.* Boston: Beacon Press.

Polsby, Nelson. 1968. "The Institutionalization of the House of Representatives." *American Political Science Review* 62: 144–68.

Powers Rawl. 1998. *Fastening Systems Handbook.* New Rochelle, N.Y.: Powers Fastening Incorporated.

Radcliffe-Brown, Arthur R. 1952 [1935]. "Patrilineal and Matrilineal Succession." Pp. 32–47 in *Structure and Function in Primitive Society.* Glencoe, N.Y.: Free Press.

Redfield, Robert. 1971. *The Little Community and Peasant Society and Culture.* Chicago: University of Chicago Press.

Roethlisberger, Fritz J., and William J. Dickson. 1950. *Management and the Worker.* Cambridge: Harvard University Press.

Rosenbaum, James. 1976. "The Illusion of Choosing Fate." Pp. 107–25 in *Making Inequality: The Hidden Curriculum of High School Tracking.* New York: Wiley.

Saks, Michael J., and Reid Hastie. 1978. *Social Psychology in Court.* New York: Van Nostrand Reinhold.

Schauer, Frederick. 1991. *Playing by the Rules: A Philosophical Examination of Rule-Based Decision Making in Law and in Life.* Oxford: Clarendon Press.

Scheff, Thomas J. 1990. "Language Acquisition versus Formal Education: A Theory of Genius." Pp. 156–75 in *Microsociology: Discourse, Emotion, and Social Structure.* Chicago: University of Chicago Press.

Shapiro, Susan P. 1984. *Wayward Capitalists: Target of the Securities and Exchange Commission.* New Haven: Yale University Press.

Shklar, Judith N. 1964. *Legalism.* Cambridge: Harvard University Press.

Simmel, Georg. 1978 [1907]. *The Philosophy of Money.* Boston: Routledge & Kegan Paul

Smith, Charles W. 1989. *Auctions: The Social Construction of Value.* Berkeley: University of California Press.

Smith, Dorothy E. 1990. *The Conceptual Practices of Power: A Feminist Sociology of Knowledge.* Boston: Northeastern University Press.

Stegner, Wallace. 1954 [1953]. *Beyond the Hundredth Meridian: John Wesley Powell and the Second Opening of the West.* New York: Penguin.

Stiglitz, Joseph. 1993. *Economics.* New York: Norton.

Stinchcombe, Arthur L. 1963. "Institutions of Privacy in the Determination of Police Administrative Practice." *American Journal of Sociology* 69(2) (September): 150–60.

———. 1964. *Rebellion in a High School*. Chicago: Quadrangle Books.

———. 1974. *Creating Efficient Industrial Administrations*. Orlando: Academic Press.

———. 1978. *Theoretical Methods in Social History*. New York: Academic Press.

———. 1990. *Information and Organizations*. Berkeley: University of California Press.

———. 1991. "The Conditions of Fruitfulness of Theorizing about Mechanisms in Social Science." *Philosophy of the Social Sciences* 21(3) (September): 367–87. Revised and reprinted in Aage Sorensen and Seymour Spilerman, eds., *Social Theory and Social Policy: Essays in Honor of James S. Coleman* (Westport, Conn.: Praeger), pp. 23–41.

———. 1995. *Sugar Island Slavery in the Age of Enlightenment: The Political Economy of the Caribbean World*. Princeton: Princeton University Press.

———. 1999. "Certainty of the Law: Reasons, Situation-Types, Analogy, and Equilibrium." *Journal of Political Philosophy* 7(3) (September): 209–24.

Taylor, Serge. 1984. *Making Bureaucracies Think: The Environmental Impact Statement Strategy of Administrative Reform*. Palo Alto: Stanford University Press.

Telser, Lester G. 1981. "Why There are Organized Futures Markets." *Journal of Law and Economics* 24: 1–22.

Telser, Lester G., and Harlow N. Higinbotham. 1977. "Organized Futures Markets: Costs and Benefits." *Journal of Political Economy* 85: 969–1000.

Thomas, Robert. 1994. *What Machines Can't Do*. Berkeley: University of California Press.

Thompson, James D. 1967. *Organizations in Action*. New York: McGraw-Hill.

Tobin, James. 1989. "Financial Intermediaries." In *The New Palgrave: Finance*, ed. John Eatwell, Murray Milgate, and Peter Newman. New York: Norton.

Treiman, Sam. 1999. *The Odd Quantum*. Princeton: Princeton University Press.

Tufte, Edward R. 1983. *The Visual Display of Quantitative Information*. Cheshire, Conn.: Graphics Press.

———. 1990. *Envisioning Information*. Cheshire, Conn.: Graphics Press.

U.S. Department of the Treasury. 1996. *Government Sponsorship of the Federal National Mortgage Association and the Federal Home Loan Mortgage Corporation*. Washington, D.C.: Government Printing Office.

Wallerstein, Immanuel. 1974–. *The Modern World System*. Orlando: Academic Press.

Watson, James D. 1980 [1968]. *The Double Helix: A Personal Account of the Discovery of the Structure of DNA*. Edited by Gunther S. Stent. New York: Norton.

Weber, Max. 1924 [1889]. "Zur Geschichte der Handelsgesellschaften im Mittelalter nach sudeuropaischen Quellen." Pp. 312–443 in *Gesammelte Aufsatze zur Sozial- und Wirtschaftsgeschichte*. Tubingen: Mohr.

———. 1954 [1924]. *Law in Economy and Society*. Edited and supplemented by Max Rheinstein; translated by Edward Shils and Max Rheinstein. Cambridge: Harvard University Press.

———. 1968 [1924]. *Economy and Society: An Outline of Interpretive Sociology*. 3 vols. Edited by Gunther Roth and Klaus Wittich. New York: Bedminster Press.

Wigmore, John Henry. 1940. *A Treatise on the Anglo American System of Evidence in Trials at Common Law.* 10 vols. Boston: Little, Brown.

Whyte, William Foote. 1961. *Men at Work.* Homewood, Ill.: Dorsey Press.

Zelizer, Viviana. 1994. *The Social Meaning of Money.* New York: Basic Books.

Zuckerman, Harriet, and Robert K. Merton. 1971. "Patterns of Evaluation in Science: Institutionalization, Structure and Functions of the Referee System." *Minerva* 9: 66–100.

INDEX